Dear Jim,

It was a pleasure
doing dinner recently.
I look forward to working
with you in the future

STOLEN
WITHOUT A GUN

Walter Pavlo, Jr., March 2002
Edgefield Federal Prison Camp, Edgefield, South Carolina

Stolen
Without A Gun

Confessions from inside
history's biggest
accounting fraud–
the collapse of MCI WorldCom

**WALTER PAVLO, Jr.
& NEIL WEINBERG**

with a foreword by **Dennis Kneale
Managing Editor, *Forbes* Magazine**

 Etika Books Tampa, Florida, U.S.A.

 # Contents

To Minna and David Weinberg

"You see, Mr. Gittes, most people never have to face the fact that at the right time and the right place, they're capable of anything."

—Corrupt businessman Noah Cross, in *"Chinatown"*

 # About The Authors

WALTER PAVLO JR. is a popular national speaker who has made keynote addresses at America's top business schools, professional societies, Fortune 500 companies, accounting firms, and federal law enforcement agencies.

His story and presentations have been featured by *Forbes* magazine, *USA Today*, *New York Times*, National Public Radio, and ABC's *Nightline*. A number of organizations incorporate his experience as the basis of case studies and documentaries aimed at educating students and business people about white-collar crime.

Pavlo holds a degree in Industrial Engineering from West Virginia University and an MBA from Mercer University. He worked in finance roles at Goodyear Tire's aerospace division and GEC Avionics before joining MCI Communications.

In January 2001, Pavlo pleaded guilty to wire fraud and money laundering and agreed to cooperate with federal investigators. He began serving a two-year prison sentence later that year.

Since his 2003 release, Pavlo has told his story as a cautionary tale to thousands of students, business people, professionals, and law enforcement officials.

Walter Pavlo Jr. is the founder of Tampa, Florida-based Etika, LLC. Additional information is available at www.EtikaLLC.com.

NEIL WEINBERG is a Senior Editor at *Forbes* magazine in New York. He focuses on investigative reporting of controversial practices in business and politics. Over the past few years he has profiled corporate, mutual fund and pension scandals, the dark side of whistle-blowing and problems with private equity and hedge funds.

A fifteen-year *Forbes* veteran, Weinberg served as the magazine's Tokyo bureau chief from 1995 to 1998 and has reported extensively abroad. Last year he received the Overseas Press Club's annual award for the best business story in a magazine. Weinberg appears frequently on *Forbes on Fox* and other TV news programs.

He holds an MBA from the American Graduate School of International Management and a Bachelor's Degree in English Literature from the College of William and Mary in Virginia.

Acknowledgments

L ONELY AS WRITING a book like this can be, the journey was enriched and the result enhanced by the honest guidance and endless patience of many friends, relatives, and harried experts.

This is a true crime story, but we have tried to paint a dramatic picture of a corporate world with which many of us are familiar, where the line between right and wrong often twists itself into a dollar sign—the perfect environment for white-collar crime.

We reached out to dozens of people, including some for whom the events recounted in these pages have been the most painful of their lives. Some gave us the cold shoulder, but many others were generous with their time, memories, and emotions. They provided the texture and depth we hope makes this a tale that transcends a memoir or confessional.

We offer special thanks to Jim and Becky Wilkie, who opened their home and their hearts to us in Atlanta. They set aside their pride and shared how this shameful episode in their lives changed them, hoping that by doing so they may influence someone else to pick the right choice over the easy one. We are grateful to Walt's dad, Walt Pavlo, Sr., for doing the same.

Thanks to the editors of *Forbes* magazine for making it possible for Neil to complete this project. That's especially true of Editor William Baldwin, who provided encouragement and book leave, Deputy Managing Editor Stewart Pinkerton, who worked out the details, and Managing Editor Dennis Kneale, who was keen on telling Walt's story from the outset and wrote the Foreword.

Our gratitude goes to the many former MCI employees, customers and others who played roles in this drama and shared their experiences. Some requested anonymity. We thank them with just as much gratitude as we have for those we can name: Ralph McCumber, Mark Benveniste, Julie Benveniste, Jack Hammer, John Paulsen, Jim Franklin, Jonathan Spear, Harvey Linder, Jim Hannon, Ian Ratner, William Jennings, and Doug Dely.

Jack Martin and Bruce Morris, two of Atlanta's most respected criminal defense attorneys, gave generously of their limited free time. Bruce led us into the dungeon beneath his building where we found some legal gems among the moldering stacks of court filings.

Three members of the federal law enforcement community, after investigating Walt's crimes and sending him to prison, agreed to explain how they did it, lending balance to our perspective. They are IRS Special Agent Patricia Bergstrom, FBI Special Agent (retired) Raymond Kyle, and Assistant U.S. Attorney William McKinnon.

Given the complexity of the financial, accounting, and legal issues in this story, we appreciate the insights of Tim Hedley, PhD (KPMG, Partner-Forensics), Eric Rayman, (of counsel, Miller Korzenik Sommers LLP), and Dan Reingold, an MCI alum, former telecom analyst and author of *Confessions of a Wall Street Analyst*. Howard Jonas, Art Levinson and Dick Martin shared insights into the telecom business that only come from true pros.

Our editor, Foster Winans, shepherded this book toward publication, polishing the manuscript and design and, most importantly, wringing out of us observations and emotions we hadn't known well enough to share.

Several people took a read and offered common-sense improvements along the way. Thanks to Michael Maiello, Gary Weiss, and Paul Witcover for sharing them early on. Also opining, proofreading, and improving were dear relatives and friends Linda Abdella, Michael Abdella, Mandy Cormier, William Duryea, Don Jones, Andrew Korman, Robin Korman, Tim Olewine, Lisa Pavlo, and Robert Sellers.

For moral support, we are grateful to Catherine Burns, Renee Haugerud, Dave Osborne, and Don Soderquist, who offered constant encouragement and reminded us that no venture worth completing is completed without pain. Thanks also to Nomi Prins for her authorial insights and sympathy.

We would be remiss if we did not save our most heartfelt gratitude for Donna Cormier and Sonoko Setaishi, the best proofreaders, reality-checkers, and long-suffering wives we could ask for. We thank them, along with Alisa, Bubby, Howie, and Mia for putting up with all the travel, and lack of it while we were writing away, late nights, early mornings, and lost weekends. We are eternally grateful for your patience, support and unconditional love.

—Walt and Neil, September 2007

# Foreword

I N EVERY BOOMING BUSINESS in most every pocket of the planet, soaring sales and profits can obscure an underbelly of unalloyed greed—wild behavior, shabby practices, stupid gambles and, all too often, chicanery so brazen as to inspire admiration for its unabashed ballsiness.

That was true in the laying of the railroads and the rise of the robber barons around the turn of the 19th century; and it was even more true at the end of the 20th century amidst the telecom boom that powered the global spread of the Internet. In the latter half of the 1990s, telecom companies in the U.S. laid enough new fiber-optic cable to spark a 50 percent increase in total route miles—and a thousand-fold increase in bandwidth, thanks to miraculous advances in the underlying technology. Yet demand rose only a hundred-fold in this time, creating an imbalance that led, inevitably, to a crushing shakeout: $1 trillion in lost stock-market value, $275 billion in defaulted debt, 225,000 axed jobs, dozens of dead companies and a handful of breathtakingly large bankruptcies.

As this roaring industry writhed in collapse, some of its excesses were exposed: Bernard J. Ebbers, founder of the moxie-fueled telco MCI WorldCom, oversaw, with temerity and impunity, the falsification of $11 billion in profits, a new record high in the annals of fraud. Such large-scale schemes, however, are an outgrowth of complicity and cooperation below, among dozens of smaller parts and bit players.

This book focuses on one of them, unflinchingly and unforgivingly: Walt Pavlo, an ambitious young career-climber who went too far.

In alternately gripping and fascinating detail, we watch Pavlo go from hopeful *wunderkind* to cynic to multimillion-dollar thief, at a time when it seemed like everyone was in on it—reseller scammers that ran up big bills owed to MCI and other majors; international-calling schemes; 900 numbers for phone sex and astrology readings; salesmen signing up unreliable carriers to spark bigger bonuses; and their bosses ignoring the abuses and benefiting from same. In the fraud triangle of rationalization (I'm underpaid, everyone's cheating), opportunity (lax controls) and pressure (I gotta make my numbers), chicanery and flim-flam flourish. This book offers an intimate look at how it happened in the last market boom and why, likely, it is already happening again.

—Dennis Kneale, September, 2007

 # Preface

THIS STORY FOUND ME one day in January 2002 as I was sorting through a pile of mail on my desk at *Forbes* magazine in New York's Greenwich Village. It arrived in a plain white No. 10 envelope with a return address full of numbers and acronyms from somewhere in South Carolina.

A psychiatric hospital, I guessed. Or a prison. Journalists get crank letters all the time from screwballs and jailbirds. The patients typically rant about conspiracies. The prisoners swear they are innocent victims of overzealous lawmen or treacherous, lying co-conspirators. Such gems usually end up pinned near our glass-walled meeting room, the "fish bowl," where they provide a few days of amusement before disappearing forever.

This letter was different. It was articulate to the point of clinical. But it also gave a few glimmers of the journey recounted in these pages of an ordinary person who got swept up in an extraordinary drama.

The author of the letter, Walter Pavlo, Jr., was a federal prisoner. He admitted he had embezzled $6 million but insisted his own crimes were a pittance compared to the financial shenanigans he had witnessed in the telecommunications business, including at his former employer MCI Communications—which by the time Pavlo wrote to me was part of a stumbling but still iconic company called WorldCom.

If Pavlo knew what he said he knew, and if he was willing to say it, and I could prove it was true, I'd have a chance to open a window into the engine room of a historic white-collar crime. Here was a rare chance to go eyeball-to-eyeball with a prisoner on the inside who sounded like he actually had more to say than "I was wronged." Besides, it was winter and South Carolina is a lot warmer than Manhattan.

I arranged a prison interview with Pavlo a few weeks later. During our hours together, he told me how he arrived at MCI a gung-ho MBA and was disgorged five years later a convicted felon headed for federal prison, his family fragmenting, his finances gone and his career over. My story, based on those interviews and follow-up research, was published in the June 10, 2002 edition of *Forbes* with a two-page photo of a sober, boyish Pavlo in his prison garb, and the headline "Ring of Thieves." The book you hold in your hands is the full version of that story.

From the start, Pavlo drew me in with his eagerness to describe what happened in a way that spared no one, least of all himself. Forthcoming, yet painfully ashamed of his own wrongdoing, he pulled back the corporate veil to show the morally ambiguous way the company had been run. He vividly described the intense pressure put on rank-and-file managers and workers to cut corners and fudge the books by bosses obsessed with reporting good quarterly earnings to justify the company's lofty stock price, and the value of their stock options.

His was an intensely intimate look at a subject that is usually viewed from afar through the lens of the courts. Within months of the story's publication, his tale of the accounting fraud he took part in helped drive WorldCom, and the former MCI with it, into the largest bankruptcy in history. Altogether, an estimated $2 trillion in shareholder value was squandered in the technology and telecom implosions.

I thought Pavlo's story would make a great vehicle to illustrate the wretched excesses and callous self-interest that helped inflate the biggest stock market bubble in history. But Pavlo was locked up far away, and I was busy covering Wall Street's meltdown.

Pavlo was released from prison in 2003 and came to see me in New York, in a dimly-lit booth in the back of Greenwich Village's Cedar Tavern, around the corner from *Forbes'* offices. I told him his story ought to be a book. He told me that, like a sinner seeking relief with each word of his confession, he had banged out a manuscript in prison in a single frenzied month. It was rough, but we decided to collaborate.

One of the things that excited me about Pavlo's story was how different it was from the broad-brush landscapes journalists typically churn out in books about the industries they cover. This, by contrast, was a story rich with detail and telling anecdotes about a uniquely American variety of tragedy. We wanted to present the story honestly and let readers draw their own conclusions about the players. The story itself struck me as both chilling and absurd. You can't make this stuff up, I thought. Or could you?

I conducted extensive research, interviewing perpetrators of the crimes described and their wives, plus the FBI and IRS agents who investigated, and the assistant U.S. attorney who prosecuted them. I spoke with defense lawyers, civil litigators, private investigators, accountants, analysts, and business people who played roles in this sprawling drama.

Working with Pavlo, I culled other information from thousands of pages of court transcripts, depositions, and other legal filings, company records, financial reports, and press accounts. Dialogue has been reconstructed from these sources and the memories of Pavlo and others involved. This is a true story. The names are real, except for those of Sean Hennessy, his wife Brenda, and a few other characters, as indicated in the text, who played sensitive but minor roles and have moved on with their lives.

This has been the toughest assignment of my two decades in journalism, but it has been a breeze compared with Walt Pavlo's. I have watched and prodded him as he has gone through an intense period of soul-searching to understand how he conned himself into believing he was justified in crossing the line, and how he found a way to survive the shame and guilt.

Walt has worked hard to explain himself and to repurpose his life. The FBI agent who investigated his crimes urged him to try speaking publicly about his case. Now Walt travels the country most of the year, addressing students and business people, offering insights into aspects of business culture that can make it easy for good people to make bad choices. We invite you to share the experience—without the consequences.

—Neil Weinberg
New York City, September, 2007

 # Author's Note

I N DECEMBER 2002, with four months left to serve in federal prison, I was contacted by FBI Special Agent Ray Kyle, the guy who had put me away. I braced myself. It turned out Agent Kyle had been asked by the FBI to round me up for a presentation, after a number of agents had read about my crimes in a feature story about me in *Forbes* in June, 2002.

I was wary, but appreciative that such an audience was interested in what I had to say. Not long afterward, there I was, sprung briefly from prison, and making my first appearance as a public speaker in front of four hundred FBI agents, postal inspectors, Secret Service workers and U.S. attorneys.

Since my permanent release from prison in March, 2003, I have addressed hundreds of audiences about my criminal past—at universities, professional societies, corporations, and big accounting firms. I can never thank Agent Kyle enough for the encouragement he gave me. I can only hope to repay the favor in some small measure by offering others a positive lesson to take away from my own cautionary tale.

Recounting my misdeeds on stage and in this book is a mixed bag. I am no longer the young man whose selfish and careless decisions fill these pages. Neil and I have tried to educate and entertain with this story, but I live always with the knowledge that my actions hurt others.

I've had to dredge up and relive the most painful times in my life, but in the end it's been a rewarding experience. Through a number of interviews, mostly conducted by Neil, I gained new perspectives on my own behavior. I am a better person for working with him, and for being forced to reflect and challenge myself.

It is our hope that as you read this story you will laugh where we laughed and cry where we cried, and then take away something that will illuminate your own life.

—Walter Pavlo, Jr.
Tampa, Florida, September, 2007

STOLEN
WITHOUT A GUN

# Diesel Therapy

T HE BUSINESS END of a high-powered rifle tracked Walt Pavlo as he stepped into the main courtyard of Jesup Federal Correctional Institution, in the piney flatlands of southeastern Georgia. The guard in the crow's nest of the main watchtower was alert. Forty felons, most violent and dangerous, were on the move. Alone among them, Pavlo looked up, like an out-of-towner gawking at the Manhattan skyline.

"Baby steps," Pavlo thought, recalling a Bill Murray line from "What About Bob?" He shuffled one chained foot in front of the other, trying to avoid any sudden moves that could be mistaken for aggression or resistance. His stomach growled. He'd been rousted from sleep at three in the morning and never got breakfast. It was ten o'clock. Already the August sun stung his bare arms, and with each step the shackles bit into his ankles and wrists.

The prisoners shuffled single file through several sally ports and gates, the only sounds were the slamming of heavy metal latches, the ever-present jingling of keys on the belts of the guards, and the squawk of two-way radios. Finally they arrived at the door of a battered, unmarked bus in which a heavy-gauge cage had been welded. Only the guards knew where it was headed that day, but it would be somewhere along the hub-and-spoke network known in prison lingo as Con Air.

"Inmate Pavlo, 52071 dash 019. Step fo'ward." A guard studied his clipboard without looking up.

"Yes sir."

"You the awdalee."

"Pardon?"

"You minimum security so you the awdalee. You give out the food on the bus." A guard cradling a sawed-off shotgun nodded gravely.

Pavlo finally caught on. As the sole inmate with minimum security status, he was to be the orderly, whatever that entailed.

The guard tucked the clipboard under his arm and unhooked his mass of keys to unlock Pavlo's ankle chains, then motioned for him to stand aside in the broiling heat, handcuffs bolted to a chain around his waist, as the other thirty-nine men stumbled up the steps into the bus.

Pavlo was glad to finally be moving, but nervous. Jesup had been his introduction to prison life. He had been on the minimum-security "camp" side. Inmates in the federal system are usually assigned to minimum security camps because they've pleaded guilty, have short sentences or are nearing the end of long ones, and are not violent. The Jesup camp was the same place Praise The Lord Club founder Jim Bakker had been locked up for fraud. It had no fence and no locks on the inner doors. Most of the population was black and in for drugs, with a smattering of mostly white, white-collar crooks like Pavlo. There were rarely more than two or three guards on duty, and they often played Gin Rummy with the inmates. It was all very civilized.

Camp time was the easiest a con could do, so nobody wanted to screw up. But occasionally some miscreant figured out a way to get more time than he already had. One obese, middle-aged embezzler had slunk off to the woods one night for an unapproved conjugal visit with his wife. The guards were waiting for him when he returned. They shackled and whisked him off to segregation—"The Hole"—a barren cell where he spent twenty-four hours a day awaiting a ride on Con Air to serve his new, extended sentence for escape, in a maximum security joint.

For Pavlo, the worst thing about his five months at Jesup had been the petty indignities. As a new inmate he got the worst job, washing dishes three meals a day. He shaved his head to avoid having to barter with another inmate for a haircut. He felt compelled to exaggerate his forty-one-month sentence when talking to men who were on the final legs of fifteen-year stretches. Jesup had felt a lot like middle school detention.

Now he was about to play nursemaid to thirty-nine hard-timers on a prison bus on the two-hundred-mile excursion to the massive

Edgefield prison complex in South Carolina cotton country, birthplace of Senator Strom Thurmond. Pavlo would have preferred to stay at Jesup, but he was eager to take advantage of a prison alcoholic treatment program available at Edgefield. If he completed it, he could shave twenty-four months off his sentence. That would mean returning home to his wife Rhoda and their two sons—eleven year-old Bubby and nine year-old Howie—in 2003 instead of 2005.

If he got to Edgefield at all, that is. Pavlo had heard stories of prisoners getting lost in the Con Air system for months, rotting in holding cells after being misdirected like lost mail to the wrong facilities and thrown into segregation while the Bureau of Prisons took its time sorting out the paperwork. Once you were on a prison bus, the legend went, only God knew where you'd end up. If you were lucky, you'd go straight from point "A" to point "B." If you weren't, you might find yourself touring the far-flung outposts of the federal prison system. It was common for an inmate being moved from Florida to New York to find himself in Oklahoma or Minnesota.

Sometimes the extra mileage was deliberate. Cons who refused to cooperate with investigators and testify against others, or filed too many nuisance lawsuits against the Bureau of Prisons, or caused some other trouble, were tagged for "diesel therapy," the torture of endless bus rides and prison holding cells. Diesel therapy was a way of making inmates disappear. No one outside the system knew where these men were. What mattered was they couldn't cause any trouble, and had lots of time to contemplate whether they might be willing to become state's witnesses or otherwise modify their behavior.

So Pavlo boarded the bus when it was his turn, praying that his paperwork was in good order, and nobody had marked him for diesel therapy. As he reached the top step his nose filled with the odors of shit and sweat.

One of the guards unlocked his handcuffs. Pavlo rubbed his chafed wrists and took the seat the guard pointed to, just inside the cage that separated the prisoners from the driver and guard. The other inmates chattered loudly behind him. Some were being moved for having beaten the hell out of one too many fellow inmates, or having been beaten up too often, or because they'd managed to scam the prison medical officers into believing they needed a change of scenery because of asthma attacks or migraines or some other excuse.

In the business world Pavlo had left behind, his youthful good looks and blond hair had given him an edge. In prison, it made him feel like a three-legged deer listening to the howl of a wolf pack. Several of his fellow travelers had been "bagged," meaning they were so prone to violence their hands had not only been cuffed and shackled to their waists but also covered with padding.

The guard slammed shut the cage door and bolted it with a padlock the size of an ax head. Then they sat there for an hour in the stifling heat and stench while the guards racked up some more overtime. Pavlo was lucky. At least he could wipe the sweat running down his face without his handcuffs digging into his wrists. Finally, the driver cranked the engine and the bus eased out onto Highway 301.

"Souf! We goin' souf!" an inmate called out.

"That mean Tallahassee," a voice answered.

"Shit, yeah!"

Pavlo turned to survey the rows of bobbing heads. For many of them, the trip was a major life event. Some hadn't seen the outside of Jesup since the forty-foot pines whizzing past had been saplings. To Pavlo, the speculation was deflating. Tallahassee was a day's ride in the wrong direction. He sighed and stared out the window at the fields of peanuts and dusty side roads as the bus wended its way through southern Georgia and crossed the border into the Florida panhandle. Everyone perked up when the bus pulled in at a couple of county jails to pick up new residents of the federal prison system.

Pavlo had dozed off later when an angry voice startled him awake.

"Awdalee! We starvin' back here. Awdalee! Yo. White muthafuckah!" Pavlo turned and looked into the scowling face of one of the inmates. "I'm talkin' to you, asshole!"

Pavlo cast a questioning glance at the guard outside the cage.

"Men must be hungry," the guard said, fishing a French fry from the bag he'd picked up at Wendy's a few miles back. "The smell don't help much. Food's in back." He jerked his thumb toward the rear of the bus.

Pavlo stumbled, swaying, down the aisle between the men to the back of the bus where the stench was even more intense. The source was a plywood plank in the floor with a hole cut in the middle and human waste sloshing around in a tank below. Right next to the splashing sewage sat a water dispenser, a stack of Dixie cups, and two cardboard boxes of Oscar Mayer Lunchables, the same snacks Pavlo had lovingly packed in his sons' school bags in his old life.

The men began shouting their preferences to Pavlo: Cracker Stacker or Fun Fuel. To avoid getting into a debate with anyone, he ripped the covers off the packages before handing them over. Then he walked down the aisle balancing a stack of the boxes and handing them out. "Steak or fish?" he joked. The inmates with bagged hands couldn't hold anything so he had to feed them by hand like a keeper at the zoo. They didn't like it any better than Pavlo–they wolfed down the food in two or three bites.

After he'd handed a Lunchable to everyone else, Pavlo was ready to sit back down and satisfy his own hunger.

"Ain't got no goddamn food!" said the inmate seated just in front of the toilet. His hands bagged, he gave Pavlo a mad-dog look. "Gimme that goddamn food!"

Pavlo returned to the back of the bus. "You already got one. See?" He pointed to a crushed container under the inmate's foot.

"That shit ain't mine. Mine's right there," the man said gesturing with his chin at the box in Pavlo's hand. Pavlo hadn't eaten in almost twenty-four hours. He weighed his gnawing hunger against the risk that if he didn't give in, the guy might catch him in an unguarded moment in a dingy lockup and…?

Pavlo sighed and placed the meal on the bagged hands of his tormentor, who crouched over and wedged the box between his mouth and the padding and tore into it with his teeth, like a jackal.

"Git'cho ass outta here, muthafuckah. Tryin' ta cheat me outta my lunch 'n shit."

"It's not lunch 'n shit," Pavlo replied, defeated but feisty. "It's Lunch a ble." Then he retreated to his seat to settle for a sip of luke-warm water.

"Got ennymore Lunchables?" asked the inmate across the aisle.

Pavlo shook his head. "All gone."

"Figures. I'm Coco. Who you?"

"Pavlo."

"No way to shake," Coco said, jutting his chin toward his bagged hands. "Wha'chu in fo?"

"Stealing money," Pavlo said, opting for the short answer. The full answer, that he had embezzled $6 million in accounts receivable from his former employer, MCI Communications, would have required much more explaining than he had the stomach for, and mark him as that much more of a freak in Coco's eyes.

Pavlo was now a citizen of a world as foreign to him as any

he could have imagined. As bad as it was, the worst part was knowing what it was putting his family through. When his wife and sons had visited him back at Jesup, the guards had searched their bags and treated them like inmates before they were allowed in to sit and wait for him at a Formica table in a barren, soul-less cafeteria. He would arrive in his green shirt and pants and try to put on a good face, telling absurd prison tales that often fell flat under the circumstances. Rhoda would prompt the boys to talk about their school activities and she'd fill him in on family gossip. Pavlo felt like a spectator in his own family's world. After such visits, he would be depressed for days.

Now he was on the road and wondered when he would ever see Rhoda and the boys again. He'd never felt so alone and disconnected from the world.

Prisoners in transit were allowed one five-minute phone call every three days. Pavlo dialed home twice from Tallahassee, but nobody answered. Calls had to be placed collect, so it wasn't possible even to leave a message. It was almost a relief. The only thing worse than isolation from his family was the frustration of such short, truncated conversations.

A week after he arrived in Tallahassee, Pavlo was awakened by a guard around 2:00 a.m. He was moved to the processing area, stripped, ordered to lean his hands against the wall and spread his legs for a body search. Then he was told to put on an orange jumpsuit, shackled and left standing around for seven hours before loading onto a bus. No special "awdalee" dispensation this time. He was just another one of the brothers. The white sheep of the family.

"Edge-feel," an inmate shouted as soon as the bus turned north. Pavlo heaved a sigh of relief.

"Heeell no," said another. "Et-lanna." Other heads nodded. Pavlo's spirits sank.

He tried to limit his motions but the bumping of the bus and the need to keep blood circulating caused his restraints to slowly ratchet tighter. By the time they arrived in Atlanta ten hours later his wrists were bruised and his ankles swollen.

"Dis da prison?" a young inmate asked. "My momma toll me it da capitol." A nervous laugh rose from the prisoners.

Built in 1900, the Big A, as the maximum-security United States Penitentiary in Atlanta was known, looked every inch the hell-hole it was reputed to be. It had housed Al Capone and been spattered with blood during the 1987 Cuban prison riots. An inner graveyard held unclaimed residents.

The bus turned into a cavernous underground garage, and the guards ordered the men into rows five across and eight deep. They were marched into a massive freight elevator. Pavlo's hands trembled. He clasped them and silently recited as much of the Lord's Prayer as he could remember from Catholic school. Tears ran down his cheeks. He tried to dry them on his shoulders since his hands were chained to his waist.

When Pavlo got to the processing unit a guard unshackled him. Blood trickled back into his hands and feet. He was led to a cubicle where a young woman in a Bureau of Prisons uniform waited.

"Name?"

"Walter A. Pavlo, Junior."

"Number?"

"52071 dash 019."

"Got AIDS?"

"No."

"Heart problems?"

"No."

"Taking illegal drugs?"

"That's a tricky one," he said.

"Yes or no?"

"No."

"Cooperating with the government?"

The question caught him off guard. He was cooperating with the government. But wouldn't the government know that? "Why do you ask?"

"Fo' yo' safety," the guard said as if he had insulted her intelligence. "Guys 'roun heah don't look kindly on snitches. If you is one, we pu'chu behind the glass. Separate from the othas."

"I'm not a snitch," he said. By prison standards he actually was but in his own eyes he was just a guy doing what he had to do to get back to his family. He remembered an ode to betrayal some daring inmate had scrawled on a wall back at Jesup.

> *Call me a snitch,*
> *Call me a rat,*
> *But call me at home,*
> *'Cause that's where I'm at.*

"No cooperation here," Pavlo said.

"Next!"

Pavlo spent the next eleven days in a cell with an inmate named Carlos who was on his way home from seventeen years in Leavenworth. Pavlo was then once again awoken by a guard in the middle of the night. He bid his cellmate a quick goodbye and stepped over another prisoner who overnight had been assigned to a blow-up mattress, known as a canoe, on the floor of the cramped cell.

Finally, after three weeks in transit, Pavlo pulled up to Edgefield Federal Correctional Institution around sunset. He was processed, sent to the "camp" side of the sprawling complex, and assigned "waterfront property," near the latrines. His first order of business was to find the phone bank and call home. "Please, please, somebody be home," he murmured.

The line clicked open and a child's voice piped, "Hello." It was Howie, Pavlo's nine year-old.

"This call is from a federal prison facility. Press one to accept the call or five to block it," a pre-recorded message interrupted.

"Dad?" Howie's voice was shaky. Pavlo felt a rush of emotion. "Howie?"

"Is it really you, dad?" Then his voice dissolved into sobs. Pavlo could hear the phone clattering, like it had been dropped.

He could hear Rhoda's voice in the tinny distance. "Is that your dad? Oh my God. Gimme the phone!" Then she was there, right in his ear. "Walt? Where are you?"

"Edgefield," he said, starting to cry. "Almost home."

 **Big Time**

WALT PAVLO'S SPIRITS soared as he cruised down Interstate 85 in his Honda Civic toward his new job in Atlanta. He checked himself in the rear-view mirror and liked what he saw–a full head of blond hair, freshly trimmed, his new red silk tie laying flat against his starched white shirt. He might not be a millionaire when he turned thirty next year, but he had arrived on the corporate scene.

He had been hired into a very sexy business by a major player: MCI Communications. William McGowan had bought into Microwave Communications of America, as MCI was originally known, in 1968 with a vision to use the fledgling provider of two way truck radios to build a nationwide long-distance telephone company. To do it, McGowan, a Harvard MBA, set up shop at 1801 Pennsylvania Avenue in Washington, D.C. and created what by his own account was "a law firm with an antenna on the roof."[1]

The venture was so dicey, and MCI came so close to bankruptcy, that on one occasion even its copy machines were repossessed. In the end, McGowan won the battle in the court room, convincing Judge Harold Greene that AT&T no longer deserved special treatment and protection as a public utility. McGowan went down in history as the David who brought down the telecommunications Goliath when Ma Bell was broken up in 1984 into a long-distance company, AT&T, and several regional bells.

Then he rode the wave, enjoying his cult status as an innovator and loading MCI up with a mountain of debt, courtesy of junk-bond king Michael Milken. That allowed it to consistently undercut AT&T on rates, and to invest in costly infrastructure like fiber optics and switching stations.

Salesmanship coursed through McGowan's veins. Early in his career, before MCI caught his eye, he was pitching shark repellent to the Navy to protect downed pilots when his product began attracting the beasts. Without missing a beat, he began selling the brass on why the Navy needed a shark aphrodisiac.[2] Under his direction, the sales-driven MCI helped build long-distance market share with compensation that was sometimes 100 percent commission-driven[3] and customer loyalty with clever promotions. One pitched free Mother's Day calls with the tag line "Give mom a priceless ring."

Under McGowan, employees were expected to work long, punishing hours, be superlative and innovative sales people, and play as hard as they worked. If you wanted to be where the action was in the new world of communication, MCI was it.

By 1992, MCI was an established upstart with about 15 percent of the long-distance market and revenues of $11 billion. As Pavlo arrived for work that July, the company's four-month-old "Friends & Family" calling plan was luring half a million households a month from AT&T and Sprint.[4] Its stock price had doubled to around $20 in the previous two years, outdoing even its own 27 percent average return during the 17 years since its original listing.[5]

The morning Pavlo had reported for work at MCI, he had carefully tucked into his new leather binder, now sitting on the passenger seat, the letter he'd received offering him $43,000 a year to be a manager in the company's Financial Services unit. At that pay, it wouldn't be long before he had the down payment to finally replace the old Honda with something new and sporty. Pavlo was feeling good.

The only imperfection seemed to be the department that had hired him—Financial Services. Accounts receivable, credit, and collections for the Southeast. He was going to be a bill collector. It wasn't sexy like sales and marketing, but he figured it was worthwhile for the money and the recognition factor on his resume. Manager I, Financial Services for MCI, had the ring of crystal and fine china.

Pavlo arrived at Ravinia, the suburban-Atlanta office park where several thousand MCI workers toiled in a sprawling pagoda-like complex. He entered the seven-story tropical atrium and took the elevator to MCI's second floor lobby. Next to the reception desk, a ticker flashed the company stock price. A photo of Bill McGowan sat on a table surrounded by flowers. MCI's visionary leader had collapsed and died of a heart attack a month earlier.[6]

Bert Roberts, Jr. was the new man at the helm. A low-key engineer, he lacked McGowan's charisma. But Pavlo wouldn't have known either man had they walked up to him and shook his hand. Pavlo announced himself to the receptionist and waited nervously for Ralph McCumber, his new boss, to come and greet him. All the other people arriving for work were crisply-dressed and moved with purpose. They looked like they were eager to get to work, and Pavlo was glad to be one of them now.

McCumber appeared promptly, his sleeves already rolled up even though it was only 8 o'clock. McCumber's thick body moved with a certain grace and authority. A Naval Academy graduate, he'd done a tour in Vietnam as executive officer aboard a 31-foot river patrol boat. He still wore his hair close, and his graying sideburns and mustache were trimmed and symmetrical.

McCumber had risen through the ranks to become a Commander and even briefed the Joint Chiefs. He'd given twenty years to the service and now, entering his fifties, MCI had become his second career.

"Welcome to MCI," McCumber said, extending a hand.

"It's an honor to be here, sir."

"Sorry I wasn't here to meet you, but some son-of-a-bitch carrier went bust owing us a million in unpaid LD."

"LD?"

"Long-distance," McCumber explained. "What, for public consumption, we refer to as our esteemed carrier clientele is actually a snake pit of thieves. The bastards collect money from their own customers, run up big tabs on our network and then head for the door like sorority sisters skipping out on the bar bill. You're gonna love it. I'll show you to the elevator. Wendy can introduce you to your people. She's your executive assistant. We'll reconvene in the cafeteria at..." he looked at his watch "...eleven-hundred hours. That's eleven o'clock to you civvies."

Pavlo found his new office at the end of a maze of desks at which some two dozen clerks sat surrounded by piles of paperwork. In one corner sat a half-dozen shared computers. This looked nothing like the gleaming conference rooms where Pavlo had been interviewed.

His assistant, Wendy, young, attractive and professionally dressed like everyone else around them, showed him to his office. The fake oak furniture was a step up from the scarred metal desk he had manned at GEC Avionics. Best of all, he had a window that overlooked Ravinia's inner gardens. Pavlo eased the door shut, sat down, and put his feet on the corner of the desk.

He allowed himself a moment to enjoy a sense of having arrived. The son of a steel worker and stay-home mom, Pavlo grew up in Savannah, Georgia and Parkersburg, West Virginia. After high school, he'd earned an engineering degree from West Virginia University in 1985, more through grit than aptitude, and then landed a job with Goodyear Aerospace in Akron, Ohio. That's where he met Rhoda Voth, a fellow industrial engineer and his future wife, while working on the Pershing II missile, jet simulator, and counter-munitions projects during the Reagan military buildup.

When the couple started dating in 1986, Pavlo could hardly believe that the athletically slim blonde beauty from a wealthy Ohio family would have given him the time of day. They were married in the Voth family's Lutheran church the following August.

When Goodyear Aerospace ran into financial trouble, Pavlo convinced Rhoda to move back South and they landed in Atlanta in the spring of 1988. He found a job at GEC Avionics and Rhoda worked as a healthcare consultant for Touche, Ross & Co., traveling nonstop every week. Pavlo filled his free evenings with night school classes and earned an MBA from Mercer University.

Their first child, Walter Pavlo, III—"Bubby"—was born in January, 1990. Rhoda quit her job and they had to cut back on some of the extras they had enjoyed as a two-income family. Less than two years later, Rhoda gave birth to their second son, Howard, and Pavlo's $35,000 salary was barely enough to pay the bills. An old Voth family friend introduced him to MCI in Atlanta and his new career in telecom.

A determination to work hard, rise fast and provide everything Rhoda and their two young sons could desire was Pavlo's driving force when he arrived precisely at eleven o'clock in front of the Masters Café at Ravinia. With original art work on the walls and understated lighting, it was several cuts above the standard corporate chow line. McCumber walked up a moment later. They filled their trays from a U-shaped assortment of kiosks, paid and sat down.

"Nice choice of ethnic foods you have here," Pavlo said.

"We inmates would probably riot if they didn't give us some variety out here in office park purgatory," McCumber said, methodically demolishing a pile of refried beans.

"The sushi bar reminds me of some of the stuff I had to hold down when clients took me out for dinner in Seoul," Pavlo said. He thought it would help to remind his new boss he was a seasoned executive.

"You wanna talk exotic?" McCumber asked. "I was on river patrol in Nam back in sixty-seven. One day we found a body on the riverbank. This big Komodo dragon was making a meal of what was left. I blew away that sorry-ass lizard with one shot. Then two of the South Vietnamese soldiers chopped off its tail. Thing fed fifteen."

"What did it taste like? Chicken?"

"Hell, no! I could barely hold it down. Surprised me, too, considering what those people can usually whip up in a pinch."

McCumber wiped his mouth with a napkin. A chill ran through Pavlo's body.

"Look, Walt. This carrier finance stuff is pretty simple. If every one of us big phone companies laid fiber to haul calls to every corner of the country, we'd all be bankrupt and the U.S. would be one big construction trench. So we use the other guys' networks in some places and they use ours in others. Our job is to track what they use and make sure MCI gets paid."

"Sounds pretty straightforward."

"The problem," McCumber continued, leaning in and lowering his voice, "is that our Friends & Family commercials aren't going to fill the network so we wholesale to competitors. I know it sounds screwy, but these guys can bring in serious numbers of minutes. The problem is they discount like hell, push down prices and cannibalize our business."

"So why does MCI do it?"

"If we don't, AT&T and Sprint will," McCumber said, chuckling. "For you and me the trouble comes when Sales recruits dirt-bags for customers. We're the ones who have to make 'em pay."

"Like who?"

"Dial-a-porn guys. Psychics. Dating services. Basic scum-of-the-earth long-distance carriers."

"Carriers don't pay other carriers?"

"I'm not talking about the big boys. They game the system too, but it's the three hundred you've never heard of that cause us to shit bricks. Most don't do a damn thing but run traffic over our network and slap their names on bills. The arcades are the worst."

"What're they?"

"Telecom's equivalent of crack houses," McCumber said. "They rent a line in a slum somewhere and charge a bunch of bastards too poor to own phones obscene rates to make calls. Their over-nineties can be killers."

"What's that?"

"Debts owed MCI that're over ninety days past due. The way we track debt is current, meaning less than thirty days outstanding. Thirty-one to sixty days get caution flags. Sixty to ninety days past due are trouble. Over-nineties are mostly dead meat."

"So what do you do about them?"

"Squeeze their balls as hard as we can. We're managing about $250 million that these guys owe us at any given time. This year we won't collect ten or fifteen million of it. That's tolerable. My fear is the way Sales is going at some point we'll have so many fly-by-nights on the network the figure will blow sky high. I must've warned management a hundred times."

Pavlo couldn't imagine a business where a $10 million dollar write-off would be good news. "What're your bosses doing?"

"Praying like hell we keep collecting and sending Sales out to drum up more of these bums," McCumber said. "First rule of Carrier Finance. Never believe a word a carrier tells you. The second rule is never believe a syllable that comes out the puke-hole of an MCI Sales rep."

The debris on his tray neatly organized, McCumber got up to leave. "Those Sales sons-of-bitches know one thing. Sign up new customers and collect their fat-ass commissions. After that, they're on to their next golf outing or some special goddamn bonus for sucking up to their bosses or they're gone. Turnover in Sales is huge. Chasing down the lowlifes they sign up is our problem. Welcome to Carrier Finance."

Shady customers. Corporate intrigue. A reptile-eating boss who could cuss like a truck driver. Maybe collections wouldn't be so dull after all.

"We'll go over your duties in detail at seven tomorrow morning."

"Yes sir."

"Another thing," McCumber said turning back. "Enough with the 'sir' stuff. This isn't the service. Ralph is fine."

"Okay, Ralph."

"I think you're gonna like this job. It's hard, but it's a great proving ground. You make it in Carrier Finance, you can hack it anywhere at MCI. And, as I told you in our first interview. I'm not planning to stick around forever."

Pavlo returned to his office filled with enthusiasm and purpose. He'd landed a big raise, joined a prestigious high-tech outfit, had a boss who was looking out for him, and he had a wonderful young family. He was living the American dream. Everything was going his way.

 # Reach Out and Touch Yourself

THE FIRST TIME he heard the word "audiotext," Pavlo thought it sounded like the term to describe a radio script for a show like *A Prairie Home Companion*. Instead, it was the euphemism in the phone business for the burgeoning traffic in phone sex, astrology, racing results, for-profit evangelism, personals, and sports scores. One company that did it all went by the generic-sounding name Telephone Publishing Corp., or TPC. Based in Marietta, Georgia, part of Atlanta's sprawl, it was the first MCI carrier client Pavlo visited.

Audiotext began to boom in the 1980s, but it actually got its start in 1927 when New Jersey Bell first offered callers the exact time of day. In the beginning, live operators—always women—answered the phones and announced the time. But sex was on the minds of many male callers, so the company instructed its operators to mimic the recorded messages that were just coming on the scene, so they wouldn't spend their shifts fending off propositions.

AT&T offered the first long-distance audiotext service in the early 1980s to poll TV viewers, using the 900 prefix to distinguish it from toll-free 800 service. Callers paid fifty cents each to vote on everything from who won the Reagan-Carter debate to whether Saturday Night Live's Eddie Murphy should boil Larry the Lobster.[1]

Following the break-up of AT&T, MCI and Sprint got into the business. In 1988, 900 audiotext calls generated an estimated $2.5 billion in revenue.[2] Even President George H.W. Bush got in the act, appearing in an ad urging viewers to call a 900 number to make contributions to the USO.[3]

The big telephone carriers hated much of the content—sex chat, psychics, and so on—but loved the money. Some companies adopted policies against carrying sexually explicit conversations and other questionable services. But the allure of big commissions and the ability of the customers to cloak themselves from detection, or in the First Amendment, made it hard to keep them out. AT&T went so far as to open an office in Chicago and staff it with employees assigned to leaf through skin magazines looking for dial-a-porn ads, then check whether they matched any of the numbers it rented out.[4] MCI ran a similar operation out of Tysons Corner, Virginia, but it was an open secret among Sales and Finance that the ban on sex chat and other lowbrow content was porous.

As Pavlo pulled into TPC's parking lot, a stocky guy in a crew cut who also looked around thirty was exiting a Mercedes 500 SE big enough to fit Pavlo's Honda in its trunk.

"Walter Pavlo?"

"Yeah."

"Harold Mann."

"Glad to meet you." They shook hands.

"Boy, are they gonna be surprised to see me this early," Mann said, checking his Rolex watch. It was two o'clock in the afternoon. Pavlo had been working for six hours. He wondered if Mann worked nights, or was just making so much money he didn't have to show up on time.

Pavlo learned on the way into the building that Mann was a Toronto native—Canada was "back home"—and he spent his summers there vacationing on a lake. Mann had gotten his start in telecom working for a Toronto phone-sex company called Denmark Dial. He had moved his family to Atlanta two years earlier, in 1990, set up TPC plus a number of other firms and was making a fortune handling sex chat, the North Dakota fishing license lottery, and fundraising for the likes of white supremacist David Duke.[5]

Mann fancied himself the architect of a vast, vertically integrated pornography empire that one day would turn him into an industry icon, like Hugh Hefner or, better yet, Larry Flynt.

"Hey, Wally," he said in the elevator on the way up. "You know how AT&T tells callers to 'Reach out and touch someone'?" Nobody ever called Pavlo "Wally."

"Yeah."

"What does MCI tell them to do?"

"Reach out and touch someone for less."

"Bingo. And my company?" Mann asked

"I haven't got any idea."

"Reach out and touch yourself!' Pretty snappy, eh?"

"Brilliant."

The elevator delivered them into a sprawling climate-controlled call center. There, dozens of TPC customer service reps worked the phones and the customers for minimum wage. Walking down an aisle, Pavlo caught a snippet of conversation.

"My name is Bambi. I'm five-foot-two, petite, and I like it rough," a heavy woman giggled into a headset.

"Check this out," Mann said, motioning Pavlo toward a thin middle-aged man in glasses.

"You sound like the man of my dreams, George," the guy was saying. "Are you as big and strong as you sound?"

Nearby sat a pale, twenty-something girl with a backpack and college literature anthology propped on her desk. "This mojo stuff is one of our top sellers," Mann beamed.

"I see danja in you future, my love," the woman told a caller in a feeble attempt at West Indian patois. "Crush dee chicken bones into dee fine powda an bury dem..."

"Ain't this a great business?" Mann gushed as he marched Pavlo to a door marked "Harold." Inside, a crystal chandelier hung above over-stuffed white leather couches. A wet bar sported a dozen decanters with engraved silver pendants identifying the booze inside. Mann's desk, big as a king-sized bed, was bare except for family photos and a phone.

The speakerphone crackled to life. "Harold. I've got Hustler on one. You gonna take it?" Gloria, Mann's motherly, chain-smoking secretary, asked via speakerphone.

"You mind?" he asked Pavlo.

"No. Go ahead."

Mann punched a button and put the call on speaker. "How's it going, Harold?" a male voiced said.

"Goin' great," Mann said. "Everything's according to plan. Except that Asian ad you ran for me last month. I know the knockers over there aren't the biggest. But damn, they look like that old Japanese saying. You know, two raisins on a cutting board. Can't you enhance that little lady's mammalian protuberances with an air brush or something?"

"Not a problem, Harold. Your fetish is our command."

"It's not my fetish. But it does bring in the business, eh?"

"I hear ya, Harold."

Pavlo was fascinated. Here was the secret of MCI's most profitable business, lonely men dialing numbers like 1-900-GET-SOME for a few minutes of imagined pleasure. The way it worked was the call was picked up by the regional Bell company switching station which recognized it by a Carrier Identification Code, or CIC, assigned to MCI, in this case 022. The call was then routed over MCI's network to one of its 50 or so 900-line clients.

The law required that the caller be forewarned that there would be a per-minute charge, usually two-to-five dollars a minute. Then the call was routed to a "phone mate." The average caller would have his "needs" fulfilled in about eight minutes, generating a charge on his next phone bill of perhaps $24.

When Mr. Lonelyheart paid his Bell company bill, the local phone company got to keep a dollar for its trouble, passing on the rest to MCI, which charged 15 cents a minute for long-distance service and another $2 or so for billing and collections. That left companies like Mann's TPC between $15 and $20 a call to cover Bambi, office rent, and Mann's high life. The problem for many of these 900-call startups was that it took the Bell companies ninety days or more to fork over their share. Many a porn kingpin had gone bust waiting for the cash to arrive.

Mann had figured out how to reverse the food chain so he got paid first. He did it by turning to the independent financing companies that had started springing up to cut into the big long-distance carriers' lucrative billing and collections businesses. The lenders enabled Mann to "factor" some of the money he was due. That meant an outside lender known as a factor would calculate how much TPC was owed by its callers and lend it 80 percent or so of those so-called receivables. When the cash eventually rolled in from TPC's callers, the factor got back its principal plus interest income that pushed the outside of the usury-law envelope. To Mann, it was worth the high finance cost to generate immediate cash flow.

By the time Pavlo showed up in 1992, Mann's revenues were running about $5 million a month on long-distance calls that cost him $600,000 to deliver over MCI's network. Pavlo figured that even after paying his phone mates and other overhead, Mann had to be clearing $20 million a year.

But there was a problem. When Mann started financing his

receivables elsewhere, he stopped paying MCI on time. Pavlo's mission that day was to find a solution.

"Quite an operation you have here," he said.

"Pays the bills, eh?"

"Except for your long distance. You know that your account is about $300,000 past due?"

Mann started leafing through a pile of messages Gloria had left on his desk.

"C'mon, Wally. You haven't even kissed me yet and you're asking for money!" Mann said, grinning. "You know as well as I do this business generates a shitload of cash, but it flows like molasses in January. I can only factor so much of it. I need terms, Wally. Gimme terms!"

"Terms?"

"Hell yeah. A discount. A reprieve. Something."

"Look Harold, I'm just trying to keep you off MCI's watch list," Pavlo said. "The last thing either of us want is for my bosses to insist on limiting your usage."

"Wally, Wally, Wally. You think I give two shits about bein' watched by MCI's bean-counters? I've had a damn TV crew following me around trying to wreck my business. I had to put a friggin' bag on my head to walk to my car. Goes with the turf."

"Look, I need a payment. You know what'll happen if I hightail it back to my boss empty-handed?"

"What? He's gonna cut me off?" Mann asked, feigning concern by clutching his chest with his hand. "That would force me to switch carriers and take at least a phone call."

"You signed a contract."

"So sue me. You can take a number and get in line. TPC doesn't have any assets. If it flies, fucks or floats, I lease it."

Pavlo felt at a loss for what to do. The last thing he'd expected was for Mann to laugh off his threats. "I really don't want to get into a pissing match with you, Harold. I've got lots of customers plenty worse than you but you're right here in our backyard. Work with me, okay?"

"How old are you, Wally?" Mann asked, grabbing a Blow Pop from his desk drawer.

"Twenty-nine."

"I'm thirty-two so we're the same generation. We both have jobs to do. Mine is to run TPC. Yours is to collect MCI's money. Since we're both consenting adults, here's what I'm gonna do." Mann leaned forward and hit a button on his phone. "Dave?"

A reply came by speaker phone. "Yeah."

"I've got a Mr. Pavlo here from MCI. Cut them a $100,000 check and bring it down here, eh?"

"Sure, Harold."

"This is to break the ice," Mann said. "You golf?"

"Now and then."

"Great. We'll go out soon."

David Wickett, a short, thirtyish geek who looked ten years younger and had no need for a razor, walked through the office door.

"Dave, this is Wally. Wally, meet my chief financial officer, Dave."

Pavlo shook the guy's hand.

Wickett handed him the check for $100,000 and left.

"There, now! You won't have to face your boss empty-handed," Mann said expansively. He walked Pavlo out of the building while continuing to sell him on the limitless potential of the tele-porn business.

"Where's your car?"

"There," Pavlo said, pointing to his Civic.

"Mmm. Must get great mileage," Mann said.

"Can't beat a Honda."

"No?"

"I'm thinking of trading it in," Pavlo said, feeling a little defensive.

"My advice is go for the absolute biggest, most expensive car the dealer will let you drive off the lot," Mann said. "That way, if you fall behind on the payments it's his problem, not yours."

Pavlo pulled out onto the highway, amazed at how Mann had maneuvered him from the $300,000 McCumber had sent him for down to $100,000. At least he still had his pants on, which was more than most of Mann's customers could say.

Biting Heads Off Chickens

I T TOOK PAVLO less than three months to become McCumber's first lieutenant. He did it by proving himself more than a good soldier. He made a habit of getting up at 4:30 every morning, quietly padding around the dark house, and pulling the front door closed behind him with his thumb on the latch to avoid waking Rhoda or the boys. Then he drove the short distance to Ravinia's empty parking lot and started his work day at 5:30. He'd have preferred to stay and have a few minutes with the boys before work but it felt like a small price when weighed against the advantage it gave him over his colleagues, and the impression it made on McCumber.

Each morning at 7:30, the two men sat at a conference table and pored over the latest traffic data reports, trolling for potential problem accounts–customers whose call volumes were spiking out of the normal range and those who were late paying their bills. The goals, set by higher-ups to measure performance and determine compensation: keep accounts that were ninety or more days late under seven percent of total receivables and bad debt write-offs under two percent.[1]

One day at the end of September 1992, on Pavlo's thirtieth birthday, McCumber began their daily ritual by saying, "You've really caught on. How long you been here? Half a year?"

Pavlo beamed with pride. "Almost three months."

"That so? Jeez, you wouldn't know it. Don't get me wrong. There're things you need to work on. But you're a fast tracker. I'm promoting you to Manager II, effective immediately."

"Thanks." Pavlo felt a blush coming on.

"Shit! You're grinning like a Navy plebe about to go on leave,"

McCumber said. "Questions?"

"No sir." Pavlo was as happy as a dog with two tails.

"The promotion means you're getting bumped up to forty-five thousand, but you probably knew that. Okay, enough pep talk. We've got work to do. Tell me about this one here, LCI. Their over-nineties are way up."

"Sales said they want to get with Brian Thompson, the chief executive, before we do," Pavlo said. Thompson was a former MCI executive vice president,[2] so Pavlo assumed there was a political issue.

McCumber looked left and right, then back at Pavlo. "Funny, I don't see anyone around here from Sales who looks like your boss. Am I missing something?"

"No sir," Pavlo said defensively.

"Okay, then you can call that son-of-a-bitch Thompson and tell him to wire us a good-faith payment today if he wants to hear a dial tone after five o'clock."

"Roger that."

They spent another half-hour parsing the sheets and then McCumber stretched and invited Pavlo outside for a smoke. Pavlo had never before taken more than a puff here and there in high school, but face time with the boss couldn't hurt, and Pavlo sensed McCumber might have something on his mind.

They rode the elevator down to the Japanese-style garden that Ravinia's builders had created by bulldozing the E.S. "Red" Spruill family farm. It was crowded with smokers exiled from their offices.

McCumber lit up a Now 100, exhaled a long, satisfying cloud of blue smoke and announced, "Management's reorganizing. We've been ordered to transfer our national accounts to Washington and Cedar Rapids."

Pavlo was stunned. It sounded like bad news. "What'll we handle then?"

"Carriers. Resellers. The 900 guys. All that shit from all over the country."

Christ, Pavlo thought. National accounts were the crown jewels of Business Services, the half of MCI that handled non-consumer operations. They were mostly major corporations like American Express, General Electric and IBM—blue chip companies that always paid their bills, millions of dollars a month, like clockwork.

Carriers, on the other hand, were a crapshoot. The biggest ones were MCI's archrivals, AT&T and Sprint. They were forever fighting over who owed what to whom for using one another's networks. The forced nature of their alliances was aggravated by MCI's antiquated billing systems. There was plenty to argue about.

The upstarts—the next rung down the food chain—were an even bigger pain. Most were just marketing outfits that resold MCI's long-distance capacity at retail—to small customers—and thus were responsible for hundreds of connect and disconnect orders a day. They were high-maintenance accounts.

Most were relatively small. Long-Distance Discount Service, known as LDDS, and from late 1994 as WorldCom, was among the biggest at $15 million a month in MCI billings. The concept for the company had been dreamed up in a Days Inn coffee shop in Hattiesburg, Mississippi by a former milk man and high school sports coach named Bernie Ebbers. Ebbers had a reputation for hardheadedness. He had fought with McCumber often over billing and collections, and the LDDS chief had threatened to take his business elsewhere unless Pavlo's boss was taken off his account. By 1992, the two had settled into an uneasy détente.

While McCumber was trying to keep MCI's customers honest and its cash flowing, the Sales people were, to Pavlo's eyes, giving away the store. MCI's phenomenal revenue growth had propelled the price of its stock, pleasing Wall Street and enriching MCI executives who had been granted stock and options as part of their compensation.

Some of the fastest growth was coming from resellers like Ebbers' acquisitive company, and that meant swelling commissions for the sales people. So the Carrier Sales department was encouraged to do whatever it took to land and hold on to these accounts. The reps handling these resellers were rumored to be taking home seven-figure paychecks, with some as big as that of MCI chief executive, Bert Roberts. The company made sure the reps knew how much they were appreciated by throwing lavish affairs for top producers where Tim Price, MCI Sales' chief, would address the troops like a sweaty televangelist stoking the fire in everyone's belly.

Sales, in turn, pulled out all the stops to get everyone and anyone they could on the network, porn touts, psychics, and other boiler-room operations included. Nobody knew the risks of easy credit better than McCumber, which, Pavlo realized, was why the carriers were being dumped on him, and why the easy money, the nationals, were being pulled. Pavlo wondered what this would do to their bad debt ratios and receivables over ninety days past due. Without the nationals, the numbers were bound to jump and that would look bad to somebody upstairs.

"Taking over carriers sounds like a beast."

McCumber nodded. "Screw up and it could cost us our jobs. Speaking of which, we need to do a RIF." He flicked the ash from his cigarette into a potted plant.

"What's a RIF?"

"A Reduction In Force under Termination Code 40 of MCI's Human Resources Manual," McCumber rattled off. "We fire people in the fall to save a few months' salary, then re-hire in January. It's an annual ritual around here so MCI can make its year-end earnings numbers and clear out the dead wood."

"How do the RIFs affect us?" Pavlo felt a twinge of anxiety.

"I just got off the phone with Doug Maine, MCI's CFO. He told me we're fine."

Phew! Pavlo thought. He liked the sound of that "we."

"All we need to do is let one person go." McCumber dropped his cigarette on the walkway and stepped on it. Then he picked up the butt and dropped it in a trash can. "A sacrificial RIF for the reorg." He turned and gave Pavlo a direct look. "Who's it gonna be?"

Eslene, one of the bookkeeping clerks, popped into Pavlo's head. She'd been struggling to keep up with her work. She suffered from vertigo and had been visibly wobbly around the office, and sometimes too dizzy to do her job. But Pavlo liked Eslene. She was fiftyish, easy to get along with, always pleasant. It'd be cruel to can her just because…

With a slight flourish, McCumber looked at his watch.

Pavlo sighed. "Eslene?"

McCumber grinned. "Right answer. Let her have one more day of innocence. Then whack her in the morning."

"Me? But I've never—"

"You're a Manager II and she's your employee. Your job's to hire, discipline, lead and, when necessary, fire. Get used to it." McCumber clapped a hand on Pavlo's shoulder. "You lemme know if you need help, okay? Oh yeah, and happy birthday."

McCumber pivoted on his highly-polished black shoes and marched off. Pavlo watched him go with a combination of admiration and shame. The man never missed a beat. He was a maestro and Pavlo the violin. He realized that McCumber had been putting on an act upstairs about how surprised he was that Pavlo, the fast-learner, had only been with the company a few months. Now he was mentoring Pavlo in how to fire people. Well, Pavlo thought, it is a core skill for a manager. But it made him queasy all the same.

|||

He arrived at work the next morning in a sour mood after a night of fitful sleep. He was the executioner, but somehow he felt more like a condemned man—condemned to be the bad guy to a nice old lady who needed her job for the health benefits, if nothing else.

The hours from 5:30 until 10, when Pavlo had determined to do the deed, were torturously slow. Finally, the clock hands ran out of minutes and he approached her desk.

"Um, Eslene. Do you have a minute?" He could barely look her in the face. His heart was thumping and he felt as if he had to gulp for air.

She smiled at him and tilted her head. "Sure."

He walked ahead of her down the aisle between the desks. Out of the corner of his eye, Pavlo spotted some of the other employees glaring at him. He was sure they were thinking, You cold son of a bitch! To hell with them! They should be thinking, Better Eslene than me!

He halted just outside his office door and turned to face Eslene. She gently grasped his arm.

"It's okay, Mr. Pavlo," she said softly. "I'll be fine."

"Sure you will." Pavlo couldn't bear it another second. "Uh, Ralph has something to tell you." He turned and led her down the hall to McCumber's office. McCumber looked up as they entered and, without missing a beat, leaped to his feet and graciously gestured to a chair.

"Please, Eslene. Sit down." Pavlo slumped into the chair farthest from her, feeling like a puppy that had just gotten caught pissing on the rug. McCumber pretended not to notice, unflustered as always.

He leaned against the edge of his desk and shoved his hands in his pockets. "As a result of an unavoidable reduction in force, your job has been eliminated." He held Eslene's gaze. "We thank you for your service. Walt will escort you to your desk to collect your belongings and help you with any last details."

To Pavlo it felt as cold as a street-corner execution—a single bullet to the back of the head. Quick. Efficient. Humane as such things go. And wrong.

Eslene stood, steadying herself on the arms of the chair. "It's been an honor working for you, Ralph."

Pavlo stood, his heart breaking for this woman, hating himself.

"Thank you," McCumber said. "Will you be needing boxes for your personal belongings?"

"No. I took most of my things home last night."

"Of course." Pavlo realized with a shock that Eslene knew it was coming. And he realized that McCumber knew she knew, which didn't bother him since such rumor-mongering helped spare everyone a scene.

Eslene turned to follow Pavlo down the hall to her desk to get her pocketbook. A frown flitted across her brow. "Are you alright?"

"Fine," he lied. At her desk he said goodbye. "Listen, if there's anything I can do for you, anything at all, please let me know."

"Nobody's died," she chided him. "Cheer up. You're going to be a great manager. Keep it up."

Pavlo slouched back to McCumber's office. "Permission requested to take the rest of the day off."

"Conscience bothering you?"

"Yeah."

"It always hurts the first time. But it's survival of the fittest, like 'Nam. Just make sure you show up tomorrow ready to bite the heads off chickens."

5 Hedge Hopping

"**H**EY, WALT."

Pavlo looked up from his desk to find Cynthia Shaw, one of MCI's top carrier reps, leaning against the doorjamb. Slim, well-proportioned, and blonde, she was known as a predatory sales animal, driven and determined to maintain her six-figure income by any means. Her intelligence and ambition were exceeded only by her stunning good looks.

Pavlo had met her at company events where she'd demonstrated her knowledge of the telecom business, and her intimate knowledge of Bernie Ebbers' WorldCom, her largest and fastest-growing account. In a culture dominated by men, many of them MBAs who'd fled the late-1980s washout on Wall Street, Cynthia Shaw stood out like a yellow Lamborghini in a church parking lot.

"Hey, Cindy," Pavlo said. "What're you doing here? Did you get lost?"

"No, I was looking for you, actually."

Pavlo's radar picked up the telltale ping of an agenda. She was in enemy waters. Why? Sales and Finance were natural adversaries, as they often are in business. At MCI, the competition was fierce. The carrier sales reps would sign up any customer with a heartbeat, and then pressure the Network Services people to flip the switch and give them a dial tone before the credit application even hit Finance's desks. It was the job of Finance to look for any good reason to turn down the business–everything from bank references to criminal background checks. Finance was the gatekeeper and the sales reps the gate-crashers.

Once customers were on the network, it was Finance's role to dog them into paying their bills on time. The reps were always promising Finance that new customers were "good as gold," and when they turned out to be slow paying instead, would try to badger Finance into giving them "just a little more time" to catch up. The reps' commission gushers depended on a liberal credit policy and on stringing along the late accounts so they wouldn't go elsewhere or go under.

"I'm surprised you even know where Finance is," Pavlo said, tapping his pen on the day's receivables aging report.

"I did have to ask, I'll admit."

"So, what's up?"

"You. I know how busy you are, but I happen to have two extra tickets to Heritage and wondered if you and Rhoda want to go."

Shaw and Pavlo worked for the same company but that was about all they had in common. She'd never met Rhoda, but MCI sales reps were skilled in the art of the schmooze, keeping track of spouses' and kids' names, birthdays, favorite wines, and so on. Pavlo was impressed. She'd done her homework. She definitely had an agenda.

The tickets Shaw was offering were for a golf tournament sponsored by MCI, the Heritage Golf Classic, held each spring at Hilton Head's Sea Pines Plantation. MCI was always throwing splashy events to show its "gratitude" to the reps and their customers. The Heritage was the most lavish of them all, a form of legal bribery known as the corporate promotional event.

MCI flew in chief information officers, communications managers, big resellers, and anyone else who had their mitts on somebody's telecom purse strings. Then they wined and dined them into submission. Pavlo had heard tales of wretched excess at these events, rivaling the kinds of Romanesque parties thrown by big Wall Street outfits in the 1980s, events with nicknames like "The Predator's Ball," where MCI's Bill McGowan had been a regular.

Inviting someone from Finance to Heritage sounded to Pavlo like asking a priest to an orgy. He already knew how McCumber felt about fraternizing with Sales. He'd chewed out Pavlo once for accepting tickets and a limo ride with some clients to a Bette Midler concert, all arranged by Shaw. "If you're going to be a debt collector, you can't compromise your independence," he'd warned. Pavlo took it to heart. But he also liked to party, and was drawn to the many temptations life at MCI offered like a bee to a snowcone.

Besides, the Heritage was an official MCI event. Even though McCumber would never go to Heritage, he couldn't squawk if Pavlo went. It would also make for a free mini-vacation for Rhoda, and the way Pavlo had been working he figured MCI owed her one.

"I'll have to check with my wife," Pavlo lied, hedging his bets. He knew Rhoda would jump at the chance to be spoiled a bit.

"C'mon, Walt! She'll have a great time," Shaw cajoled. "Hotel. VIP tent. Rounds at the Hilton Head National Golf Club. Parties and after-parties and after-after-parties. By the time it's over, you'll want to get back to the office just for some rest."

"I suppose it'd be a chance to talk business with clients."

"Okay, then. It's a deal!"

"Well, I have a lot of work but...I guess I owe it to Rhoda." That was for sure. He'd been feeling guilty not only about leaving her all the child-raising chores, but also for marrying her away from her monied family. Rhoda's father had been in the manufacturing business in Akron, Ohio, supplying the big tire makers. She had grown up playing with the children of other wealthy industrialists while their parents swatted golf balls at the city's exclusive Portage Country Club. Rhoda would fit right in at the Heritage.

And then there was a certain, sweet irony in his spending a couple days at Hilton Head. He'd grown up a few miles away, in Savannah, on the other side of the manicured hedges that separated the haves from the have-nots. He would now get a chance to call some of his old friends and brag a little: "Yeah, I have to go to this company thing at Hilton Head."

On the way, he and Rhoda could drop off the boys with his mother near Atlanta.

"Great. I'll make the arrangements," Shaw said, closing the deal. "The foursome will be you, Rhoda, Harold and Karen."

"Who?"

"The Manns," Shaw said, her long lashes batting slightly.

Mann was the late-payer with the boiler-room operation, one of Shaw's fastest-growing accounts. Pavlo had been monitoring Mann's account—TPC—and it was back up to a $300,000 tab, not quite big enough to cause panic. But if he did start squeezing Mann to get caught up, the guy might bolt and Shaw would be out her commissions. Big ones at that. At MCI, growth was everything, and it was rewarded through the company's commission structure. For someone like Shaw, the rewards were greatest for doubling revenues with a client like Mann.

"I just hope Harold sucks as bad as me at golf," Pavlo said.

"You'll be fine." Shaw flashed him a mischievous smile. "Oh, by the way, Harold asked me to give you this." She pulled an envelope out of her shoulder bag, handed it to Pavlo, then turned and waltzed out. Inside was a check from TPC to MCI for $25,000, and a scrawled note: "See you in Hilton Head. Harold."

|||

As the days ticked down to the Heritage, Pavlo grew nervous about going. McCumber had grudgingly granted him permission—but docked Pavlo vacation days. His real worry was whether he'd come off as the poor cousin in front of the millionaire Manns and MCI's high-and-mighty. The Pavlos had recently stretched to buy a new home in St. Marlo, a gated community in Duluth, Georgia, an up-and-coming suburb of corporate strivers. Most of the rooms remained unfurnished.

But Pavlo put all that behind him when they got to Hilton Head and found themselves feasting on fresh Alaskan crab, drinking champagne, and being served by an army of crisply-suited waiters. It was all mesmerizing and intoxicating—easy to forget a lot of things when lounging in the lap of luxury.

Mann and his wife turned out to be charming conversationalists. They made it easy to spend the weekend together without feeling the urge to talk about such unpleasantness as delinquent bills. But it did strike Pavlo as absurd to hear Mann, only a few years his senior, talking about his 6,000 square-foot home in Atlanta's exclusive Baldwin Farms neighborhood; his East Cobb Equestrian Center in Roswell, where his dozen jumpers and hunting horses lived better than most humans; or how the Manns always escaped the hot Georgian summers by retreating to their Toronto home and Canadian lake house. Pavlo recalled the spreadsheet sitting on his desk with a column of numbers under the heading: "90 to 120 Days."

In the end, nothing mattered, not even Pavlo's incompetence with the little white ball. The weekend felt like a double date. The Pavlos laughed a lot, loved with renewed passion, and came home feeling pampered, refreshed, and optimistic. When Pavlo marched into the office the following Monday morning ready to tackle the world, McCumber wasted no time taking the spring out of his step. "I hope you didn't make any promises you can't keep." It was back to work.

At the end of 1992 and the beginning of 1993, the Atlanta finance unit had to juggle the day-to-day credit and collections work with the chaos of transferring the national accounts to other offices, and taking over the carrier accounts itself. McCumber's new Carrier Financial Services operation had a tight budget that precluded hiring full-timers. They were already down one since Eslene was let go, so they had to resort to temps. Fortunately, there were plenty with experience around, mostly Yankees fleeing the recession-battered Northeast.

Pavlo and McCumber turned their attention to getting to know their three hundred or so carrier customers, most of which made their livings piggybacking on MCI's network and reselling long-distance service under their own names.

Phone sex and other caller-pays 900 services made up the rest. Altogether, carriers did about $600 million in revenue in 1993, up an impressive 20 percent over the previous year. Although these customers represented only five percent of MCI's $12 billion in annual sales, the margins were huge—some more than 50 percent, several times the profit on most corporate and consumer accounts. MCI was charging 900 customers as much as 28 cents a minute for service it could deliver for about a nickel.

As a result, the corporate chiefs, eyes always on the stock price and therefore on MCI's earnings reports, had a special fondness for carrier sales. No one wanted to disturb the goose laying the golden eggs.

For McCumber and Pavlo, one of the biggest challenges in keeping Carrier Finance healthy was dealing with MCI's patchwork accounting system. Telecom billing was a complex nightmare under the best circumstances, involving the aggregation of billions of transactions calculated down to the last second. MCI's meteoric growth rate forced it to allocate the bulk of its capital to building out its national fiber-optic network. Updating and upgrading its billing systems got short shrift. The accounting function was so dysfunctional that in 1988, when the company launched a toll-free 800 service, it ended up having to give it away for free for a few months because it lacked the ability to figure out what customers owed.[1]

When Carrier Financial Services was set up in 1992, each of the thousands of daily orders to credit or debit carrier accounts was still being written out by hand as a "journal voucher" to verify the transaction. Staffers handed each one to a clerk who typed it into the accounting system. All told, it took MCI sixty days after month's end to get carrier bills out. Since clients were given another fifteen days to pay, that meant invoices were seventy-five days old before they were even due.[2]

For corporate accounts, the creaky system was serviceable since their usage didn't change much month-to-month. But the Sales reps had locked many of the carriers into "ramp up" contracts, which penalized them if they didn't grow fast enough. That meant a long-distance reseller might not receive a $100,000 January bill until March, by which time it might be running a million dollars in monthly traffic. That often left McCumber and Pavlo no way of knowing how much the company's riskiest customers owed until it was too late.

Pricing was an even bigger mess. MCI rarely charged carriers its published prices, known as tariffs. They were merely a starting point for negotiations. Instead, Sales lured carriers with what MCI called Special Customer Arrangements, or SCAs.[3] Each carrier contract spelled out incentives for the customer to increase minutes used, and penalties for falling short.

It fell to Finance to cobble together customized spreadsheets to track the plethora of payment plans. For McCumber's and Pavlo's people, that meant creating invoices one account at a time using incompatible spreadsheets and payment software. It would have helped immensely to consolidate the entire operation in one MCI office, but the system was too "fragile," as McCumber put it, to do so quickly.

The result was widespread errors. Carriers had learned to raise petty discrepancies as excuses for making partial payments on invoices, or none at all, and to hold on to MCI's cash. The problems were so systemic that MCI printed an Arbitration Rule Book to send to carriers "to assist you in resolving your billing dispute with MCI."[4]

Then there was some carriers' bizarre practice of selling minutes for less than they were paying MCI for them. Pavlo called one such customer who was having a hard time keeping up with his payments and the owner told him, without laughing, that his company planned to make up the shortfall on volume.

His claim wasn't as absurd as it sounded. When carrier clients ran up big debts, MCI frequently renegotiated their contracts to avoid tarnishing its own books with unsightly bad debt write-offs. The customers often walked away not only with lower long-distance rates going forward but forgiveness for past bills. Sometimes MCI forgave old debts altogether simply for a promise of future business.[5] Since MCI's long-distance rates were themselves moving targets, it was hard to tell whether a customer who was offering low-ball retail prices intended to rip off MCI outright or was merely gaming the system the company itself had created.

Even when customers played it straight, the manual nature of the work made it a major feat just to apply their payments correctly. The money they sent in rarely matched the invoices Pavlo's people had sent out. Single checks for millions of dollars would have to be split among thousands of sub-accounts. As the department closed its books each month, millions of dollars typically sat around without a proper home. Such vagabond payments, known as "unapplied cash," rose to more than $50 million dollars some months.[6] It was an accounting nightmare.

Finance was supposed to collect millions more from clients listed as "unknown."[7] The mystery billing became necessary when MCI Sales reps, in their zeal to book new business, told Network Services to turn on circuits for customers without filing paperwork.

Before MCI consolidated carrier accounts in McCumber's department, responsibility had been assigned to regional offices MCI had been writing off about two percent of carrier revenues a year as uncollectible. Now that they were all under one roof in Atlanta, with 1993 revenues of $600 million, that same ratio would represent $12 million in bad debt. To show the cop was on the beat, McCumber set a goal of reducing it to $11 million for the year.[8]

To do this, he ordered his finance troops to take the fight to the enemy. Pavlo began leaning on delinquent carriers as soon as the month ended, and even before MCI's bills had been generated. If Sales could hook up customers before they had a billing code, Finance could badger them before knowing how much they owed. Bad debt would never stay below McCumber's new, more austere write-off ratio if Pavlo sat around twiddling his thumbs.

He took to the task with a passion. He pushed delinquents to commit to monthly payments or made them obtain letters of credit, property liens, or put up other collateral. He also turned his attention to the decrepit state of the department's accounting processes. Many of Carrier Finance's analysts were still using handheld calculators. Pavlo put together a $50,000 budget to buy computers and train the staff to use them. He hired a programmer to customize software that shortened the time it took to figure out how much a carrier client owed from six weeks after the billing period closed to two.

Even though Pavlo was logging long hours, he was getting professional satisfaction for the first time and, best of all, McCumber noticed. He promoted Pavlo another notch and wrote a glowing performance evaluation that said Pavlo "consistently exceeds" expectations. "Walt has a clear view of what needs to be done, whether it is reducing [overdue debt], negotiating a settlement, or producing an invoice... with a keen sense of providing customer service."[9]

Pavlo wasn't being much of a family man, often going days without seeing the boys for more than a stolen moment here or there. But he felt he was being a good provider by striving to get ahead. If he kept at it, he'd move up the corporate ladder and become the guy pushing the buttons. Then he'd have the time and the money to be a good father and husband. He was certain it was only a matter of time and hard work.

Making The Numbers

WHEREVER MCI did business, it did so in fancy digs. Its choice of a site to relocate Carrier Finance in early 1994 was no exception. Pavlo's new place of work was a 63-acre office campus fifteen miles due north of downtown Atlanta, in Sandy Springs. Concourse, as the complex was called, had an artificial lake, a luxury athletic club, and an upscale hotel. Its twin, 34-story, green-glass towers dominated the area's skyline.

McCumber leveraged the move to gain control of the parts of the carrier billing operation that had been handled out of offices in Chicago and Arlington, Virginia. He now was responsible for collecting three quarters of a billion dollars a year from MCI's carrier customers. His department's running balance of accounts receivable, which was the amount its customers owed it at any given time, was averaging around $400 million.[1] McCumber's goal was to finally establish a modern, integrated system out of the company's existing patchwork of spreadsheets and antiquated billing processes.

The stakes were enormous, as was the pressure to perform. In the eyes of the world MCI was valued for growth, period. By the end of 1993 it was reporting annual revenue of $14 billion, up from just $5 billion five years earlier. Amid fierce industry competition, however, its earnings had lagged, growing only 50 percent to $581 million. Yet Wall Street still had great expectations and had pushed up MCI's stock price four-fold to $25 over the same period.

MCI had been growing like a weed, but only more of the same would satisfy—and enrich—its executives, employees and investors. With long distance prices tumbling 10 percent or more a year, the only way MCI could achieve that growth was by evolving into something different.

To all the big U.S. long-distance carriers, that meant weaning themselves from the hyper-competitive domestic market by pairing up with European and Japanese carriers. The Holy Grail was the lucrative, multi-billion dollar business of providing big corporations one-stop shops for global telecom services—one throat to choke, in industry parlance.

Overseas, AT&T was leagues ahead of everyone else. MCI tried to close the gap in 1990 by partnering with British Telecom to lay a high-capacity cable under the Atlantic. Then, in mid-1993, MCI announced it was cozying up to its UK partner by selling 20 percent of itself to British Telecom. The move brought in a sorely-needed $4.3 billion in cash for further network expansion.

Early in 1994, MCI announced an audacious $20 billion, six-year initiative called networkMCI, aimed at creating a single communications platform that would deliver computer signals, video and voice calls over a single network—the Internet.[2] With so much cash flying out the door, and long-distance rates going ever lower, the pressure to cut costs was incessant.

To do its part, Carrier Finance used its move as a pretext for another round of layoffs. Pavlo had grown a thick skin by then, so firing people was no longer the stomach-churning experience it had been the first time. Besides, his bigger problem was keeping competent people. Half his staff were temps, and turnover was running 100 percent a year.

Criminal elements, meanwhile, were starting to become a serious problem. They were discovering creative ways to exploit MCI's clumsy and inefficient accounting systems with "bust-out" scams. Sales had begun signing up companies who resold MCI's minutes on calling cards in inner-city neighborhoods at rates far below their invoiced costs. The resellers would unload as many of these calling cards as they could for cash. By the time MCI got around to asking for its money, many of these customers were into it for millions of dollars. Then, instead of trying to negotiate down their bills, the resellers would bust out by folding up shop and leaving bankrupt shells with no assets to collect.

Many otherwise legitimate 900 customers, meanwhile, had decided to cope with increasing competition and falling rates by "cramming," or padding, bills with bogus minutes. Some billed twice for the same call. Others foisted charges on people who'd never used their service.

The big regional phone companies, like Bell South and GTE, began to receive angry calls from customers whose bills showed the bogus charges. The Bells, rather than try to sort it all out, adopted a policy of reversing 900 charges for anyone who asked and then deducting them from their payments to the 900 call vendors.

Word soon spread through the kinky caller community that full credits were available to those who complained legitimately or otherwise. Within a few months, charge-backs jumped from one or two percent of the typical 900-call company's revenue to half or more. Entrepreneurs who'd grown rich overnight, people like Harold Mann, began going under just as fast.

On the receiving end of all this mayhem, McCumber and Pavlo watched with dismay as con artists began to run wild and clients collapsed. Only a miracle could keep Carrier Finance from blowing past its $12 million bad debt ceiling for 1994.

Pavlo's new system for tracking traffic allowed McCumber to identify trouble sooner and try to keep the damage from becoming catastrophic. But it wasn't enough. So he and Pavlo took to giving some clients big discounts if they paid in advance.[3]

Even so, they were increasingly being out-gunned. By the time most resellers found their way onto McCumber's priority list, they were so deep into MCI that the only sensible thing to do was pull the plug on them. Unfortunately, the harsh reality of telecom was that once the product, a phone call, was sold there was no way to repossess it. That meant cutting off customers almost guaranteed to push them over the brink into bankruptcy and leave nothing for anyone to collect.

When they couldn't squeeze any cash out of delinquents, McCumber and Pavlo turned to MCI's Accounting department for guidance on how to handle their debts. Accounting was under the same pressure from the executive suite, which was under pressure from the board of directors and Wall Street, to report earnings each quarter that would support the company's lofty share price.

McCumber got together with Accounting to buy a little time to restructure the numerous carriers with big past-due balances. He needed a way to keep them alive until he and Pavlo could work out new payment plans. One method McCumber and Accounting agreed on was to get a handful of the delinquent customers to sign promissory notes—legally binding promises by clients to pay back their debts over time.

The notes bought Carrier Finance breathing room to work out terms with its clients. An added accounting benefit was that since the promissory notes represented customers' obligations to pay MCI, they were categorized as assets on the company's books. That meant the bad debt was shifted off Carrier Finance's reports, making it look like McCumber and Pavlo were cleaning up troublesome accounts. It didn't seem to matter that there was no precedent to predict whether or not these debts would actually be collected. In cahoots with Accounting, Carrier Finance accepted a $3.5 million promissory note from a client named Voicecom. The customer managed to pay $100,000 a month for ten months before defaulting on the remaining $2.6 million.[4]

Through promissory notes, persistence, and minor slights of hand, McCumber and Pavlo managed to keep Carrier Finance below $12 million in bad debt for 1994. They would need to pull more rabbits out of the hat to achieve an encore in 1995. They sat down on the first work day of the new year to assess the potential damage and come up with a strategy to manage it.

Pavlo gave McCumber the final tally for 1994:[5]

"Legal's closed 81 claims for which we're trying to recover $11,678,375.96."[6]

"What'd we get back so far?" McCumber asked.

"Only $139,925."

"Figures. How about the arcades?" McCumber asked, referring to outfits that sold high-priced calls *a la carte* to inner-city residents.

"Of the $2 million or so they stuck us for, we've gotten back $3,000. I don't know how Legal got even that much, unless they pawned some guy's Rolex."

"Bastards just disappearing on us again?"

"Yup. Legal can't even locate most of these guys." Pavlo rattled off a list of usual suspects, companies with suggestive names that came and went before they could get caught with their hands in MCI's cookie jar–Good Times Telecom, American Inmate, and Telecarribean. "It's a long list. We did get a lead on one of the arcades, Hasan Travel."

"The one that burned us for seven hundred grand last year?"

"Yeah. The good news is we found the owner. The bad news is he's been indicted. Maybe we can get something through government restitution."

"Yeah, right."

"Legal's still working on some bigger accounts, too. Fantasy Telecom, Transworld, Telelatinos, Universal Lifestyles. Don't even ask what they're selling," Pavlo said. "They owe us $581,000 and they're gone. We can't find the company or its owners."

"You got more of those?"

"A few."

"I shudder to think what Sales is gonna dump on us this year. How are you on people?"

"I lost two temps last month to full-time jobs in other departments."

"Get some new heads in here. We gotta keep the paper flowing. What's next?" McCumber tossed a stress ball in the air.

"Unknown accounts. I've got two people tracking down clients with over $100,000 balances that Sales put on the network but didn't bother to identify."

"The 'unknowns' are down, so it must be working. Stay on top of it."

"On the over-90s, WorldCom's still the worst. It's bitching about our billing and dragging its ass in paying. I might have to pay them a visit."

"How much they got over ninety? A few million?"

"Yeah. I could always apply that double payment they screwed up and sent in."[7]

"I don't want to do that bastard Ebbers any favors but that's not our money. Leave it alone," McCumber said. "You got any good news?"

"Inphomation! The guys running Psychic Friends Network.[8] Gotta love those Dionne Warwick commercials. They're still sending in $250,000 a month like clockwork."[9]

"At $3.99 a minute, they should be able to pay something.[10] What else you got?"

"Ogden,"[11] Pavlo said. "It was a big holding company in janitorial services and airport fueling that decided to try its hand at telecom resale. They owe us about $1.2 million. They're off the network."

"You sent them a disconnect notice?"

"No. Someone hacked their switch and ran up an extra several hundred grand. They called me asking to disconnect. I was thinking of cutting them a break."

"Screw that. They got deep pockets. Let 'em pay."

"Shouldn't I give 'em a few hundred grand off? The rates we gave them were really high."

"I can't believe we're having this conversation. They're big boys. They signed a contract. Get the money."

"Okay."

"I also want you to go to Toronto to see TelRoute," McCumber said.

"Why? We disconnected them last year. I heard they're not even operating."

"They're not. But the owner, Doug Lloyd,[12] has some fancy restructuring plan he's presenting to creditors. It's probably bullshit, but they owe us, like, a million for their U.S. traffic. I think that makes us number two after Bell Canada."[13]

"What am I supposed to do?"

"Just listen. If Lloyd's got some cash we might let them back on. If not, no deal."

"I'm there."

McCumber invited Pavlo outside for a smoke. After two years on the job, Pavlo–who had been a serious athlete in high school and college and never touched tobacco—had become a regular smoker. He hid his habit from friends and family but couldn't kick it. He blamed the stress of work, and the constant company of a committed smoker like McCumber.

He hated himself for corrupting his health and being unable to quit. He was starting to doubt himself about the work, too. A small voice in the back of his head was trying to be heard. It was warning Pavlo that some of the corners he was cutting could lead to trouble. Writing essentially worthless promissory notes, for example. But he trusted McCumber's judgment. Besides, he had too much work to do to stop and contemplate. It was easier to ignore the small voice.

 **Target Man**

PAVLO FLEW to Toronto and found himself at the poshly decorated offices of the troubled carrier TelRoute. There, he listened to the president, Douglas Lloyd, earnestly describe a restructuring plan that offered little and promised more of the same. The company owed about $3.5 million to Bell Canada, which was apparently willing to go along if the other large creditors—most importantly MCI—would too. Pavlo was asked to present MCI's position.

Unmoved and unconvinced by Lloyd's breathless optimism, he rose and took the podium. "I appreciate Mr. Lloyd inviting me here to discuss TelRoute's situation, but I can state that its restructuring plan is completely unacceptable to MCI. I frankly don't see how this company's going to be turned around."

Lloyd, who was seated in the first row of chairs, jumped up and lunged toward Pavlo. The other TelRoute executives near Lloyd restrained him as Pavlo stepped away from the microphone and took a seat next to the lawyers from Bell Canada, who were shaking their heads in disbelief.

TelRoute's attorney, realizing its last-gasp restructuring bid had failed, announced that if MCI was pulling the plug, the company had no choice but to liquidate. The small group of creditors agreed to meet among themselves in a conference room. When Pavlo entered, one of them already had his briefcase propped on the wet bar and was filling it with bottles of liquor. Others were sticking crystal glasses and coasters in their suit pockets and rifling through the cabinets. This was not the liquidation procedure described in Pavlo's MBA classes.

McCumber shook his head knowingly when Pavlo told him what happened, then offered him an "attaboy" for having the good sense to stop the bleeding. Carrier Finance took a $1.5 million hit.

With the bad receivables piling up, McCumber decided to set up a "high-risk" SWAT team. He put Pavlo in charge of about twenty analysts and three collections managers—a quarter of Carrier Finance's staff. He anointed Pavlo the department's "target man,"[1] personally responsible for collecting from the worst offenders. This was in addition to running the department during McCumber's frequent travels, negotiating payment terms with customers, and cooking up new ways to secure MCI's money.[2]

Pavlo discovered a productive ploy–showing up unannounced at industry trade shows where carriers assembled to hype themselves and lure independent sales agents. One of the most colorful characters at the shows was James R. Elliott, chairman of Westchester, Illinois-based Cherry Communications. His company's booth was staffed by bikini-clad Cherry Girls who handed out Cherry beach towels, flip-flops, golf balls and, most popular of all, Cherry panties.[3]

Behind the scenes, things were not so cheery at Cherry. Elliott had previous convictions for mail and wire fraud, and making false statements.[4] He had run afoul of the Federal Elections Commission in 1992, for using company resources to pressure employees to attend a Republican fund-raiser.[5] Cherry's license had been revoked in California for "slamming,"[6] the practice of switching customers' long-distance providers without their permission. Cherry had a reputation in the business of running up large balances with carriers and then haggling over the bills until the creditor capitulated and reduced its indebtedness.

Pavlo showed up for his first conference as MCI's target man at the Walt Disney World Swan and Dolphin hotels in Orlando. The event was run by a trade group known as America's Carriers Tele-communication Association. He couldn't help feeling like the proverbial party pooper, working the poolside cocktail binge the first night with a list of attendees, a note pad, and an aging report showing which customers owed MCI how much for how long. The more inescapable truths he had at his fingertips, the less room customers had to wriggle out of their obligations. Since he had spoken with most of his delinquent clients only by phone, Pavlo sidled up to MCI Sales reps asking them to identify his prey. After two days working the trade show floor, and endless cocktail parties, Pavlo proudly walked away with $2 million in checks.

As he began to make the rounds of conferences, he started

bumping into his counterparts from the collections departments at AT&T, WorldCom, Sprint, Wil-Tel, and SP Telecom, the forerunner of Qwest. They swapped war stories and discovered it was in everyone's interest to share intelligence. A group of them began compiling a National Telecommunications Data Exchange[7] to track the dozens of resellers applying to hop onto the big networks each week.

It was like a terrorist watch list, flagging companies that had caused mass destruction to the income statements of one big network operator after another. The resellers' counter-move was to put their accounts in the names of wives, girlfriends and drinking buddies. The resellers always seemed to be one step ahead of the collections people. MCI's debt woes, like those of its competitors, continued to grow.

|||

One of Pavlo's most bizarre "targets" was Caribbean Telephone & Telegraph, based in Detroit but with a big operation in New York City. On a steamy July day in 1995, he made his first visit to the Big Apple, already feeling like a lost kitten in a jungle full of predators when the cab driver turned off Broadway and cruised down a pot-holed side street. He thought the driver had made a mistake, but in broken English he insisted that the graffiti-covered door on the building with the rusted fire escape matched the address Pavlo had given him.

Caribbean Tel was a big buyer of international minutes. It resold them as pre-paid calling cards that entitled users to a set amount of long-distance or international talk time. The calling card business was booming and when it came to growth CT&T was a model customer. It had gone from a run rate on MCI's network of a few thousand dollars a month a couple years earlier to $10 million by mid-1995. It was high-profit business, about 50 percent—if MCI got paid. Calling cards also opened a market to millions of immigrant callers too poor to own their own phones who could now dial home regularly. The big carriers hoped that the pre-paid cards would cut into the billions of dollars a year they were losing to "call-sell" thieves—guys who stole access numbers from credit card callers and then rang up huge bills re-selling calls at pay phones.[8]

By the time Pavlo came around, CT&T's unpaid balance had jumped to $25 million, more than that of any other upstart reseller. The situation was dicey because CT&T used local distributors who were themselves millions of dollars in hock to CT&T. For all Pavlo knew the distributors might also be owed millions by the beer and cigarette deliverymen rumored to be reselling the cards to urban delis and bode-gas. Since the CT&T food chain was all cash, it was virtually impossible to track, much less collect from.

McCumber had been lobbying to pull the plug and a few times thought MCI would begin blocking calls carrying Caribbean Tel's ANIs, or automatic number identifications. But then he would discover it was still on the network. Sales had its spies and invariably had used its clout to keep them operating.

Pavlo approached the battered steel door of the five-story building and pulled on the handle. It was locked. A row of buttons to the right had names scrawled on little tags. The top one read "CT&T." He pushed the button.

"Yeah," a voice answered.

"Walt Pavlo here. From MCI."

"Who?"

"The finance guy from your telecom company. I'm here to see…"

"Bzzzzzz." It took him a second to realize he was being buzzed in and he pulled the door open. His nostrils immediately filled with the stench of old urine. In the entryway a bum was curled up on the floor, snoring. Pavlo sidled past, breathing through his mouth to stifle the stench. He pulled up the heavy iron gate on a freight elevator, being careful to avoid getting grease on his new suit, Hermes tie, and gleaming black loafers.

"We aren't in Kansas anymore, Toto," Pavlo muttered to himself.

The elevator hummed and shuddered several floors, stopping abruptly and disgorging him into a hallway with a reception opening in the wall of thick bulletproof glass. A young woman peered out through the greasy window.

"You da MCI guy?"

"Yes, ma'am. Walt Pavlo. Here to see Jim Franklin."

She nodded toward a door, reached under her desk and a buzzer sounded. He let himself in to a small lobby where two swarthy, bulky men lounged on a ratty vinyl couch that had been repaired with duct tape. They looked up at him with barely a flicker of interest. Each wore a leather jacket and had a nine-millimeter Glock semi-automatic pistol parked in front of him on a battered table. Pavlo felt like he'd stumbled onto the set of a cheap action movie.

"Walt?" a man's voice called from his right.

"Yes sir."

"Jim Franklin." Short, bald, with a trace Midwestern accent,[9] Franklin looked nothing like a calling card kingpin, let alone one catering to expatriate Caribbeans. Pavlo knew from his research that Franklin had cut his teeth in the business in San Francisco, running operations as diverse as a porn line and a Dial-A-Santa service that children could call and listen to pre-recorded Christmas stories for 50 cents each.[10]

"What's with the heavy armor?" Pavlo asked as they walked down a narrow hallway.

"This place belongs to our distributor here in New York. He's putting a lot of cards on the street and dealing in a lot of cash. A bit of protection can't hurt," Franklin said. "Besides, they're pussycats."

"Gotcha."

"Your timing is great, Walt. As you'll see, the cash flow is pretty damn good right now."

Franklin opened an unmarked door. Inside, a large table was covered by a mound of cash. A woman was separating and stacking the bills by denomination. Two other women carried the stacks to counting machines, which bundled them in wrappers marked $1,000 each. A kid with a broom stood nearby sweeping up the currency that fell to the floor.

"We're up to a million already this week," Franklin said, motioning to four large duffel bags near the door into which the women were stuffing the counted and wrapped bundles of cash.

The receptionist entered the room with a large paper bag in each hand. "From the 145th Street route," she said dumping two new piles onto the table.

Pavlo was dumbfounded. "Is it like this every day?"

Franklin nodded. "Same in Detroit, Miami and soon in L.A."

"That's amazing. Especially considering how much you owe us at the moment."

Franklin shot Pavlo a sideways glance. "How much I owe you?"

"Twenty-five million, Jim."

Franklin made a face. "Can't be that much. I only have invoices for about $10 million. You better check that."

"If we cut you off today, $25 million's how much you'd owe," Pavlo said, using one of his standard implied threats.

Franklin shrugged. "I'll have to get with my accountant and get back to you."

New day, same bullshit, Pavlo thought. "Here's a better idea. How 'bout you count out a hundred thousand." Pavlo imagined how the bag screeners at La Guardia would react to a knapsack full of cash. "I'll give you a receipt, take it back to Atlanta and credit your account."

"Can't do it," Franklin said. "This isn't even my money. It's our distributor's."

"You owe us too much, Jim. This can't go on much longer."

Franklin held his hands out in supplication. "What do you expect me to do? I can't pay you until my distributors pay me. That takes time. You guys've made things a lot worse, too, by locking me into rates that're double street prices."

Pavlo winced. Franklin had him there. The tsunami of cash business in the calling card game had sparked an all-out war between MCI and its rivals to sign up customers like CT&T. One outfit, Teleperranda, was wreaking further havoc by selling its phone cards at a fraction of their wholesale cost. MCI's rapacious sales reps, meanwhile, had locked CT&T into a ramp-up contract that assessed penalties if it didn't meet ever-rising volume quotas. The only way Franklin could get lower rates was to run more minutes over MCI's network, so he had opened the floodgates.

Franklin no doubt understood that MCI would either have to renegotiate CT&T's contract or risk bankrupting him and ending up with nothing.

"You setting your own rates now?" Pavlo asked.

"I'm in business to make money," Franklin said. "Just like MCI."

"That's why I'm here. To talk money. How MCI can get what we're owed so you and your distributors can stay in business."

"Fine. Just give me a minute. I've got an urgent call to make."

Pavlo wandered back to the lobby and waited for an hour perched on a wobbly folding chair, his leather briefcase on his lap, eyeing the artillery on the table and the two security men who took turns dozing off. Finally, the receptionist came in and announced that Franklin had been called away to an "urgent meeting." Pavlo swore under his breath.

"He said to tell you he'll ring you later at your hotel for dinner." She pushed a button that set the door buzzing. Pavlo was excused.

He slouched down the broken sidewalk to the nearest intersection and hailed a cab back to his hotel, breathing a sigh of relief when he walked back into the elegant, air conditioned lobby. He ordered a bottle of wine from room service and settled in for the wait.

He called the CT&T office once every hour, hoping to catch

Franklin off guard and shame him into keeping his dinner date. Now he understood why those attorneys had been packing their briefcases with wine and trinkets at TelRoute. It infuriated him that people who carried on like they were captains of industry turned out to be nothing better than ex-porn operators with grand ambitions.

He made his last call to Franklin before the evening news and then decided to retreat to a nice solo dinner out. Another day wasted, he thought. At least he had seen the money, even if he couldn't get his hands on any. He couldn't shake the image of all that cold cash in big stacks on the table, and bags bulging with it on the floor. And the kid with the broom to sweep up the leftovers!

It had been exactly three years since he started with MCI and looking back on it the whole journey had been one bizarre twist after another. Pavlo had earned his MBA aspiring to the Harvard Business School utopian vision of the corporation as a community, run by thoughtful innovators striving to do good while doing well. He imagined his fellow MBA graduates toiling away in such a world, working with sane people in efficiently-run businesses, enjoying carefree weekends indulging in fun hobbies like sky-diving or trout-fishing, or just playing with their kids and loving their spouses. He was only thirty-two years old and he'd already seen enough of the underbelly of the corporate beast to know that none of them would ever believe him if he told them what was there.

At least it had been an education and, in an odd way, he looked forward to the next twist, like watching a really bad car wreck in slow motion. As long as McCumber held the steering wheel, the worst thing anyone could say about Pavlo was that he worked his ass off and tried to be a dependable copilot.

Change of Command

T HE TWISTS kept coming.

Hi-Rim Communications was a subsidiary of a penny-stock company called Teletek that was based in Nevada and appeared to be running a high-octane version of a bust-out scam. Instead of retailing long-distance service through its calling cards, Hi-Rim turned out to be fronting for other prepaid card firms not even authorized to use MCI's network. As its usage soared, Hi-Rim balked at making its payments with a smokescreen of specious complaints about MCI's invoices and network deficiencies.[1]

Hi-Rim Vice President Wayne Godbout was a master of nerve. After repeated promises that a check was in the mail, one day he gave Pavlo a FedEx tracking number to prove that a check was actually in the mail. The package arrived at MCI's Concourse offices the next day, empty.

Target Man Pavlo traveled to Hi-Rim's Las Vegas headquarters in October 1995, by which time it was in hock to MCI for several million dollars. He was greeted by Godbout with an obscene, high-volume rant about screwed-up bills and dropped calls. Pavlo played the patient but persistent parent. When Godbout calmed down, Pavlo invited him out for a round of golf the next morning, thinking he might accomplish more on neutral territory. Godbout accepted the invitation but didn't show up for the tee time. When Pavlo phoned Hi-Rim's office, Godbout's secretary told him the boss had taken off on a week-long business trip. "No, he didn't leave a number where he can be reached." Pavlo returned to Atlanta feeling like a failure.

Pressure to cope with such problems without taking big write-offs forced McCumber and Pavlo to become ever more creative. Cam-Net Communications Network Inc., a long-distance startup in Vancouver, was another fast-growing customer that began short-paying invoices and quickly ran up a $1.7 million tab.

After months of brush-offs, McCumber and Pavlo were convinced Cam-Net was never going to pay down its debt. Cutting it off was an unappealing option. Even if Sales didn't block the move, disconnection would almost certainly drive it out of business, force MCI to pursue legal claims in a foreign country and leave it with nothing.

McCumber and Pavlo needed some other way to protect their employer's interests. Fortunately, Cam-Net was still a going business with shares that traded on the Toronto Stock Exchange. Wary of McCumber's heavy pressure to pay up and threats to disconnect his firm, Cam-Net's chairman, Daryl Buerge, proposed giving MCI $2 million worth of stock to collateralize its debts. Short of alternatives, McCumber ran the concept past his protégé.

"That's brilliant!" Pavlo said excitedly.

"I'm not sure this entire company's worth $2 million, but work out the details," McCumber replied.

Pavlo arranged for Cam-Net's finance execs to issue MCI $2 million worth of unrestricted stock. Pavlo signed a side agreement that stated MCI would not unload its stake for one year to avoid putting selling pressure on the share price. If the share price was lower when the year was over, Cam-Net would pay MCI the difference between the original $2 million value and the amount MCI realized by selling its shares in the open market. If the stock's value rose, Cam-Net could repurchase it for $2 million and pocket a profit. To MCI it wasn't as good as cash in the bank, but Pavlo was proud of having crafted such a creative deal. He also felt confident Cam-Net's stock would soar, making MCI's collateral ever more secure and him look ever smarter. After all, tech was heating up. A little outfit named Netscape had recently gone public and seen its stock jump 150 percent before lunch.

With the Cam-Net details worked out, MCI allowed it to continue using its network as long as it paid its new bills on time. Pavlo didn't know precisely how Accounting was booking its past-due debts and the stock MCI held as collateral, but as long as nobody was on his case he was content to let things ride. His confidence got another boost when Cam-Net sent McCumber a certificate for the two million shares precisely as promised.

Even before McCumber had a chance to turn it over to the company's Treasury office, he showed up at Pavlo's office door with a sour look and a copy of the *Wall Street Journal* under his arm.

"Smoke?" Pavlo read the intense look on his face as a command rather than an invitation.

"Sure."

When they were outside and had lit up, McCumber handed Pavlo the newspaper, folded to a short item on an inside page. "We got a problem."

Pavlo read the headline:

> *MCI COMMUNICATIONS INC.: Cam-Net*
> *Communications To Sell 6% Stake to Firm*[2]

"What the?…" Pavlo said.

"Holy shit's more like it," McCumber growled. "Cam-Net sand-bagged us. They're spinning the deal as a vote of confidence by MCI. That's the good news. The bad news is that MCI's already got a partner in Canada. Stentor. This makes it look like we're screwing its sister."

"Whoa," Pavlo managed. "Are we…you and me…screwed? Royally?"

"I'm not sure how it's gonna break, but I'll take the hit," McCumber said.

Pavlo felt like an idiot. He had crowed to Rhoda the night before about pulling off the most brilliant deal of his career. Now he might get fired. When he got back upstairs to his desk, the phone was ringing.

"Mr. Pavlo?"

"Yes."

"Please hold for Mr. Crane."

Pavlo's scalp and scrotum crinkled. Jonathan Crane was President of MCI International. Now he really needed a cigarette!

"Pavlo?" a man's voice barked.

"Yes sir."

"Who the fuck do you think you are pulling this shit with god-damn Cam-Net?"

"Well sir…"

"Cam-Net, for Christ's sake!" Crane said with disgust, like he'd just discovered he'd stepped in dog shit.

"We…I…was just trying…"

"Pavlo, Stentor just spent a half hour tearing me a new asshole. Why the hell wasn't I consulted?"

Pavlo had to fight to keep a whining note out of his voice. "We were trying to secure MCI's interests, sir. Cam-Net owes us a lot of money and…"

"Jesus friggin' Christ, son! Do you have any idea the mess you created?" He ranted on for another minute and then slammed the phone down.

Pavlo could hear McCumber's raised voice down the hall, laying into Daryl Buerge, Cam-Net's chairman. Pavlo went to a terminal on one of the clerk's desks and called up Cam-Net's stock. It had popped 11 percent that morning, to $1.59 a share.[3] At least MCI's option to sell the shares back to the company was in the money.

It took a lot of phone calls and eating a lot of crow, but McCumber managed to calm the waters both with MCI's Crane and with Stentor. As Pavlo had predicted, the stock did well over the next year and MCI got its $2 million back. Then, some of their colleagues had the gall to gripe that he and McCumber had left money on the table when the stock rose further.

MCI was lucky to get anything, as it turned out. In the fall of 1996, Cam-Net's Buerge was charged with conspiracy to commit securities fraud[4] and ended up on the lam.[5] The company later went bankrupt.[6]

McCumber and Pavlo had won a battle, but by the end of 1995 they were losing the war. Franklin's Caribbean Tel was at risk of burning MCI for $50 million. Godbout's Hi-Rim looked likely to whack it for $20 million in usage, plus millions more in contract penalties. More than a dozen other carriers were also flat-lining for a total of $50 million. That meant they had certified dead money totaling $120 million. And that was just what they knew about. Who could say what new disasters lay ahead?

The department's mandate in previous years had always been to keep bad debt below two percent of revenues "come hell or high water," as McCumber put it.[7] For 1995, revenues were on target to come in at around $1.1 billion.[8] Two percent of that would mean writing off no more than $23 million. Yet the guys running Business Services, the half of MCI under which Carrier Finance fell, had committed it months earlier to a bad debt budget of just $10 million. That was $2 million less than the previous year, although revenue was up 60 percent.[9] In contrast, the $120 million or more in bad debt McCumber and Pavlo were sitting on represented over 10 percent of revenues. Booking it would involve fessing up to a total meltdown. Their bosses weren't about to let out such ugly truths so late in the year.

Instead, they decided to delay big write-offs at least until 1996.

That made McCumber, the former Navy Commander, a pawn in a high-stakes game of cook-the-numbers. He was called into a sudden rush of closed-door meetings with higher-ups. Good soldier that he was, he came out tight-lipped about his distaste for the orders he was being given. But Pavlo could tell the fight was going out of him. Their old-style sit-downs, in which McCumber had mentored Pavlo by discussing the issues of the day and how to handle them, gave way to brief meetings and edicts.

McCumber wanted out. He had been laboring 60 to 80 hours a week for five years to prevent slime-ball carriers from fleecing MCI. By late 1995, Sales' quest for commissions, and senior management's for growth, were completely overwhelming his efforts. His wife was ill and his doctor was warning that stress threatened his health, too.

When McCumber brought up his plans to leave the department, Pavlo wasn't surprised. His boss had been grooming him to take over Carrier Finance's day-to-day operations. McCumber was also already holding down what was supposed to be a second full-time job inside MCI, running a more laid-back unit called Contract Development Services. McCumber began spending less time in Carrier Finance and more in his other post while continuing to provide Pavlo some guidance, and adult supervision, until another director took over his duties. Pavlo didn't blame McCumber for making the move. Chasing carriers around the country was a young man's game, and McCumber already had a nice Navy pension. He had done his duty at MCI, too, and could now hang on a few years longer in an easier job as the value of his stock options grew into a cozy retirement cushion.

As fast as Pavlo had progressed, he felt unprepared to inherit Carrier Finance's day-to-day workload. He had been popping the occasional Prozac to calm his jittery nerves. Now, if McCumber was worried enough about its problems to leave, Pavlo knew he should worry, too. He asked to transfer with his boss but McCumber resisted. Carrier Finance needed him. McCumber promised his protégé a special "out-of-policy" raise to $62,784 to make it worth his while to stick around.

Pavlo was anxious about the prospect of losing his mentor. But he was also excited. Ready or not, this was the chance he'd been waiting for his whole career.

 **Young Turks**

THE RELAXED GOLFING weekend that Pavlo had enjoyed with Harold Mann and their wives had evolved into a professional friendship of sorts. Pavlo found Mann at times exotic and eccentric and, at others, sleazy and amoral.

Mann was still in the 900 sex-call business—Denmark Dial—and had proved to be a valuable resource, willing to do "a little checking around" when Pavlo was trying to divine what some of MCI's other customers were up to. The two men would occasionally have lunch together and one day in late 1995, Mann invited Pavlo to Rio Bravo, an upscale Mexican restaurant, telling him he had a new friend that Pavlo "must meet." Pavlo assumed Mann had an agenda, but he expected it to amount to little more than the latest industry gossip.

Mann was dressed as usual in a custom-made double-breasted jacket over a brightly-colored, open-collared shirt, looking like a Vegas high-roller. Seated with him was a young man about Pavlo's age—early thirties—wearing a crisp gray suit and an earnest face.

"Walt, this is Mark Benveniste of Manatee Capital," Mann began. "Mark, Walt Pavlo of MCI."

"Nice to meet you," Pavlo said, shaking hands. "Do I know Manatee?"

"Probably not," Benveniste said.

"But you should," Mann broke in. "It's got the recipe to turn MCI's carrier meltdown into a money machine."

"Really?" Pavlo allowed himself a small silent sigh. His lunchtime would be sacrificed to some cockamamie scheme.

"Walt, it's a terrible human tragedy what's happening in this industry," Mann said with characteristic sarcasm. "Charge-backs have turned most of the 900 business into toast. The long-distance resellers are getting desperate, too."

"So what's your point?" Pavlo asked.

"The money these days is in financing. The tougher things get, the more important it is to gain control of the money and get paid quickly."

"True. But the last thing any of MCI's customers want is for us to take control of their cash," Pavlo said. "MCI is already playing banker to enough of these guys as it is."

"That's why Mark's plan for Manatee is so brilliant. He'll take control of the cash and make sure both MCI and your carrier customers get paid fast. Everyone's happy so everyone plays by the rules. It's human nature."

Pavlo immediately concluded that Benveniste was a bright guy but couldn't imagine he was going to offer up a silver bullet solution to MCI's carrier problems here at Rio Bravo. Might as well hear him out though, Pavlo thought. After all, Mann liked the idea, and he knew the business well enough to have made a fortune off it.

"It's simple, Walt," Benveniste began. "The resellers like to bill through the big regional phone companies. It makes them look legitimate to have their charges appear on a bill from a Bell South or a PacTel. But those guys take 90 days to pay. Meantime, your reseller customers have a hell of a time paying you."

More preaching to the choir, Pavlo thought grumpily. He took a deep draft of his Diet Coke.

"Enter Manatee," Mann piped up, tapping out a drum roll on the tabletop while looking over Pavlo's shoulder. "Look how hot that hostess is Wally!" Pavlo hated being called Wally almost as much as the way Mann was always shamelessly hitting on women.

"We'll pay MCI up front," Benveniste said, starting to sketch a box with arrows on a piece of paper to illustrate.

"I'm listening."

"We do thorough due diligence on every long-distance discounter and 900 customer we finance. Then, once we get their call records each month and calculate how much they have coming from the Baby Bells, we pay them most of it within seven days, and collect when the Bells pay up."

"Okay. So Manatee's a factoring company," Pavlo said with a slight shrug.

"Precisely," Benveniste said.

Pavlo had pitched McCumber and his boss, Ernie Lederer, a Finance vice president, the year before on the idea of MCI getting into factoring-style financing to limit bad debt and carve out for himself some new turf to oversee. His superiors had listened and then shot down the concept. Pavlo remained convinced it would work but had moved on to more urgent matters rather than fight an uphill battle to get it approved. Now, he thought, might be his chance to set up a factoring program externally. First, he needed to know more about Benveniste and the people behind him.

"So what's the deal with you, Mark? How did a buttoned-down guy like you ever get in this business?"

Benveniste said he was a lawyer, and had worked for an Atlanta firm after graduating with honors from American University Law School. He'd met a guy named Jack Hammer—"Swear to God, his real name."—when Benveniste's brother was dating Hammer's daughter. Hammer operated government-subsidized apartments through his Atlanta company, Housing Systems, Inc. Benveniste happened to run into him again when Benveniste's firm was hired to represent Hammer in the sale of Arlington Memorial Park, a cemetery in Sandy Springs, Georgia. Hammer sold it for $30 million in stock to Service Corporation of America, a funeral home franchiser.

Benveniste said Hammer had met the owner of a small Miami-based 900 outfit who complained about how hard it was to keep his business going while waiting for the regional phone companies to pay him. Hammer smelled an opportunity and set up Manatee Capital Corp. to finance telecom receivables. Hammer was an entrepreneur who spent half his time in Miami Beach. He was sufficiently impressed by Benveniste to offer him a full-time position as general counsel of his real estate empire, and as the head of his new venture, Manatee.[1]

Benveniste started with a 10 percent equity stake, and the promise of much more if all went well. He dove into the work and, early on, ran into Harold Mann.[2] Mann was launching another offshoot of his company and needed financing.

Benveniste had signed Mann up, agreeing to lend him 85 percent of his receivables, once they had been "scrubbed" of questionable accounts.[3] Between interest and fees, Manatee stood to make a lot of money if the company could sign up enough cash-hungry telecom customers.

"So how's it working with your existing customers?" Pavlo asked.

"We've been doing this for months with Harold here. It works,"

Benveniste said.

"Sure does," Mann confirmed, shaking the ice in his empty tumbler to get the attention of a passing waitress. "I bet a hundred bucks I could get that hostess back to my office."

"We could work out a deal where we finance every under-capitalized reseller on MCI's network. It would solve the problems Harold tells me you're facing in the market," Benveniste said. "Manatee would be the one waiting for the phone companies to repay our loans plus interest."

"What kind of interest?"

"Up to 36 percent annualized," Benveniste said. "Most carriers gladly pay it to get their money up front."

"That's hefty," Pavlo said.

"You know as well as I do these guys aren't triple-A credits," Benveniste said. "And, according to Harold, you have a few customers who are definitely high-risk."

Pavlo chuckled. "A few? We've got over $100 million categorized as high-risk, and probably just as much more that isn't but should be. How much you guys have to lend?"

"We've got a $10 million line of credit with NationsBank," Benveniste said. "We can ramp that up to…whatever."

Pavlo was warming to Benveniste. He was quick, articulate, and, like Mann, had an aura of financial success, but without Mann's crude behavior. They agreed to meet again, maybe get in a round of golf. Pavlo thought the factoring idea was worth considering but he would have to think about it. Benveniste picked up the tab and excused himself.

"Pretty nifty, eh?" Mann said as he and Pavlo left.

"It's got potential. God knows, with my boss Ralph McCumber on the way out I could use some outside help. I've got shitloads more work."

"More money too, I hope."

"A bit."

"What're they paying you now? Two, three hundred grand?"

"Dream on."

"How much?"

"What's it to you?" He was embarrassed to say.

"I'm just a guy who's lookin' out for his friend."

"I'm at sixty-three." Pavlo blushed a little as he said it. "But my stock options could be worth a lot some day."

"Congratulations!" Mann said, shaking his head. "Look, Wally.

Let's do this deal. I'll make it worth your while."

"It'd be worth my while if it got MCI's bad debt problem under control." Pavlo felt the hair standing on the back of his neck. Worth MY while? What did Mann mean by that?

"Think about it, eh?" Mann said, clapping a hand on Pavlo's shoulder. "This could be big. And I'm not just talking big for MCI, okay?" He winked.

On the drive back to his office Pavlo didn't need a calculator to see what Benveniste and Mann were so hot about. If MCI factored $100 million in risky accounts, Manatee could gross close to $20 million a year in interest and fees, and probably net half that after its own financing and administrative costs.

If Pavlo helped them pull the deal together, Mann had dangled the possibility of something. What it might be he could only guess—a new job with one of Mann's companies, or with Manatee itself. He imagined what it would be like to be pulling down twice or three times what MCI was paying him for all the grief he had to deal with day in and day out. With McCumber phasing out of Carrier Finance, the burden of how to deal with the $120 million debt disaster was now settling on his shoulders. How the hell were they going to dig themselves out of a hole that big?

While Pavlo pondered factoring as a way to save the day, MCI had its own ideas of how to handle the growing problem of bad debt—hide it. McCumber told Pavlo that the Finance chiefs had decided to shift the Caribbean balance to a promissory note. Pavlo was shocked. They'd never accepted a promissory note for more than a few million. CT&T owed $55 million.[4] It was a big enough number that it could raise a red flag with MCI's outside auditor, Price Waterhouse, and with Wall Street.

"Is CT&T putting up collateral?"

"There is none."

"So we're writing a promissory note we know is total bullshit with nothing to back it up? This is really screwed up, Ralph."

"Every organization's screwed up," McCumber said with a wave of his hand. "At least nobody's getting killed over it."

"Killed, no. But you're leaving. What happens to me if the auditors dig into this shit?"

"CT&T and Hi-Rim were on my watch," he said. "For you the note's a chance to start over."

"So you're saying this is right?"

"No, I'm not saying it's right. I'm saying don't worry about it.

You're never going to see it in writing, but you've been told this isn't going to stick to you. So just hang in there."

Pavlo was confused. McCumber had always sorted through the fog of war and come up with ways out of the tightest jams. Now he just seemed to be throwing up the white flag. "Hang in there when we're whitewashing a $55 million debt? I don't see how you can—"

"Don't tell me what I can and can't do!" McCumber barked. "Orders are orders. You've got yours."

It was a horrible moment for them both. McCumber didn't like the deal any more than Pavlo. But he was an expert at picking his battles, and this was one he had decided he couldn't win, at least not with a frontal attack. The next day he told Pavlo to put together figures for the upcoming year, including an accurate debt forecast, Caribbean Tel and all. It was going to be very ugly.

|||

Christmas came and went with Pavlo and Rhoda doing their best to put on a good holiday for the boys without busting their household budget. It was a stretch and the new year dawned with Pavlo in a funk. Another year and his workload had only gotten worse, while his salary was stuck.

The first business day of 1996, AT&T shocked Wall Street and the telecom industry by announcing it would cut 40,000 jobs, one of the largest corporate work-force reductions ever, and take a $6 billion charge against earnings.[5] The problem was competition. Like the first blast of Arctic air in the winter, the news felt like a harbinger for an industry struggling to adapt to a harsh new environment.

The next day, January 4, 1996, Pavlo got to work on McCumber's assignment. "Aging Information and High-Risk Accounts" was the spellbinding title he put on his budget memo.[6] By "high risk" he meant accounts he was almost certain would become uncollectible. He forecast that this figure had hit $88 million in 1995. That did not even include December usage figures, which were not yet available and likely would have added tens of millions of dollars more to the previous year's figure. Pavlo emailed his estimate to Don Lynch, a senior vice president of Finance, to Jim Folk, the newly appointed VP of Revenue Operations, and to McCumber.[7] The task was one of his last under McCumber, who moved on to his new position.

The response to Pavlo's email came a month later when he was summoned by James Wanserski, who was scheduled to take over for McCumber. Wanserski was an accounting graduate of Rockhurst University in Kansas City who'd come to MCI in 1991 as a result of its acquisition of Telecom USA. He was in his mid-forties and a sea change from McCumber.[8]

Wanserski was cordial but aloof, even socially clumsy. Pavlo couldn't imagine him fraternizing with the troops over beers after work.[9] Where McCumber kept a to-do list on a single sheet of paper, and chewed out Pavlo if he didn't do the same, Wanserski carried a bulging catalog case, the kind airline pilots tote around. Sometimes he traveled with two. His office was such a mess, Pavlo had to clear a stack of papers from a chair just to sit down.

"We need to talk about your bad debt projection," Wanserski began.

"It's a big number," Pavlo admitted, "but I ran it by Ralph and we talked with Accounting about stretching out the pain over a few months. We're in a gray area, but I don't think anyone's gonna accuse us of breaking the rules."

Wanserski ignored Pavlo's remark. "Your bad debt budget for 1996 has been set at $15 million."*

Pavlo couldn't believe it. First, his bosses had shoved 1995's bad debts into 1996, and now they were telling him to shove everything under the rug. He decided to push the issue further.

"What about CT&T? It's a $55 million corpse. If our budget's $15 million, where do I bury that? And what about Hi-Rim and the rest?"

"Management knows all about CT&T and Hi-Rim," Wanserski said. "Just set them aside and attack the rest of the customer base. Maybe things won't be as bad as you think."

"Excuse me for saying this, but there aren't gonna be any happy surprises. We're lucky to recover five cents on the dollar once debt's 90

---

* This statement is disputed by James Wanserski in *Financial Executive,* Mar. 2006. In his Aug. 6, 1998 deposition, Wanserski stated "I don't recall what the budget was but it would have been much higher than that ($15 million)." Ralph McCumber testified in his July 15, 1998 deposition that there was no bad debt "ceiling" but the department was given a "goal" of $15 million in 1994 or 1995. James Folk testified in his deposition July 29, 1998, "There is a plan that is put together for the company that has within it a target for what our bad debt is going to be," and that such a plan existed at the beginning of 1996.

days past due. I doubt we'll get that much from these crooks...er... customers."

"Whoa, Nelly," Wanserski said waving both hands in the air. "You can check the Cowboy McCumber act at the door. We have our budget. Let's just work with it."

Pavlo sighed. "Yes sir." He stood to leave.

"You know, you should give the guys running this place a little more credit. Rumor is, MCI's in play as a possible takeover target," Wanserski said. "We need to do our part and make these numbers. If we can just hang in there, it will be worth our while. So hang in there, Walt. Okay?"

Pavlo had heard takeover rumors before. There was constant gossip in the office about anything that could boost the stock price. Wanserski's boss, Jim Folk, had taken to sending out inspirational emails quoting rosy forecasts issued by Jack Grubman, Salomon Brothers' renowned telecom analyst.

Pavlo was unmoved by all the enthusiasm. His bad debt problem was bulging at the seams. He would have to go back to his desk and wrestle with the usual suspects and try to perform some more hocus pocus.

|||

Soon after, Pavlo attended the monthly meeting of senior Finance managers. Pavlo referred to the group as the Young Turks since, with McCumber no longer around, the most senior managers attending were in their early thirties.

Alex Harriman*, the senior manager from Accounting, ran the meeting from the head of a gleaming conference table. The head of Planning was there to work up financial forecasts and tell the group what numbers their bosses expected them to hit. A Business Development manager reported on new contract signings. Marketing discussed new products in the pipeline. And Carrier Finance's Walt Pavlo was there to go over looming disasters.

"Congratulations, guys. December ended a good year on an excellent note," Harriman began. "But this year's looking tough. Why don't you begin by telling us what Business Development's got in the works."

"I've put together a spreadsheet of accounts we're negotiating with," Business Development's Art Russell* said, passing around

* Pseudonym

a handout to the senior managers and a dozen or so assistants who'd tagged along. "Of the eighty or so in total, a little over half are renegotiations."

"Any big incentives that we need to know about?" Harriman asked, grimacing. By January, 1996, long-distances prices had fallen by almost half since the break-up of AT&T a dozen years earlier.[10] The giant regional Bells, which had been prevented from offering long distance services, were lobbying hard to get into that market. All signs pointed to more deregulation, more competition and ever lower long-distance prices.

Business phone customers were making the most of the uncertainty by playing big carriers against one another to win price cuts. To keep clients, MCI Sales had been badgering Russell's group for lower-priced contracts. The price declines, in turn, hurt profit margins, which was Harriman's problem.

"WorldCom," Russell said. "With all their damn acquisitions, they're starting to act like the class bully. We're giving them a $30 million re-signing bonus."

"When's that going through?" Pavlo asked. His Carrier Finance group would have to make the accounting entries to reflect the discount.

"Probably this month," Russell said.

"We can't take the whole thing in one month," Harriman broke in. "It'd blow Carrier segment margins all to hell. Let's spread it out. Like $10 million a month until it's done."

"Fine with me," Pavlo said, "We'll credit $10 million a month starting in February."

Russell ran through a long list of such renegotiations, all involving rate cuts. Then Marketing's Rick Knight detailed MCI's latest "switchless" resale campaign. It was designed to drum up new business with resellers who hadn't invested a dime in a phone switch or other physical equipment. All they needed was an MCI contract and some salesmen. McCumber had opposed switchless resale as a bad credit risk. Now that he was out of the picture, Marketing had succeeded in pushing it through.

"Okay, Walt. I hope you're going to be more gentle than McCumber was," Harriman joked.

"I'll try. Carrier Finance ended last year looking great on paper, but a lot of our problems got pushed into 1996."

"How much you writing off for 1995?" Russell asked.

"Ten million. It's a record low."

"What're you looking at this year?"

"Including last year's rollover, it could be $120 million. Or more."

Pavlo could feel the air being sucked out of the room.

Russell was the first to break the awkward silence. "Where the hell did that come from? You guys asleep over there or what?"

"Hey, don't blame us," Pavlo said. "We weren't the ones pushing Caribbean Tel. We just got stuck with its $55 million bill that's never going to yield a dime."

Harriman chimed in, "We're building CT&T into the numbers later in the year."

"Not one of our finer moments," groused Knight from Marketing.

"So what're you doing to make sure there isn't gonna be another Caribbean Tel?" Russell asked.

"Taking a closer look at our big accounts. Who we let on the network. Even if Sales doesn't like it," Pavlo said. "Especially the pre-paid card guys. They've been ramping up like hell and with all the damn cash they deal in, collections is a nightmare."

"It's not just CT&T?" Russell asked, incredulous.

"I wish. We've got about $20 million in exposure to Hi-Rim out of Vegas. I've made a couple trips out there and don't have a good feeling. Someone upstairs better decide what to do about that one soon or it's gonna get a lot worse."

"Damn. I never even heard of them until a couple months ago," Harriman said.

"There're more pre-paid card guys popping up in New York and South Florida," Pavlo plowed on, glad for the chance to get some of this off his chest. "We dropped a few after they missed their first payments. That cut our losses to a million or so each."

"Wasn't long ago when a million was a lot," Russell said.

"I also sent a memo to Lynch, Folk, and McCumber," Pavlo added. "I told them we're looking at $88 million in bad debt this year and things have started looking worse since then. Usage for some of these guys has been spiking by millions each month."

"Jesus! There's no way we can report all this stuff all at once," Harriman said.

"What can I write-off?" Pavlo asked.

"You got any small accounts gone bad?"

"Small, medium, large. Take your pick. Something for everyone."

"Do a million or so for January. We'll worry about the rest later."

"Got it," Pavlo said, wondering how he'd managed to miss the section in his old grad school accounting textbook on how to hide bad debt write-offs by stringing them out over time.

Pavlo left the meeting with a clear mandate–delay issuing credit memos to good accounts (like the WorldCom $30 million discount) and write-offs to bad ones. He would brief Wanserski, but Pavlo had the distinct impression his incoming boss wanted to leave the mundane details to his staff.[11] It would be up to Pavlo to figure out how to carry all the bad debt on their books. He'd have to get even more creative.

The $10 million management had let him write off the previous year[12] had been a fraction of the true bad debt. His $15 million budget for 1996 was equally ludicrous. Harriman had given him marching orders, but Pavlo didn't work in Accounting. McCumber had dismissed factoring as unworkable but now that McCumber was leaving, Pavlo had to start thinking for himself. If MCI's meteoric rise had taught him anything, it was that desperate times call for creative responses.

Since Pavlo had first met Mark Benveniste, they had gotten together a few more times to discuss a possible factoring deal. Pavlo never disclosed the meetings to anyone at MCI. He figured his best shot would be to work out all the details first, and then present the financing as a *fait accompli*, the only option left.

The Manatee deal was looking increasingly workable. Pavlo would identify MCI resellers who needed financing and steer them to Manatee, which would pay MCI in a week instead of in three months. Collecting would then be Manatee's problem. Pavlo figured he could even sweeten the deal for resellers by offering them MCI's standard 2.5 percent discount for early payment.[13]

The only problem, and it was a biggie, was that Benveniste was insisting MCI guarantee the loans Manatee made to MCI's clients. He made it clear that without MCI's guarantee, his boss Jack Hammer, and his bankers, would never lend the kind of money MCI's resellers needed. Benveniste argued that the loans were safe since Manatee would control the money; and that MCI should be willing to assume some risk, anyway, to get paid up front.

Pavlo conceded the point but he knew he'd never get MCI management to sign off on such a guarantee. He didn't even know whom to go to for approval, but they probably far out-ranked Wanserski or Folk.

Knowing this, Pavlo kept playing along with Benveniste,

hoping a solution would present itself. He also agreed to meet with Manatee's bankers from National Bank of Canada, which had teamed up with NationsBank recently as Manatee's lenders, to see if there was a way to make it work. He'd gauge how keen they were on the deal and take it from there.

Benveniste set up the meeting at the Georgia Club in Atlanta's Galleria mall with National Bank of Canada. Pavlo and Benveniste arrived to find Roger Smock, Senior Vice President and General Manager for U.S. operations,[14] waiting at a large corner table. Smock, a devout Mormon, looked every bit the seasoned banker in his suit and crisp white shirt. Seated around him were the bank's Atlanta branch head, Frank Johnston, Senior VP Vernon Woods, and two VPs.[15] Pavlo was impressed. He must be doing something right to attract this deep a team.

"I can't tell you how much we've been looking forward to this meeting," Smock began. The young execs around him nodded like bobble-heads. "We think Manatee and MCI are onto something big."

"I couldn't agree more," Pavlo said, suddenly feeling self-confident and in charge. "It amazes me, with telecom growing so explosively, that no major carrier has developed a wholesale financing program. National Bank of Canada is getting in on the ground floor."

"That's precisely the sort of opportunity that appeals to us," Smock said, allowing the waiter to clear his salad bowl.

"I think about it like the auto industry," Pavlo said, borrowing a line he'd heard from Harold Mann. "General Motors doesn't earn a dime making cars. The money's in financing." Smock's lackeys nodded and scribbled furiously on their legal pads.

"So how much financing you figure MCI's wholesale market can accommodate?" Smock asked.

"Ballpark, I can see us doing $100 million our first year. Maybe three times that in a year or two, if all goes well."

Smock's eyebrows arched. "That's a big number, son. Our line of credit with Manatee's only $10 million."[16]

"Is that all the money you have up in Canada?"

It was a joke, but the bobble-heads looked up in shock. Then Smock chuckled. "Of course we've got the money, Mr. Pavlo. That's not the issue. The issue is the right relationship."

Pavlo spent the next two hours so busy answering questions along with Benveniste he hardly touched his steak. The bankers seemed to hang on his every word, impressed with his command of the details.

For the few questions to which Pavlo did not have answers, Benveniste backed him up seamlessly.

When the meeting finally broke up and he was pulling on his suit jacket, Smock leaned toward Pavlo and said privately, "I don't mind telling you, telecom financing is very attractive to us. Mark's done a great job growing Manatee so far, and if MCI's involved we could all take this to an entirely different level. But it's also new to us, and we'd feel a lot more secure if MCI were behind loans to your customers."

Pavlo was pumped. He'd had these bankers from Canada eating out of his hand for two hours. He was their man, their ticket to big new sources of revenue and profit. "We're willing to stand behind them one hundred percent," Pavlo said without a second thought. There, he'd done it. Why not a loan guarantee? His bosses wanted solutions. He was providing them.

 **Solutions Provider**

P AVLO AND HIS STAFF faced the job of massaging the numbers once again in February to satisfy their bosses, as they had been doing every month now for some time. Pavlo achieved the desired result by ordering a stack of pizzas to keep his accounts receivable managers, mostly temporary help, fed while divvying up the month's loot in such a way as to make the department look good. It was, Pavlo observed, not unlike—and about as professional—as a frat-house poker game. The only thing missing was the beer.

He'd met with his managers earlier in the day and gone over which customers were expected to send in last-minute payments and which were in trouble. The party began when the staff sat down to figure out how best to apply the payments received during the month, being as accurate as possible.

Under pressure from above, Pavlo interpreted "as possible" as a license to engage in what is known as accounts receivable "lapping"—the posting of one customer's payments to another's account to hit certain targets. It was an accounting abomination, but effective.

In the case of MCI, the corporate headquarters set various financial "targets" without explicitly telling anyone to do anything unsavory to hit them. It was then left to functionaries like Pavlo to make their numbers by deciding, for example, how much deadbeat debt would be written off each month, and how much would stay on the books a little longer pretending to be collectible, or by recording some payments—temporarily, of course—where they would look the best instead of where they belonged. That way, Pavlo could write off bad debt over time, or at least push it into the future.

One of the biggest fudges involved Ebbers' WorldCom. The company's monthly bill with MCI was running between $50 million and $60 million a month. WorldCom was gaming MCI by mailing it a paper check on the last possible day.

The huge, last-minute payments wreaked such havoc with Carrier Finance's over-90 day balance that Pavlo started flying a clerk to Jackson, Mississippi on the last day of the month to sit in WorldCom's lobby and wait for the check to be handed to him. The clerk would then rush a fax of it to Carrier Finance, which would use the documentation to justify posting the sum to WorldCom's account as if the cash were in the bank. MCI referred to the phantom money as "placeholder credits."[1] His workers called them The-Check's-In-The-Mail deposits.

Pavlo knew that in a legit operation, this kind of prank would blow up when it hit the Accounting department. But at MCI, Accounting obliged Carrier Finance's creativity. Pavlo persuaded the bookkeeping people to post the phantom payments under a special "reason code" called "cash in transit."[2] When the real check arrived, Carrier Finance deposited it and the Accounting staff would reverse the first entry just long enough for the real check to clear. This bizarre charade allowed Carrier Finance to hide in plain sight tens of millions of dollars from WorldCom's over-90-day balance.

Pavlo was sticking his neck out, but he was confident WorldCom was good for the money. His staff was so impressed by the technique that it began to spread like wildfire. By early 1996, they were offering check's-in-the-mail credits to any customer that produced a fax of a real, cashable check and a Federal Express tracking number to prove it was on its way.

The next unexploited opportunity was found in the millions of dollars in vagabond payments Carrier Finance received each month. Sometimes customers sent them in to profit off of MCI's inefficient accounting system, and sometimes the system simply wasn't up to figuring out where they should go.

Either way, MCI had millions in "unapplied cash" sloshing around, waiting until someone could figure out how to apply it to the right accounts. One manager reported with pride that he had used this accounting gap to "clean up" about $4 million in bad debt accounts.[3]

This ploy worked because the following month, when the loose cash got properly assigned to the account of the customer who paid it, the old bad debt it was covering for would go back on the books as a spanking new balance that wasn't even due yet.

Instead of gaming the system, MCI Finance had turned the

system into a game, going so far as to send around a monthly internal report, grading departments on how well they did in sticking to their "aging" numbers.[4] Pavlo got a hearty pat on the back from his superiors, and he passed on the favor by praising his staff for their heroism in battle.

When the accounts receivable lapping party was finally over and everyone had left, Pavlo wandered into the now-empty and cluttered conference room. It stunk of greasy cardboard, he had a headache, and he was sinking into a foul mood. He craved a drink. He shuffled back to his office, flung himself into his desk chair and gazed out the windows of his tenth-floor corner office at the downtown Atlanta skyline in the distant haze.

Three and a half years before he'd been a new-hire manager. Now, at thirty-three years old, he was master of MCI's carrier portfolio, overseeing more than $2 billion in annual revenues,[5] and a hardened veteran in the art and science of squeezing money from the toughest clients. His office walls were plastered with photos of him doing the grip-and-grin at golf outings and yacht races in the company of telecom muckity-mucks with faces as flushed as a monkey's ass. In the warren of cubicles and computer screens toiled his army of eighty mostly young, bright, ambitious men and women who reported to him and sought his sage counsel, just as he had McCumber's.

He was by most measures a success, but he hated it. He was a bill collector in a corporate ghetto, and he had become an accounting alchemist, expected to pull ever larger rabbits out of his hat. Positive reinforcement was driving him—hit your numbers and we love you. Miss them and...he didn't want to go there. Too many people above and below him, and at home, were counting on him.

He should have quit, but he'd been raised Catholic and acquired an inner voice that whispered anytime he thought of bailing, "Always finish whatever you start." He rationalized that quitting would be disloyal to Rhoda and the boys. And then there were the stock options and the buyout rumors. If he left, he might miss out on a big payday. He needed to hang in there until...

There was the other thing—the seed planted by Harold Mann had germinated in his mind. "I'll make it worth your while," he'd said. He and Mann had become buddies. Mann wasn't perfect, Pavlo knew, but he was charismatic, fun to be around, and the kind of person who made things happen by sheer force of will. Pavlo could learn a few things from him, and maybe make some real money for a change. Judging by the way Mann lived, his business ventures minted the stuff.

Pavlo wondered how long he could hold out. His heavy travel schedule was taking a toll. He loved being with the boys but was so busy he missed Bubby's sixth birthday because he had to brief senior executives in the company's Reston, Virginia headquarters about Carrier Finance's deteriorating financial situation.[6]

He missed Valentine's Day with Rhoda because he had to be in McLean, Virginia for a big meeting with a delinquent account that was accusing the company of billing screw-ups. From there he flew to New York to visit a calling card outfit that was behind. It was his fifth trip to New York in a year but Pavlo had yet to see Times Square, Wall Street, or the Statue of Liberty.

At his office in Atlanta, he was constantly on the phone and being paged. Rhoda was doing her best to grin and bear it, but they hardly spent any time together anymore and Pavlo could feel her growing resentment and discontent.

At the end of February, Pavlo flew to Miami Beach for an industry conference.[7] It was a light-duty trip to a warm, exotic location. All he had to do was attend a few events, catch up on the latest industry gossip, and have dinner with a customer—Robert Hilby. A Mormon who taught Sunday school, Hilby had worked with Harold Mann a few years back. He claimed to have soured on sex-chat after Mann took him on a marketing swing through Los Angeles where the first stop was *Hustler* magazine.[8]

Hilby persuaded Mann and a handful of other 900 impresarios to back him in a new company catering to the "wholesale" side of the business. Telemedia Network, Inc. as it came to be known (TNI), bought long-distance minutes from MCI wholesale and resold them to 900 information providers.

Hilby thus could argue that he was only providing a dial tone, not the smut itself. His role model was another Mormon named J. Willard Marriott who'd famously declared it wasn't his business to regulate what happened inside his hotel rooms.[9]

But the money was so good that Hilby found himself a loophole. A TNI affiliate offered callers a chance to speak with "the beautiful blonde women of Sweden" or told them the "snow bunnies are all tied up" but that the caller could hang up and have the bunny call back—collect.[10] Inconveniently for Hilby, the Federal Communications Commission bans such return-call schemes and later fined him $49,000.[11]

Hilby was personally pocketing half-a-million dollars a year from TNI by 1995,[12] and that May he bought out Mann's interest by giving him $600,000 worth of free long-distance to use in his own 900 businesses.

TNI itself was running a monthly bill of about $1 million with MCI, and by February of 1996 had a $2 million past-due balance.[13] Pavlo was usually the last person delinquent clients wanted to break bread with, but Hilby had asked for a meeting a few weeks earlier. Hilby's account belonged to Cindy Shaw, the sexy sales rep who'd scored Pavlo the Heritage golf tickets. She arranged the dinner in Miami with Hilby at Joe's Stone Crab, the legendary seafood haunt at the tip of trendy South Beach.

The place was packed when Pavlo arrived with Shaw. Hilby was waiting by the door. He was tall, lumpy, and just disheveled enough that Pavlo had no problem imagining him sitting on a park bench talking to the pigeons. He disliked Hilby, a know-it-all who owed MCI $2 million.

The waiter brought a tray with three crab claws on it, "so you can see our medium, jumbo, and large sizes and decide how to order." Then he left. Pavlo and Shaw watched with quiet amusement as Hilby tucked his napkin into his shirt, reached for a claw, cracked it, and began munching.

"Bob," Shaw laughed nervously. "I don't think you're supposed to eat those. They're for show."

"What! To show you how to eat 'em. Ha! They're free! Want one?"

"No thanks." Pavlo said. "But thanks for getting together with a boring old collections guy when you've got someone as attractive and capable as Cindy here to look after you." Pavlo was laying it on thick. He was curious to see just how dim Hilby was.

"Collections. Right." Hilby wiped a greasy hand on his napkin, missing a finger and streaking his Hawaiian shirt. "Things're pretty tight at TNI and I know we've fallen a bit behind, but Frank's gonna get that squared away." Frank Pazera, a former rival of Pavlo's at MCI, had left to work for Hilby at a salary Pavlo was certain was a multiple of what he had been making. Having dismissed the trivial matter of $2 million, Hilby plowed on.

"What I really want to talk with you about is Simple Access. It's a web hosting company I'm starting in San Francisco."

Shaw gave Pavlo a bright-eyed look and said, "Simple Access will run its traffic over MCI's network."

Pavlo scolded himself for getting snookered like that. He should have made a few calls before agreeing to meet this guy. He had his hand in one of MCI's pockets and now he was trying to get it in another. Of course Shaw was leading the cheers. For her, Simple Access would mean more fat start-up commissions.

Pavlo must have made a face because Hilby quickly piped up, "I can assure you Simple Access is well funded."

Sure it was well-funded, Pavlo thought. It was probably where the $2 million had gone that Hilby's other company, TNI, owed to MCI. Pavlo had no energy to get into an argument, at least not until he'd had a couple of drinks.

"Excuse me for a moment, gentlemen," Shaw said. "I need to powder my nose." As soon as she left, Hilby leaned forward, his chin glistening, and said, "Come by the hotel after dinner. I want just you and me to talk about Simple Access."

"Okay, Bob," Pavlo said, lighting a cigarette. He knew he was being set up for some kind of a pitch. He hated having to spend a minute more with Hilby than absolutely necessary but figured he would give the guy a quick "no" to whatever he proposed and call it a night.

After dinner, Shaw left for a bar where some of her customers were having a get-together. Hilby and Pavlo shared a cab up Collins Avenue to the Fontainebleau Hotel where Hilby had enthroned himself in a suite—two floors with its own staircase—bigger than Pavlo's entire house.

"Cigar?" Hilby asked, holding out a Cuban Cohiba.

"Whoa. Very cool."

"I've got connections." Hilby motioned for Pavlo to follow him out on the penthouse balcony where they settled into a couple of chairs, lit up, and enjoyed the gentle night breeze. The view was picture perfect—the Fontainebleau's sparkling blue pool in the foreground; the palm trees, beach and surf in the middle distance; and the stars shimmering in an inky-black sky over the Atlantic. Hilby handed Pavlo a crystal tumbler and poured into it from a bottle of 12 year-old Glenlivet single-malt scotch.

"How'd you fair in your Bermuda yacht race?" Hilby asked.

Jesus, Pavlo thought. This is even more of a set-up than I thought. MCI had sent Pavlo to Bermuda with a bunch of coworkers as part of a team-building weekend. They spent their time aboard a pair of Catalina 47 yachts. Hilby had probably gotten Shaw to tell him a few things he could use either to put Pavlo at ease, or shake him up.

"Great," Pavlo said, allowing a hint of annoyance into his voice.

"Made me feel like a Kennedy."

"It's always nice to live well," Hilby said. "Which brings me to the subject of your future."

Pavlo was suddenly jerked back from the pleasant haze the Scotch was producing. "Oh-kay," he said.

"The 900 business is over. And even if it isn't, I'm sick of it. Simple Access is my fresh start. Eyeball traffic's growing at amazing rates on the Internet, and one of the best ways to monetize clicks is web hosting."

"Sounds capital-intensive to me."

"That's why it takes some brains to run it," Hilby said. "What would you think about heading finance and operations for Simple Access?"

"Well, I've never really given a lot of thought to leaving MCI," Pavlo lied. In fact, he had long hoped one of MCI's more upstanding customers would spot his talent and lure him away from his $63,000 salary with a big raise. Hilby, living like a *rajah* and apparently using MCI's money to start a new business, had not come to mind as a candidate.

"You could run things out of Atlanta for awhile," Hilby went on. "Then move to San Francisco if you want. It's up to you."

It sounded like a farce. "I'm flattered," Pavlo said.

"I'll pay you a $100,000 signing bonus, $200,000 a year and give you 10 percent of the company."

Pavlo paused to pull on his Cohiba and expel a huge cloud of expensive blue smoke.

"That's just for starters," Hilby said. "Your real payoff will come when we take Simple Access public. Your 10 percent will be worth millions."

Pavlo allowed himself another pregnant pause to wallow in smugness and ponder whether this was a legitimate offer. If Bernie Ebbers could start WorldCom out of a hotel, maybe Hilby would lay a golden egg with Simple Access. In telecom, anything was possible. "You're really thinking big."

"It's a huge opportunity. Huge," Hilby said, spilling a jigger full of expensive Glenlivet on the end table as he tried to freshen his drink. "I don't need an answer right away. Talk to your family. Think it over."

"I'll do that," Pavlo said.

Hilby's offer sent Pavlo back to Atlanta the next day with a bounce in his step. The first chance he got, he went to see Wanserski to talk about his compensation. MCI's salary-increase cap punished those who had started out at low levels and rose quickly through the ranks. His senior manager salary had been capped at $63,000, while others who had arrived at MCI after him, with the same rank, were earning as much as $90,000. The scheme was so screwy that Pavlo had been forced to offer lower-level newcomers as much as he was making to attract them.

"I know your salary's an issue and I want to fix it," Wanserski said brusquely. "But given all the problems in Carrier Finance, the timing's not right."

Pavlo sighed audibly. "The problems aren't in Carrier Finance. Bad debt's gone through the roof because someone's decided to let every scumbag with a pulse onto our network."

"That's not our call, and I'm making changes to improve things. Give it some time."

"I don't know how time's going to magically rid us of all our bad debt, but I've done everything McCumber and you have asked me to. Plus some. Without me, things would be a hell of a lot worse."

"Hold on there just one minute. I think your promotions and job evaluations have given you proper credit for your efforts. As soon as things look up, I'll push for more. You're young. You can do big things at this company. Just show a little patience."

"I appreciate it," Pavlo said, thinking Wanserski's logic was penny-pinching bullshit and that his boss had no intention of seeking a raise for him any time soon.

He was worn out with the whole thing. Pavlo and McCumber had fought for years to hold the line against the carriers who were screwing up their budgets. Finance had been consistently trumped by Sales, or Corporate Finance execs trying to manage quarterly earnings and the stock price, or for all he knew by Chief Executive Bert Roberts himself. He felt like Wanserski was blaming him for the problems and, the way things were going, he was afraid they'd hang a lot more on him if he didn't come up with a fix—fast.

Now that they were facing a crisis, the order had come down that no customer would be "permitted to deteriorate,"[14] to run up any further debts. Henceforth, it would be "zero tolerance" for the company's credit junkies.[15] He was instructed to tell clients that they were— really, this time—expected to keep current with their bills. New customers would have to put up a cash deposit or other collateral to get a dial tone.

These were all great ideas but none of them was going to change the fact that they were trying to shoehorn a giant-sized bad debt problem into a miniature budget.

At least Caribbean Tel was no longer his problem. MCI had shifted a chunk of its mammoth debt to a $10.25 million promissory note.[16] The company had also dropped off Carrier Finance's aging debt reports, indicating it was no longer even on the network. Pavlo had heard that the company had stopped distributing its calling cards in February. Now it was the subject of yet more heated, closed-door discussions between McCumber, who still had a hand in winding down the debacle, and his bosses. Pavlo assumed Caribbean Tel had become a flat-liner and MCI would get burned for $55 million. Hi-Rim was already over $25 million and would be close behind.

All of which led Pavlo back to Hilby's offer. He decided he was best off heeding his parents' admonishment: Anything sounding too good to be true probably is.

He would stick around MCI and move ahead with the Manatee plan. Pavlo had spent untold hours working out the details with Benveniste over a couple months, and he had a good feeling about the setup. If it worked, he'd be hailed as a financial genius. Even if it didn't, his connections would surely lead to a job offer he might actually consider, or something else that would make it "worth his while."

During all his discussions with Benveniste, Pavlo never once mentioned it to anyone at MCI, let alone getting someone up the ladder to approve it. Instead, he allowed Benveniste to proceed as though Pavlo had the blessings of MCI Chief Financial Officer, Doug Maine, himself. The day finally arrived when all the legal paperwork had been finalized and printed, ready for signatures.

Pavlo felt a twinge of guilt about how he was handling the Manatee arrangement. But it was easy to justify his decision to go it alone. MCI not only didn't have written policies about what types of contracts Pavlo could and couldn't approve, its guiding light, Bill McGowan, had once even threatened to fire anyone caught writing a systems and procedures handbook.[17]

Unofficially, only company officers were to sign such important contracts. That would have taken forever and probably killed the financing entirely. Pavlo managed to blow past his misgivings by reminding himself that everyone at MCI was on the make. Sales sneaked deadbeats onto the network. Finance wrote worthless promissory notes. Accounting created the bookkeeping to hide MCI's past-due balances.

The company credo seemed to be, "Better to beg for forgiveness than ask for permission."

The Finance Agreement outlined the terms under which Manatee would lend to MCI's reseller customers, and included an Indemnity Agreement under which MCI guaranteed up to $40 million in loans of any customers that defaulted.

National Bank of Canada signed separate agreements to finance Manatee. The bank's own policy required that loan guarantees be accompanied by a certificate of a corporate representative's authority to act, and a legal opinion supporting that authority.[18] But this time, all the bank did was have a loan officer call MCI's switchboard to verify that Pavlo worked there.[19] That call, along with Pavlo's Georgia Club performance in front of Roger Smock and his National Bank of Canada bobble-heads, was the sum total of the banks' due diligence.

So he blithely signed the papers on behalf of MCI, documents to back transactions that could put the company on the hook for $40 million. It was a big moment in Pavlo's career. He had negotiated a major contract that could pull MCI's bacon out of the fire, all by himself, without even telling Wanserski.

Pavlo stuffed the signed documents in the envelope. He felt sure this was a good deal. At least as good as Cam-Net's. Besides, business was booming. MCI's formerly pissant little rival WorldCom was now a member of the mighty S&P 500 index.[20] Demand for bandwidth was infinite. So he'd signed a little loan guarantee. What was the worst thing that could happen? MCI would get stuck for debt it wasn't going to collect anyway? More likely, it would be bought out and all its dirty little secrets would be buried forever. Fuck 'em all! Pavlo thought.

Putting the Cat on the Roof

EVEN AS PAVLO WENT AHEAD with the Manatee financing, he continued to mull Hilby's offer. Hilby might not have the money he was bragging he'd pay. Simple Access might go bust. But a $100,000 signing bonus would make up for a lot of potential risks. Pavlo figured the smart thing was to check out Hilby. Nobody was better qualified to render an opinion than Harold Mann. He and Hilby had been partners in TNI until Hilby bought Mann out. Pavlo called Mann and set up a lunch date.

Pavlo arrived first and killed time browsing the *Wall Street Journal*. He noticed an item about MCI's new Internet 2000 initiative. The company planned to spend $2 billion over the next four years tripling its network capacity.[1] It was all part of a myth propagated by WorldCom and swallowed whole by the U.S. government, no less—that bandwidth demand was doubling every hundred days. Who cared if it was bullshit? The important thing was the lift it gave telecom stocks.

Mann arrived, they ordered drinks, and Pavlo started right in.

"I want to talk to you about a business opportunity."

"Outstanding. You're never gonna make the big bucks with your nose up some bureaucrat's ass at MCI," Mann said. "But you can't bail from MCI now that this Manatee thing's in the works, okay?"

"A man's gotta keep his options open," Pavlo said.

"Where's the offer at, Wally?"

"Simple Access."

"Bob-fucking-Hilby's Internet thing? Have you lost it? You told me yourself he's paying MCI late. He'll be out of business in a year, max." Mann put his right hand in the air and snapped his fingers. "The burgers here are unbelievable. Just like the waitresses' behinds, eh? Are you an ass man?"

"I know Hilby's a low-life," Pavlo said. "But with what he's offering, and what I'm earning at MCI, he could pay my signing bonus and go bust in a week and I'd still be ahead."

"What're you making again? One-sixty?"

"Very funny, Harold. We've been through this before."

Mann laughed. "Sorry. I didn't mean it that way."

Of course you did, Pavlo thought. "Anyway, it pisses me off 'cause I've got people working for me makin' as much as I am."

"Gotta love the way these big companies exploit labor. Gives a struggling entrepreneur hope," Mann said. "Look. Fucked up as things are at MCI, do yourself and me a favor. Stay away from Hilby. This telecom financing thing's gonna take care of both of us. But you gotta stick with MCI. Just hang in there."

"If one more person tells me to 'hang in there' I'm gonna heave on 'em. Besides, it could be a lot of hanging. Now that I've signed it, even if this Manatee deal takes off—and I mean if—it's gonna be at least a couple months. I've got carriers blowing up every day."

"We don't even gotta wait for Manatee. Just stay put at MCI, eh? I'll get back to you soon. Look. I gotta go, but buy yourself a nice lunch." He stood, patted Pavlo on the shoulder and left. Sticking out from under his newspaper was a one hundred dollar bill.

Over the next couple of weeks, Hilby called Pavlo to update him about the grand plans for Simple Access, but he wasn't pushing hard for an answer. Pavlo guessed that he wasn't quite finished milking TNI for startup money. As long as Pavlo was at MCI, then TNI would stay on the network.

Meanwhile, Pavlo and Mann were talking regularly. Mann expressed sympathy for Pavlo's dilemma, and seemed genuinely interested in trying to help. When Mann suggested another lunch, Pavlo accepted with hopes rising.

"Hilby owes you $2 million, right?" Mann asked.

"Yeah. About that."

"Suppose you put the heat on him to come up with the whole $2 million fast."

"How fast?"

"A week. No. Two weeks. You tell him either he pays up or he's fucked. You'll disconnect him."

"There's no way he's gonna come up with that kinda cash that fast."

"No, but he'll bust his ass to come up with enough to keep TNI alive. Then I'll be there for him."

"What does that mean?" Pavlo wondered why the hell Mann would do anything to help Hilby?

"I tell Hilby I'll take over his $2 million debt to MCI. In exchange, he's got to give me an upfront fee for structuring the deal and pay back the rest over time. Could you pressure him first?"

"I could. But why should I? When Hilby pays you, are you gonna pay MCI?"

"Not necessarily," Mann said slyly, sipping his drink.

"What the hell does that mean?"

"Don't worry about that for now. Just pressure Hilby. Do it for yourself. If he settles up with MCI, it means he's got a big stash somewhere and you should take that Simple Access job. If he doesn't, and I know he doesn't, then we have the makings of a lucrative new venture."

It was one of those moments when Pavlo saw in Mann something to envy. He was a master at business warfare. He knew how to work systems and people. Why had he even thought for a second about accepting Hilby's offer? But what was this "lucrative new venture"?

"I guess there's no harm in putting the thumb screws to the fat fuck," Pavlo said. "I do it to dozens of others every month."

Mann grinned. "This is perfect. Everything's going according to plan. Just do your job and leave the rest to me, eh?"

He was intrigued by what Mann had up his sleeve. He had no doubt that somewhere down the road there was a pot of gold with his name on it. But he couldn't figure out how it was all going to play out.

|||

Zero Tolerance might be MCI's new policy, but nobody seemed too anxious for Pavlo to actually implement it. It seemed to be more of a bargaining ploy. After all, unplugging delinquent customers involved the same calculus as before: Sales fought it with a rear-guard action, and cut-off customers became a stain of red ink. Pavlo decided that if he was going to club Hilby with the Zero Tolerance thing, he'd better let Wanserski in on it first.

"Jim, I think it's time we made an example of a delinquent carrier," he said one morning in Wanserski's hopelessly cluttered office. "It might scare the others into line."

"Interesting idea," Wanserski said. "I'm tired of all this non-sense as well. But we've got to keep Sales in mind. And your budget. Maybe a small account."

"How about TNI?"

"Sure. Who's TNI?"[2]

"They're a 900 consolidator over in Marietta. A smut whole-saler of sorts."

"I've never cared for that industry. What's our exposure?"

"They're behind about $2 million."

"Those cheats!"

"I think we should demand a million within seven days, and then weekly payments of $100,000 until they're current."

"And if they refuse?"

"We disconnect. No one's gonna shed a tear over a 900 outfit going out of business. We'll just write it off."

"I guess Sales couldn't make too much of a stink about one that size. But you'll check with Harriman in Accounting first, right?"

"For sure."

"Fine. Let's get on this TIN thing."

"TNI," Pavlo corrected.

"Right, TNI."

If Hilby paid, Pavlo would head off to an Internet career in San Francisco. If not, he'd stay put and see where Mann led him. Or he could just stick with MCI and get his kicks torturing resellers, wait-ing for the payday when MCI was bought out. That April, two pairs of regional phone companies, Bell Atlantic-NYNEX and Pacific Telesis-SBC, announced merger plans,[3] and AT&T's equipment arm, Lucent Technologies, did the largest public stock offering in history.[4]

Like a cold-blooded assassin, Pavlo planned when and where he was going to ambush Hilby. He'd scored an invite from Cindy Shaw to MCI's skybox at Fulton County Stadium for the opening game of the Brave's 1996 season. It was a good score. The Braves had won the World Series the year before. He asked Shaw to have Hilby join him,[5] knowing Hilby would jump at the chance to see the game and find out whether he'd hooked Pavlo with his offer.

Once they got settled in and had their drinks and cigars, Pavlo began, "I know this isn't the best place to talk shop, but I thought I should give you a heads up about MCI's new Zero Tolerance policy."

"Sounds like a program for drunk drivers," Hilby said, chuckling as he shoved half a hot dog in his mouth.

"Actually, it's for carriers. We're not letting guys run up debts anymore. You've got to pay off what you owe right away and start keeping current."

Hilby stopped chewing. Then, muffled through his mouthful of food, he said, "Or what?"

Pavlo felt a rush of adrenaline. "Or we're gonna play hardball, no pun intended. I just figured I should let you know."

Hilby swallowed the bolus of food and washed it down with a pull of Scotch. Then, with studied casualness, he said, "You give Frank a call tomorrow. Tell him what you need. I'm here to watch the game. And another thing, Walt. I'm gonna need your answer on Simple Access pretty soon."

Pavlo chuckled to himself. He couldn't wait to tell Mann. It was high-stakes poker. He was pretending to bluff, while almost certain that Hilby was drawing dead.

"Not a problem, Bob."

The next morning Pavlo called Frank Pazera at TNI.

"We've been friends for a long time so this is difficult," Pavlo lied to his old colleague. "The big dogs're all over my ass to get some accounts paid down and TNI's first on their list." Actually, it would have been more like fifty-first if such a list existed, but Pavlo was going for dramatic effect.

"Shit!" Pazera spluttered. "I knew this was gonna happen. I told Bob to... Never mind. What're we talking, Walt?"

"They want a million by next week and $100,000 a week until you're current."

"That's impossible and you know it. What about a note or something like we used to do when I was there? Work with me here!"

Pavlo leaned back in his chair and put his feet up on the desk, enjoying the moment. "I'd love to help, Frank, but it's out of my hands. This is coming from the top."

"I don't know what to tell you. Let me get with Bob and see what we can do."

"You do that. But I've got to formalize this. I'm over-nighting a demand letter with the payment terms and consequences for failure to comply."

"Consequences? What consequences?"

"Disconnection."

"Jesus! I'll be in touch," Pazera said coldly.

Pavlo hung up and decided to go downstairs for a smoke. He knew it would be a matter of minutes before his phone rang with Hilby on the other end fuming. This way he could let the call go to voice mail and make Hilby sweat and swear. He detoured by Wanserski's office on the way out.

"I've just gotten off the phone with TNI and I expect the owner to call back soon."

"Bully for you. They going to pay up?"

Pavlo almost envied Wanserski's naiveté. Carriers never sent in big checks just because MCI asked. "They're looking into it, but I'm not optimistic. We need to keep the pressure on. You could help."

"Sure."

"I'd like you to play the bad cop on the call. 'We've got this new Zero Tolerance policy' and all that."

"As long as it won't take too long. I've got an appointment to get my allergy shot."

"Nah. Just a few words showing we mean business. The important thing is they come from a director."

"Right-o," Wanserski said.

Pavlo got back from his smoke to find a message from Hilby saying he was in San Francisco and was sure they could "work something out." He left a number.

Pavlo went into Wanserski's office and put the call through on the speaker phone. Hilby would understand that Pavlo couldn't let on that he and Hilby had been hobnobbing, so he put on his professional tone, enjoying the irony of the moment.

"Mr. Hilby? This is Walter Pavlo at MCI. I have James Wanserski, director of the Carrier Finance Division, here on the speaker phone."

Hilby hesitated for a moment. "Hello, gentlemen."

Pavlo launched into a diatribe about TNI's contractual obligations, reading aloud the language in Hilby's agreement under which MCI could have terminated TNI long ago. Wanserski piped in with a surprisingly spirited little sermon on the seriousness of the situation. Hilby, sounding stunned, said he'd talk with Pazera and get back to them.

Pavlo thanked Wanserski and double-timed back to his office to call Mann and brag about his performance, and his strategy of dragging Wanserski into it. Mann had a good laugh. He said he'd call Hilby late in the day, to avoid the appearance of a planned one-two punch, while leaving Hilby too little time to find another escape.

But Hilby called Mann first. Pavlo didn't know it at the time, but Mann owed Hilby more than $600,000 for telephone usage in addition to the $600,000 in credit that Hilby gave him when he bought Mann out of TNI. One of Mann's objectives now was a squeeze play on Hilby that would cancel out Mann's debt to TNI.

As much as Pavlo had enjoyed skewering Hilby, Mann's pleasure was heightened by knowing the cards in everyone's hand. As he took the call his voice was brimming with bravado and good cheer. "So, Bob. What're you doing out there in Fag Francisco?"

"Working," said Hilby, sounding morose. "Listen, I'm not gonna sugar-coat this Harold. My dick's in a wringer. MCI's cracking down and I don't have the cash to pay 'em."

"Bummer, eh?" Mann said.

"Frank says you still owe me $619,000. I need you to come up with some of it now so I can throw MCI a bone."

"Gee, Bob. I'd love to help, but—"

"Harold, they're gonna disconnect my ass. I'm gonna lose the whole fuckin' company."

"Settle down, buddy." Mann called out to his secretary, "Gloria, bring me another soda, eh? Now, where were we, Bob?"

"Me getting disconnected."

"Oh, yeah. Right. Listen, MCI's played this game before."

"It's different this time," Hilby said, his voice rising slightly. He had good reason to think so. Pavlo was the MCI guy threatening to drive him out of business—the same one he had offered a $300,000 job.

"How much you into them for?"

"Two million, or somewhere near it."

"Bob, Bob! That's a damn shame. You've really let the company go to hell since I left."

"I'm not gonna get into that!" Hilby barked. "You owe me money. I need it!"

"Well, let me think now. Maybe I can help. Tell you what. Have Frank send me a statement of what I owe you and what you owe MCI. I'll make some calls. See what I can do."

"Alright," Hilby said, heaving a great sigh. "I'll be back in Atlanta tonight. Can we meet?"

"Sure. Swing by my office. We'll talk."

Mann hung up and immediately dialed Pavlo. They agreed to meet at Taco Mac, which was far from MCI, and close to Mann's office.

"Here's the deal," Mann said. "I tell Hilby he has to sign a $1.5 million promissory note with a new company I'm setting up."

"I told you he owes us $2 million."

"Humor me, Wally. My new company takes over TNI's debt, eh? In exchange, TNI pays me $300,000 up front for putting the deal together, plus regular monthly payments."

"Can he come up with the upfront money?"

"He can scrounge up three hundred grand if it's that or watch his cash cow croak."

"Lemme make sure I have this straight. Hilby pays you $300,000 up front. Then the monthly payments go to MCI?"

"I was figuring it'd be a wash for MCI," Mann said coyly.

"Meaning what?"

"Is Hilby planning to pay MCI?"

"He's better than most about paying something. But if you're asking whether we'll ever see the $2 million he's behind on, I doubt it."

"Then, if we don't pay MCI, it's not really out anything." Mann batted his eyes for effect. "I mean, you can't steal money MCI wasn't going to get anyway, right?"

Pavlo felt a flush rising up his neck. He shook a cigarette out of his pack and lit it, trying to keep his hand from shaking.

"You got one going already, Wally."

Pavlo blinked. He stubbed out the burning cigarette in the ashtray.

"Okay, Harold. Let's have it. Where's Hilby's money going?"

"Where do you think?"

"You tell me."

"What is this? Twenty questions?" Mann laughed. "How 'bout if the money goes to us? Fifty-fifty. That's a hundred and fifty grand up front for you and a comfy stream of cash to follow."

Holy shit, Pavlo thought. The guy's an evil goddamned genius! Mann knew exactly what was going on at MCI. Deadbeat balances were being shoved into every hidden corner and crevice they could find. Who'd miss a lousy $2 million if MCI wrote it off or shifted it onto one of those worthless promissory notes that were piling up in Accounting? And who was going to feel sorry for Hilby for being shaken down for a few hundred grand?

A hundred and fifty thousand dollars! It was the sort of big score Pavlo had been dreaming about.

"I see," was all he could manage to croak out. Then he thought about how many customers there were like Hilby, destined for bankruptcy but anxious to suck MCI's dial-tone teat as long as possible. Any one of them would do just about anything to keep their own cash cows giving milk.

"You know, Wally, we could turn this into a regular production line," Mann said, reading his mind. "Hey, don'cha love the boobs on the waitresses in this place?"

"Could you elaborate?" Pavlo asked.

"I think it's the low-cut Mexican necklines. Keeps their hooters nice and perked-up."

"I mean elaborate on turning this into a production line."

"You ever hear the one about the two brothers and the cat?"

"No."

"There's these two brothers, Jim and Bill. Jim asks Bill to keep his cat while he's away. Jim gets back, calls Bill and asks about the cat. 'She's dead. A car flattened her,' Bill says.

"Jim's devastated. 'You could've broken the news to me a little more gently!' he yells.

"'Yeah? How?' Bill asks.

"'Well, first you could've said she's stuck on the roof. Then when I called back that she'd jumped to a tree. Then that she'd fallen out of the tree, run into the road, and gotten killed by a car.'

"Bill says, 'I'll remember that. By the way, how's Mom?'

"'She's on the roof,' Jim says."

"Very funny," Pavlo said. His heart was pounding. Mann was proposing a felonious scam, illustrating it with stupid jokes. "What's the point?"

"We gotta take our time. Put the cat on the roof. Like you did with Hilby at the Braves game. You set up carriers by threatening to disconnect 'em. Then I come along and save the day. Give 'em the 'ol one-two," Mann said.

"There's one problem. If we pocket Hilby's money, pretty soon MCI's gonna shut down TNI for not paying the debt he thinks you're gonna cover. Then he's gonna say you were supposed to pay it and we're fucked."

"As far as MCI's concerned TNI will be a model client," Mann said. "You already told me all the ways you guys're making other carriers' debts disappear. Just make TNI's disappear. Apply some of that unapplied cash or whatever shit it is you guys do. You gotta admit. It's for a great cause, eh?"

"It isn't that easy, Harold."

"Hey, you're a smart guy! You telling me you can't hide a $2 million needle in MCI's $2 billion haystack?"

"That's the easy part. But what you're suggesting is...you know...wrong." Pavlo couldn't say the word out loud: "criminal."

"Spare me the sermon, Wally," Mann said, waving a hand. "Hilby and the rest of 'em are out-and-out deadbeats. You guys at MCI aren't any different. Just better dressers."

"C'mon, Harold."

"C'mon, my ass! You guys're cookin' the books over there and you know it. Everybody cheats. That's the way the world works. Your problem, Wally, is that you haven't figured out how to make money at it."

Mann's twisted logic made perfect sense. Money, tons of it, was being manipulated, lied about, misused, misplaced, stolen. By everybody. Pavlo knew the whole world didn't work that way, but his did, from the corporate chiefs above to the scumbag customers below.

If MCI had been paying him what he was worth, treating him fairly, he reasoned, he'd have less to complain about. But he was getting screwed, too. Sixty-three thousand dollars a year to play nanny to two billion! MCI had driven him away from his family and into the arms of cigarettes and booze. "They" were cooking the books and he was helping "them" do it, while enjoying none of the benefit.

The scheme Mann was describing, Pavlo told himself, was no worse than what MCI's customers were doing to MCI, or what MCI was doing to its shareholders. Embezzlement was the legal term for Mann's proposal. But it wasn't like he was going to trick old ladies out of their savings or bash anyone over the head. It was victimless embezzlement—unless you counted hustlers as victims. Pavlo had no trouble drawing a straight line, through all the twisted logic, from his misery to Mann's solution.

"Let me think about it."

"Fine. Think about it. But take it from me. This is a rare opportunity, Wally. You wanna make some serious money, this is your chance."

His head spinning, Pavlo rushed home from work that evening to make Bubby and Howie's T-ball games and treat them to McDonald's for dinner. After he had bathed them and read them a bedtime story, he went into his den, opened his laptop, and launched the receivables database, running various screens to see which and how many customers fit Mann's profile: shady operators behind on their payments. There were dozens.

He leaned back, listening to the quieting house. Rhoda was folding laundry and watching a re-run of *thirtysomething*. The boys were growing up fast. This was his chance to have the cash to enjoy life instead of constantly stretching and feeling like the pauper and poser in his gated St. Marlo neighborhood.

With the kind of money Mann was talking about, the Pavlos' vacations would no longer consist of visits to relatives in Ohio and Georgia. After years of toil, he would finally be able to treat Rhoda and the boys to some of the pampering that his crooked clients enjoyed, and that he personally experienced on MCI's dime when he had to travel on behalf of a company he had grown to despise. Instead, Pavlo would be able to fly his family off to luxury resorts.

He didn't think of himself as a materialist, but he was tired of striving and worrying. He could do better and, with Mann's deal, in a year or two–it wouldn't work without him at MCI–he could quit and do something he enjoyed and have a life. He'd grown up with a father who for years had dragged his family from one backwater town to the next in search of jobs. He owed Rhoda and the boys more than that. Much more. And he deserved it.

"Fuck it!" he shouted.

"What's that, honey?" Rhoda called from the living room. "Did you say something?"

"It's nothing. I'm fine."

He copied the spreadsheet into a new folder titled "Mine" and turned off his computer. He went down to the kitchen, opened a can of beer, and took a long, refreshing swallow.

He hadn't felt this good in a long, long time.

# Don't Worry Baby

PAVLO CALLED MANN at home early the next morning. "Debt doesn't just evaporate," he said. "If we're going to do this, I'll need someone on the inside. An analyst."

"Fine. But keep the party small, eh? The less the merrier."

"I've got someone in mind."

"Get 'em. This is perfect. This deal is going down!"

From the moment Pavlo realized he needed a co-conspirator to pull off the TNI deal, Sean Hennessy* popped into his mind. He was smart, aggressive, young and unashamedly ambitious. He had ruddy Irish cheeks, smiling Irish eyes and was on the make in the way of a strapping, mid-twenties fun-seeker. It also didn't hurt that he was flat-broke.

Hennessy had brought to MCI a strong Massachusetts accent and a spunky New England working-class attitude. He'd just graduated from college, in the middle of a recession, and with some buddies decided to check out the scene in Atlanta, attracted by the prospect of a Southern adventure, cheap living, and a town where there were still jobs. His father had given him an aging Ford Tempo for the trip, but it died soon after he arrived and went to work for MCI. He bummed rides to work for awhile, then commuted by a bus route that took the long way around to get to his cubicle in MCI's Concourse office. He shared an apartment with four other guys, but even so, his MCI salary didn't go far after making his college loan payments.

Hennessy was two links down the food chain from Pavlo, so the two didn't have a lot of contact. But Pavlo had seen enough of him

* Pseudonym

to form an impression that he was a bright kid with a sardonic wit and a healthy disrespect for authority. Hennessy was one of MCI's financial plumbers. He knew which levers to pull to post customer payments, issue credit memos and, when necessary, "improve" invoice dates or apply loose cash to help the team make the numbers at the month-end lapping parties.

Pavlo worked out the various scenarios in his head. If he approached Hennessy and was rebuffed, he'd laugh it off as a dark joke, a hypothetical. After all, everybody was scheming and he wasn't exactly proposing they steal from the collection plate.

If Hennessy took the bait, could he be trusted to keep his mouth shut and play the part of the good soldier? Pavlo would have to feel him out on that.

On a crisp, sunny Friday afternoon in April, 1996, Pavlo stopped by Hennessy's cubicle and suggested they go out for a beer. "My treat. I've got an idea I wanna run by you."

Hennessy responded like a puppy chasing a tennis ball. "Alright, Pavlo! You bet!" He always used Pavlo's last name in the way of teenage jocks. "Everybody's going out to American Pie after work anyway. We can meet there. What's up?"

"I'll see you there."

Pavlo had butterflies in the stomach as he drove the short distance to the singles bar in suburban Sandy Springs, parked, and walked into a storm of loud voices and pounding music. The place was full of twenty-somethings on the make. At thirty-three years old, he felt like an old man. He'd be seen as the boss making a pity visit to the factory floor.

He stopped and said hello to a couple of the other young analysts, then spotted the burly red-head and motioned Hennessy away from the crowd to a booth.

"So what's up Pavlo?" Hennessy blurted, already a bit tipsy.

Pavlo lit a cigarette and motioned to the waitress, who took their beer order. The DJ was playing some old seventies disco tunes, remixed with a techno beat. Pavlo felt like he'd wandered into a high school prom dance.

"Okay. I'm working on a deal that could have a significant financial upside for MCI...and its participants."

"Fuck MCI," Hennessy shot back. "What's in it for the participants?"

"I knew you were a real company man," Pavlo said, laughing.

"Could be many thousands for each of us."

Hennessy's eyes lit up.

"Who's *us*?"

"An associate. Me. Maybe you."

"Yeah? And the catch is?"

"It's risky," Pavlo said, launching into the spiel he had practiced on the way over. "This is not an official MCI program, nor one that's been explicitly authorized by senior management. Actually, there's a chance that, while in my estimation it would not burden MCI with additional financial liabilities, it could be construed otherwise and expose those who execute the transaction to sanctions. Possibly including dismissal or something more severe."

Hennessy looked at his boothmate for a moment, brow furrowed. "Okay. I don't have a fucking clue what you're talking about. How 'bout you cut the shit and give it to me straight?"

Pavlo was wary. "You know TNI?"

"That scumbag Hilby's outfit?"

"Yeah. That's the scumbag I had in mind. Well, I told Hilby today that if he doesn't cough up a million bucks by next week, and a hundred grand a week after that, we're gonna disconnect his ass. An associate of mine..." Pavlo glanced over his shoulder to see if anyone was sitting in the booth behind him. It was empty. "...has offered to take care of his MCI debt if Hilby will make regular payments to him."

"So what's the upside?" Hennessy asked. "Your associate's still on the hook to MCI."

The waitress delivered their beers. Pavlo waited until she left to continue. Then he leaned toward Hennessy and lowered his voice a notch.

"That's technically true, but what if TNI's debt sort of, you know, went away. I mean, we both know Hilby's gonna stiff us anyhow, so MCI wouldn't really be out anything more than it was to begin with."

Hennessy guffawed, his face lit up, and his head bobbed. "Yeah. It wouldn't be hard, Pavlo. That's for sure. How much we talking?"

"Two million."

"Are you shittin' me? Hilby's up to that much?" Hennessy chugged a long draft from his beer, licked his lips, and flashed Pavlo an ear-to-ear grin. Pavlo heaved a silent sigh of relief.

"Sean, we could do one of these a month." Pavlo sat back and lit another cigarette.

"What kind of fee you asking TNI for?" Hennessy's demeanor

quickly shifted from amazement and delight to details.

"My associate's asked Hilby for three hundred thousand up front and monthly payments of $140,000 to extinguish the debt."

"And if Accounting happens to notice that money's been misapplied?"

"We say someone screwed up and fat-fingered it, or we can put a promissory note in place. I haven't figured it all out yet." Pavlo could hardly believe the way he was talking. Or the amounts. He and Hennessy shared working-class Catholic backgrounds. They were in the first generation in their families to go to college and wear ties to work. Now they were planning to give in to the basest temptation of corporate life—pure greed. "I don't know yet how much we'll get but I'll take care of you. I promise."

"Just what I always dreamed of. To be a kept man." Hennessy smiled. Pavlo could feel the vibration of Hennessy's nervously twitching leg under the table. "Lemme think about it," he said.

Pavlo had a moment of panic. He'd spoken about something so venal out loud. It was a bell that could never be unrung. Had he misjudged Hennessy? Would he shoot his mouth off in a drunken fit of enthusiasm, or turn him in when he sobered up?

"Sure, Sean. But this is between us, right?"

"Oh, I'm gonna go straight to Wanserski," Hennessy said, rolling his eyes. "Of course it's between us, Pavlo. Like I said, fuck MCI."

Pavlo drove home with the landscape awash in the golden glow of a spring sunset. He was both exhilarated at how easy it had been to seduce Hennessy, and horrified that he'd done it. It made him feel powerful and benevolent to be helping a kid get a leg up in life, and it made him queasy wondering what might happen, what could go wrong. But he also felt confident Mann knew what he was doing. The worst thing that could happen was Accounting would notice some of the money missing, Pavlo would blame it on yet another screw-up and have Hennessy cover their tracks by misapplying money from somewhere else. Even then, they'd walk away from the Hilby sting with a wad of cash.

When Hilby got back to Atlanta, his Saturday meeting with Mann bore no resemblance to a gathering of old chums catching up on things. Hilby was all business and Mann all scamming. Mann started by declaring confidently that he had the pull at MCI to get it to accept a "sizable" discount on the $2 million that it was demanding Hilby pay immediately. After the discount, Mann would pay the balance himself. He was so confident, in fact, that he could negotiate MCI's "rack rate" way down that Hilby would have to pay him just $1.5 million over time to cover the debt. As part of the deal, Mann said Hilby also had to forget about collecting anything for the $619,000 worth of telecom charges Mann's companies had rung up on Hilby's tab.

With no viable alternatives, Hilby agreed. Mann said he would forward documents to formalize their agreement the following Monday. Then he strode out to his Mercedes 500, drove off and, speaking into the mic nestled near the visor, called Pavlo to brag.

"Wally, you're consorting with one bad dude. It was like taking candy from a baby. MCI should give us an award or something for settling up the TNI account."

"I take it that all went well," Pavlo joked. "When's he gonna call me?"

"First thing Monday, probably. Act surprised," Mann said. "Gotta go."

Sure enough, at 9 a.m. on Monday, Pavlo's office phone rang. "Walt, I think we're in good shape. I've found a wealthy investor interested in TNI. We need to meet to discuss how it'll help MCI."

Pavlo was having more fun than a kid pulling the wings off flies. "With all due respect, Bob, there's nothing to discuss. Wanserski was very clear. You pay what you owe us or we disconnect TNI and sue you. End of story."

Hilby let out a huff of exasperation. "Look, Walt. You and me... I mean, we go back a..."

"Hey, Bob. That was then. This is now. It's outta my hands. Let me know what TNI is gonna do so I can let my legal department know."

"Walt, Walt! Slow down. Lemme explain."

Hilby repeated the deal Mann had offered him. Pavlo couldn't help thinking that only in the insane telecom business would such a story evoke anything other than derisive laughter. Pavlo was supposed to buy the notion that Hilby's ex-partner, who didn't trust him, was suddenly eager to put up over a million dollars to bail him out, with no due diligence. Even if Pavlo bought it, the deal should have struck Hilby as too good to be true. But once again, Pavlo had a front-row view of the blinding powers of desperation and greed.

"So, Walt, you can see why it makes perfect sense to bring Harold into the picture. Everyone will be better off financially."

You can say that again, Pavlo thought. Just then, Hennessy stuck his head in the door of Pavlo's office carrying a cup of coffee and a handful of papers. Pavlo waved him in with a wink.

"Interesting Bob," Pavlo said. "Bob, I've just been joined by our director, Jim Wanserski, and am putting you on the speaker phone." Hennessy pointed at himself with questioning eyes and pushed the door closed. Pavlo nodded.

"Hello, Jim," Hilby said nervously.

"Afternoon," Hennessy replied.

Pavlo quickly outlined the deal Hilby had described while Hennessy cut in a few times with "right" and "I see."

"I'm for running this up the flagpole, if that's okay with you Jim," Pavlo concluded, giving Hennessy a thumbs up.

"Sure," Hennessy said.

"You hear that Bob?"

"Yeah. You're running it up the flagpole," Hilby said.

Pavlo motioned for Hennessy to keep silent. "Look, Jim had to step out. But I wouldn't dick around if I were you, Bob. You're scheduled to make your next payment to MCI this Friday. I think I can buy you until early next week. If MCI does go along with this thing, which I'm not saying it will, when could you have an agreement in place?"

"Today."

"That would certainly be in time. I'll get back with you." Pavlo hung up.

"You heard it first, Sean. Hilby's in. How 'bout you?"

"I did a little research," Hennessy said sorting through his loose papers. "The 900 accounts are so fucked up, you could hide the Titanic in there. Juggling a few million in cash and credits without anyone noticing won't be a problem."

"When will you be ready?"

"This ain't rocket science. Call Hilby and let's get in the soup," Hennessy said, waving the papers in the air.

Hennessy was psyched about the accounting challenge, as if it were some extra credit school project. But Pavlo decided to play out the charade and "run it up the flagpole." A few days later he called Hilby. "Bob, I have good news. It's a go. If the TNI debt's satisfied, we're happy at our end."

"Thank fucking God," Hilby breathed. "Fantastic. This is a great deal for all of us. Great."

Pavlo stifled a snicker. "I need for you to send me a copy of the papers you're signing with Mann." Pavlo had helped Mann draft them but the show must go on.

"You got it, buddy."

"Someone's on the other line, Bob. But let's close this by Friday."

Pavlo immediately called Mann to tell him the cat was dead in the road. Mann had already set up a Delaware corporation to handle their new "financing" business. He dubbed it Orion Management Services, reflecting his fascination with astrology, which Mann looked to for financial rather than metaphysical insights. Mann had a glossy brochure put together, replete with a stylish logo of the mythological warrior and the claim that the new venture "provides a solution to telecommunications companies that experience resource constraints, debt concerns or poor cash-flow." Mann owned 100 percent of Orion but agreed he and Pavlo would each share 47.5 percent of its profits and Dave Wickett, Mann's baby-faced financial guru, the remaining five percent.[1]

Pavlo felt like he was holding a winning lottery ticket and was champing at the bit to cash it in.

He and Hennessy got to work on the mechanics of their operation. Pavlo was in charge of collecting MCI's money and deciding–using MCI's creative accounting methods–how the cash was posted. The dual responsibilities had been handed to him to increase efficiency, but the system was utterly lacking in prudent checks-and-balances. It was, in fact, an invitation to commit fraud.

Hennessy's method of acting on the invitation was simple. The regional Bells sent Carrier Finance about thirty invoice sheets each month showing payments MCI was supposed to credit to a couple of dozen still-active 900 content providers. Hennessy had discovered about twice as many inactive 900 accounts, and that MCI was sitting on about $3 million in cash whose owners were unknown.

Hennessy took one of the invoice sheets used for the active accounts to Kinkos and had a clerk run off copies. He then filled them in with the names of inactive 900 customers and created fictitious credit memos.

He handed the sheets to Miss J., a clerk in Carrier Finance, who typed the figures into the system. As soon as the credits appeared in these small inactive accounts, Hennessy transferred the funds to TNI to retire some of its $2 million debt. The transactions required "journal vouchers" to show each had been approved by a supervisor. Hennessy got some of the approvals from Pavlo. The rest bore the name of Wanserski, thanks to MCI's practice of accepting email printouts as certified documents. All he had to do was cut and paste from a legitimate email, print it out, and, presto–the boss had signed off without knowing it. Pavlo and Hennessy dubbed the ploy their ATM machine. It would be another week or so before they saw actual folding money from the deal, but Pavlo already felt the bulge in his wallet. A few days later, he arrived home at seven o'clock, early by his usual standards. Bubby and Howie were rough-housing in the living room. Rhoda was paying some monthly bills at the corner desk. Pavlo walked up behind her and dropped a music CD in front of her.

"Beach Boys Greatest Hits!" Rhoda smiled up at him. "I love the Beach Boys, Walt. But we don't own a CD player."

"We do now."

"Oh? Where?"

"In the driveway."

Rhoda turned and gave him a skeptical look. He could feel the grin practically leaping off his face. She jumped up and dashed down the stairs. The boys, sensing something was up, followed her out the door to the garage. Feeling like a benevolent potentate, Pavlo sauntered after them. Rhoda was teary-eyed and the boys squealing with delight. Just outside the door, the lowering rays of the sun glinted off the bright red paint on a brand new BMW 318i convertible.

"I'm awfully sorry, Rhoda, but they were fresh out of mini-vans. Besides, you're way too sexy to drive a family bus."

"Oh, Walt! It's…it's just… But where…? How…?"

"Don't worry about the how. Let's go for a ride!" Pavlo said. In a move straight out of Mann's playbook, he had leased the car for $500 a month.

The family piled in and set out on a spontaneous adventure, cruising the Georgia back roads, enjoying the spring evening. Pavlo and Rhoda held hands like they hadn't in months. Love and money were in the air, along with the sweet scent of honeysuckle. The Beach Boys crooned from the CD player, "Don't Worry Baby:"

> *Well its been building up inside of me*
> *For oh I don't know how long*
> *I don't know why*
> *But I keep thinking*
> *Something's bound to go wrong*
>
> *But she looks in my eyes*
> *And makes me realize*
> *And she says "Don't worry baby"*
> *Don't worry baby*
> *Don't worry baby*
> *Everything will turn out alright.*

 **Hog Sty Bay**

THE YOUNG TURKS meeting for April 1996 produced a fresh wave of grim news. Hi-Rim had been disconnected the month before, sticking MCI with $27 million in unpaid network usage plus $8 million in penalties.[1] That was on top of Caribbean Tel's demise. Pavlo reported that the Zero Tolerance policy was unenforceable. Just tapping the brakes would result in unplugging a lot more carriers.

To lighten the mood, Pavlo added with as little spin as possible that Bob Hilby had managed to pay off TNI's entire $2 million balance. He was amazed at how easy it was to slide such news about a chronically delinquent customer past the staff. No one asked for a copy of a check or wire transfer, or any other proof. It was a bizarre and uneasy feeling, being able to steal in plain sight.

Similarly, Hilby had swallowed Mann's story without a burp. Pavlo would have expected Hilby to show more interest in how this was all being handled, but Mann had worked him into a corner and Hilby had dodged a bullet. That was enough.

Among Pavlo's more legitimate initiatives, National Bank of Canada and Manatee's Benveniste had accepted without question that he had the authority to sign MCI's loan guarantee.

He was beginning to feel bulletproof. He decided to "introduce" a second troubled MCI customer to Mann. Telecom Management Systems, Inc. was a discount reseller near Malibu, California doing only $300,000 a month on MCI's network. But it had gotten behind a few years earlier and issued MCI a $1.6 million promissory note.[2] Now it was starting to fall behind on both its current invoices and the payments against the note. All the signs were there that this was another company busily digging its own grave.

The note was personally secured by the owner,[3] but foreclosing on the company and trying to collect such a debt would be messy, expensive and in the end was likely to be fruitless.

Pavlo had flown out to see the owner, Deborah L. Ward, who threw up the usual smokescreen about MCI's inaccurate invoices. When he threatened to disconnect her, she managed to cough up a few weekly payments, but then nothing. So he arranged a conference call with Ward and Douglas Dickson, her chief financial officer and "life partner," which Pavlo gathered was Californian for common-law husband. He gave the sermon about their obligations and MCI's power to put them out of business. When Ward sounded like she was about to burst into tears, Pavlo switched gears and tone.

"Have you ever thought of bringing in outside investors, Deb?"

"Why? You know someone who'd be interested?"

"Well, I know a few guys who're always looking for the right opportunities."

"We're definitely interested," Dickson almost shouted.

"Definitely," Ward agreed.

"Okay. I'll ask around. See what I can do. No promises."

Pavlo passed on the hot lead to Mann, who let them stew for a few days and then called Ward. He told her that he'd heard good things about her company and might be interested in investing.

Within an hour, Dickson was on the phone to Pavlo, bragging, "We have a new investor. Someone who sees big potential here and is interested in taking a significant position."

"Is that right?" Pavlo said. "Gee, that's great."

"Sure is. His name's Harold Mann. I'm not sure if you know him but Harold's a great guy. Very trustworthy."

"Yeah, I've heard of him. He's got a good reputation. I hope it works out for you." Like shooting fish in a barrel, he thought. Mann is truly an evil genius.

Mann sent his financial sidekick, Dave Wickett, to California to go over TM Systems' books. Dickson insisted MCI have a presence at the meeting, so Pavlo gave Hennessy a free junket to Malibu. Wickett reported back that the company was floundering mainly because Ward and Dickson were taking big salaries for themselves, and paying salaries to Ward's mother and sister.[4] Pavlo studied their usage and became suspicious that they were siphoning off funds to launch a junk fax venture that specialized in polluting the world with mortgage pitches.[5]

But none of that mattered much, except to prove that Ward and Dickson were destined for bankruptcy court one way or the other. The cat was on the roof. Next Mann went to visit the couple and charmed them with tales of his world travels, his wine collection, and his East Cobb Equestrian Center. By the time he got to the "loan fee" of $175,000[6] and the $22,000 a month they'd have to pay to Orion Management to get rid of $2 million in debt, the only thing they wanted to know was where to sign.

To make sure Ward and Dickson didn't cheat him, Mann insisted they turn their revenue over to Benveniste's Manatee Capital to collect. Manatee, Mann explained to them, would make sure both MCI and Orion got paid.

Pavlo had crossed another line. For the first time his legitimate efforts to help MCI by offering its clients financing through Manatee were getting mixed in with his illegitimate efforts to help himself via Orion. Having made the move, Pavlo had yet another "Aha!" moment about Mann. Like a mobster, Mann had gotten control of a company, its assets, and its cash flow, which he would then methodically milk dry.

As far as MCI was concerned, Manatee was still an invisible partner. Pavlo worried that some earnest young Carrier Finance analyst would go to one of his bosses a month or two down the line asking why the checks paying the bills for TM Systems had the name Manatee on them.

Pavlo decided that he needed to somehow manipulate MCI management into blessing the arrangement. Who had the most to gain? Sales and Marketing. Whatever it took to keep customers plugged in and generating commissions was all they cared about.

In theory, signing up deadbeat clients did reps no good since they were supposed to give back commissions on bad debts. In practice, once commissions were paid out it was almost impossible to reverse them. Sales reps would threaten to quit the company or convince their superiors, who also got paid based on sales, to find an excuse to over-rule any give-back requests.

With the number of customers in trouble growing, Pavlo had been having plenty of run-ins with Sales. The Caribbean Tel debacle had given him some moral authority, proof that Sales had been overly aggressive in pushing the customer's agenda. Pavlo had started demanding that reps get new customers to put up deposits equal to three months' estimated usage before they could get on the network.

Relations between Sales and Finance, always testy, deteriorated into trench warfare.

The brilliance of Manatee—so long as no one stumbled on Pavlo's freelance loan guarantee—was that it solved Finance's and Sales' problems. Pavlo began the process of creating the aura of legitimacy about Manatee by approaching Marketing Director Leonard Dedo who was in charge of new promotions. Pavlo presented the Manatee program to Dedo as having been developed inside MCI. "We this..." and "We that..." Dedo never once asked who "we" were.

"Brilliant," he declared. "For once Finance is helping push sales instead of holding us back. Dan's gonna love this." Daniel M. Dennis, Dedo's boss and president of Carrier Marketing and Sales, had been with the company since the days when it was run by Bill McGowan. Dennis had clout.

With Dedo on board, Pavlo had no trouble convincing Dennis that Manatee was a great innovation. He even asked Pavlo to come up with a name for the Manatee program that would fire up potential customers and MCI reps.[7]

Pavlo met Benveniste for drinks and after a suitable amount of liquor, they came up with a name they believed struck the perfect balance between financial propriety and fast money: Rapid Advance.

The reps loved it. MCI Marketing turned Rapid Advance into the centerpiece of a big push to drum up new business in April, 1996.[8] That included "switchless" resellers—the group hopping on MCI's network without owning a penny's worth of their own gear. They were like junkies and Rapid Advance was their high-grade heroin.

To get Rapid Advance off the ground, MCI Marketing and Manatee each chipped in $60,000 and hired Atlanta ad agency Adair Greene.[9] It came up with a Rapid Advance logo showing a green dollar sign zipping along and the snappy slogan "Answering the Call for Instant Capital." A Rapid Advance CD-ROM went to customers bragging that the program "enabled unlimited growth." Soon, Rapid Advance coffee mugs, stop watches and banners were popping up around Concourse and MCI was marketing it nationally under the "SensiBill" moniker.[10]

Launching a program to lure new, fly-by-night customers with instant cash flew in the face of MCI's Zero Tolerance policy. But Rapid Advance was no more loopy than the other schemes management had been cooking up by 1996 to maintain MCI's growth-stock mystique. They included paying $682 million for a satellite TV license in January, the $2 billion Internet 2000 initiative unveiled in March, and a multimedia joint venture with News Corp., dubbed SkyMCI, announced in April.[11]

With Marketing and Sales on board, Pavlo headed off to Accounting to get the computer "reason codes" Carrier Finance would need to accept money from Manatee. Accounting approved them without batting an eye. When all the pieces of the puzzle were in place, Pavlo sent a fax to MCI Legal in Washington, D.C. Its eleven pages included the contract he had signed for Manatee's bank financing, minus the indemnity clause he had signed putting MCI on the hook for guaranteeing Manatee's loans to carriers. Missing too was his signature, which he figured would help him disavow ownership if Rapid Advance ever went south.

On the cover page he wrote, "This is a great opportunity for us to get out of the business of being the 'Bank' and be assured of prepayment."[12]

Pavlo also sent Legal a list of the computer codes Accounting had assigned for Manatee and a stack of Marketing's paraphernalia. He figured the more paperwork, the more legitimate the program would look and the less attention anyone would pay to the details. Legal never responded, so Pavlo forwarded a copy to Benveniste with what appeared to be a handwritten notation from an MCI attorney—but which Pavlo had scrawled himself—dubbing the contract "Approved as written."[13]

Pavlo was proud of himself for having covered all the bases. He even allowed himself the delusion that, in the end, it would be MCI's fault if the whole thing collapsed. After all, people with more authority than him had signed off and it was Legal's job to respond. Its silence was golden.

Marketing and Sales were so bowled over by Pavlo's brilliance that they invited him to present Rapid Advance to a group of MCI customers and reps at the Palm Springs Marriott during the Telecommunications Resellers Association conference in early May, 1996.[14] He accepted the invitation, but worried how Wanserski would react when he learned for the first time at the conference that his collections lieutenant had achieved rock-star status.

They met at the conference in front of MCI's booth on the trade show floor. Wanserski got there first. Behind him, a banner the size of a stretch limo displayed Rapid Advance's speeding dollar graphic with Manatee's and MCI's logos emblazoned in one corner. The knots in Pavlo's stomach unwound when Wanserski said he would be leaving the conference before the big Rapid Advance rollout Pavlo would be hosting on stage the next day.[15]

|||

The ballroom of the Palm Springs Marriott was packed with about 200 MCI vice presidents, directors, sales reps and carrier customers, plus Manatee's Mark Benveniste. When Pavlo took the podium, he put up a viewgraph illustrating how money would flow under Rapid Advance. Then he spent a half-hour explaining that, under the program, Manatee would calculate how much resellers were expected to have coming in from clients each month and quickly forward payments to them and to MCI. Manatee would then pay itself back by collecting money from end-users. He decided to end by boiling down the financing scheme to its essence.

"With Rapid Advance," he said, "MCI is putting money in our customers' pockets and, for those of you who work so hard to sell, in your pockets too." Dozens of hands shot up.

"Who's eligible for Rapid Advance again?"

"Any reseller with a revenue stream Manatee can collect," Pavlo said.

"How will this affect our commissions?" a rep asked.

"Customers who stay in good standing throw off more commissions."

"What if customers don't pay?"

"Since Manatee will control the call records and have legal rights to collect from end-users, I don't see that happening," Pavlo said.

"Are you available for meetings to go through the program with customers?"

"You bet," Pavlo smiled.

He had done it! He had gotten Sales to make Rapid Advance its own by pounding away at one simple idea: Rapid Advance meant more money quicker. Nobody in the Palm Springs crowd could argue with that.

Two days later, on May 9, Hilby formally signed his deal with Orion Management.[16] But before he started making payments, Hilby wanted a letter from MCI confirming that Orion had taken care of the $2 million owed MCI.[17] Recalling something he'd read in John

Grisham's novel *The Firm*, Pavlo avoided making blatantly fraudulent declarations about money being "credited" to TNI's account, or its debt having been "paid off." Instead, he sent Hilby a letter stating MCI appreciated his diligence in reducing TNI's debt to "zero dollars."

He told Mann to tell Hilby only that he was going to "settle" or "assume" TNI's debt with MCI—not that he'd actually paid it. Mann ignored Pavlo's advice and instead embellished the charade by presenting Hilby with a letter stating he would wire MCI $2 million on TNI's behalf by 2 p.m. on May 10, 1996.[18]

So he would not have to share the fruits of their labors with Uncle Sam, Mann arranged for an IRS tax dodge by having TNI's payments received by an entity called ACC Telemedia, in the Cayman Islands. Orion started operations with a $300,000 upfront payment from Hilby to ACC's Cayman account, and then Hilby began sending in his $140,000 a month.

Hilby assured Mann he would also meet with Mark Benveniste within a few days and hand over control of TNI's receivables to Manatee. Hilby never followed through, but with $300,000 in the bag and $140,000 a month to come, Mann wasn't sweating those details.

The day Hilby sealed his deal, Mann called Pavlo to preen about how he had twisted Hilby around his pinkie. He also said he had made reservations for Pavlo, Rhoda, and Mann's wife, Karen, to spend the weekend with him in Grand Cayman so he and Pavlo could divvy up the loot. Under the circumstances, Pavlo could hardly refuse.

The last remaining base to touch was Wanserski. Pavlo had a lunch date scheduled the following day with his boss to give him an update on the department's troubled accounts. When Pavlo told him that Hilby's TNI was no longer among them, Wanserski clapped his hands with delight.

"Good job, Walt! A few more like this and we'll really be cookin' with gas." This guy was a real piece of work, Pavlo thought. McCumber would never have bought such a tale. His old boss's bullshit detector would have gone berserk. Wanserski had turned out to be the right boss at the right time.

That Friday, in mid-May, he and Rhoda dropped the boys off with Walt's mother and drove out to Atlanta's Hartsfield International Airport to claim their first class seats on a morning flight to George Town. Pavlo was dimly aware of the Cayman Islands but knew nothing about them.

A British Overseas Territory ranked in the top ten for GDP per capita in the world, Cayman was a tax haven and had a reputation for money-laundering. The secretive money flows and favorable tax treatment had attracted thousands of companies to incorporate there, along with hundreds of banking, trust, and insurance firms. Mann had been there numerous times, and on the rental jeep ride into town he showed off his local knowledge by suggesting they snorkel in Sting Ray City, dine at Chef Tell's Grand Old House, enjoy the tarpon feeding at The Wharf, and the sunset views of the cruise ships pulling in from the Hog Sty Café. Pavlo was stunned by the natural beauty and understated elegance emanating from an economy built on tax dodgers, drug dealers and the other filthy rich.

Mann had booked a large condo at the Coral Stone Club, in the center of the world-renowned Seven Mile Beach. Outside their back door glittered a private pool and beyond it the azure waters of the Caribbean.

Rhoda had been excited by the break from her routine, but she was beginning to get suspicious about the sudden shift in Pavlo's attitude about money. After years of living within their means, suddenly there was a brand-new BMW in the driveway–leased, but new–and now first-class seats and a luxurious weekend getaway.

When she asked him where the money was coming from, Pavlo told her that he was involved in some extracurricular business with Mann that was paying off. Like everyone else, she was inclined to believe good news, and after nearly nine years of marriage and two sons she had no reason to doubt him. Besides, it was hard to quibble with the perquisites of their new lifestyle.

Pavlo and Mann dropped off their bags, left their wives to freshen up, and headed to Foster's, a local grocery, for Scotch, Red Stripe beer, and Cohiba cigars.

The men enjoyed a night of partying with their wives, and then retired for the night. Rhoda was exhausted and quickly fell asleep. Pavlo was wound up and restless. As the first glow appeared in the sky signaling the coming dawn, he walked the beach in shorts and bare feet, carrying a tumbler of Kahlúa and coffee and puffing on a cigar, pondering the bizarre path that had carried him a world away from his roots.

There was no going back now. He had crossed too many lines. He felt a mixture of terror, guilt, and rage. He hated MCI. He hated his customers. It seemed to him like the one person he respected at MCI,

McCumber, had abandoned him in the heat of battle.

That had left Pavlo at the mercy of senior Finance managers who had pledged undying loyalty to The Plan, as MCI's strategy for posting impressive numbers was known. That, in turn, had put him in a no-win position. By not allowing his department to fess up to the $120 million or $200 million or however much its bad debt had spiraled to, and without actually saying as much, Pavlo's bosses had left him with the distinct impression he had no choice but to cook the books. Or he could quit. But without another job to go to, that would have been tantamount to admitting defeat.

After a big breakfast, Pavlo and Mann dropped off Rhoda and Karen on Cardinal Avenue in George Town for some shopping and headed to the offices of International Management Services, Limited (IMS), one of the Cayman's many "management companies" that set up partnerships, corporations, and bank accounts for people who need to be invisible to authorities elsewhere.

Mann had used IMS in the past to create companies, recruit directors, and open bank accounts where he could hide his cash. IMS's offices in Harbour Centre were simple but offered a monster view of Hog Sty Bay.

As they walked into the lobby, Mann pointed to five plaques on the wall, inscribed with the names of companies unfamiliar to Pavlo. "These are all mine," he said. Mann had explained that they were going to see Michael J. Howard, who'd been in offshore banking since the early 1980s.[19] Howard was a director at IMS and of scores of other companies it had helped set up, including Mann's five.

One of Howard's most recent directorships was of ACC Telemedia, the firm Mann had minted the week before to handle the TNI deal. All it had taken was a phone call from Mann with a company name and a fax to Howard to confirm the details.

A secretary led Pavlo and Mann into a small conference room where they were greeted by a trim, well-dressed Englishman. "Welcome back to Grand Cayman," he said, shaking Mann's hand.

"Good to see you again," Mann said. "This is my partner, Walt Pavlo. He's working with me on some new projects. Call him Wally. Wally, this is Michael Howard."

"Walt's fine," Pavlo said.

"Mr. Pavlo, it's a pleasure."

"Wally here works at MCI, the big American phone company," Mann said. Under the circumstances, Pavlo would have preferred that

Mann leave out the reference to his employer, but Mann was in charge. "We've arranged for ACC Telemedia to help expedite payments from some of MCI's clients." Mann pushed across the table to Howard the $300,000 cashier's check that TNI had made out to ACC, and its freshly signed promissory note.

"Very good," said Howard.

"It's our expectation that ACC and Orion, its U.S. affiliate, will be instrumental in helping MCI improve collections. Damn these mints are good." Mann grabbed another handful of candy from a bowl in the middle of the table. "Can you get these in the States?"

"I believe so," Howard said.

"Great. Where was I?"

"ACC and Orion."

"Right. As compensation for its work, we expect ACC to receive regular wire transfers in accordance with the payment schedule on Attachment A of the promissory note I've given you."

"That explains the $140,000 we received this morning," Howard said. "Barclays called asking what to do with it."

Mann shot Pavlo a sly wink. Hilby had come through on his first monthly installment.

"You can leave it in ACC for now," Mann said. "I'll get with you next week about where to put it from there."

Howard stood."I'll get your traveling cash, gentlemen." He returned a minute later with two stacks of a hundred one-hundred-dollar bills each, plus two thousand dollars in fifties. They'd each be leaving with $11,000 cash. Mann explained that they'd have to spend more than a thousand each over the weekend to be able to arrive back in the States under the $10,000 cash reporting rule.

"Wally will be setting up his own corporation," Mann told Howard, pulling up his T-shirt and stuffing his cash into his swimsuit pocket. Pavlo had to work to get his giant wad into the pocket of his khaki shorts. Jesus, he thought. Right out of *Miami Vice*.

Howard nodded and pulled a pen and pad from his jacket. "What shall we call the corporation, Mr. Pavlo?"

"Parnell Investments," he said. "That's P-A-R-N-E-L-L." He'd been thinking about the name since the night before when Mann told him he'd need to come up with one. Parnell was the Savannah street on which Pavlo had grown up. It was where a bully named Johnny Clayton had whipped his six year-old ass until he fought back with a bicycle pump. It would be Pavlo's reminder of how far he had come.

"I'll have it done immediately," Howard said.

Pavlo wrote his name and Social Security number on Howard's notepad and gave him his driver's license to copy. He became beneficial owner of Parnell Investments, a limited liability corporation based in George Town, Grand Cayman. He was now officially an international money launderer.

Mann instructed Howard to deposit $80,000 into Parnell and $80,000 into another entity named Coby Investments from Hilby's $300,000 down payment. The remaining $140,000 was to be deposited into yet another newly-established firm, The Holding Company. Mann's game was to transfer cash out of the Cayman companies as quickly as possible after it arrived from the States. That would make it harder to track the transactions in case anyone took an interest.

The $22,000 in cash they'd just received had come from yet another Cayman account. Nothing, Mann knew from experience, inspired business partners like big stacks of bills. As they drove back to the Coral Stone Club in their Jeep, Pavlo pulled out his $11,000 and riffled the paper. He let out a loud whoop. "Thank you for doing business with Orion, or Parnell, or whoever the fuck it is," he laughed.

"This is just the start, Wally. What's our next deal?"

"TNI's done and we've got TM Systems in the hopper. I've got a couple more in mind. All the same or bigger than TNI."

"Cool. I'll set up a company here named MTC II to handle TM Systems. After that, let's take time to put the cat on the roof and do one a month. I wouldn't want to get greedy. Might attract attention."

"I've got to take care of Hennessy, too. He did all the footwork in the office for TNI."

"What's he want?" Mann asked.

"A few thousand in cash, and six more to pay off his new car would probably make him a very happy camper."

"I'll take care of it as soon as we get back," Mann said. "I've got a new office in the Olde Towne complex just off Johnson Ferry Road. I figured it'll give us a place to hang our hats and a U.S. address for appearances."

Pavlo's mind was racing. "Do you realize that if we do ten of these deals, we'll have over $2 million in the bank and a hundred grand a week coming in. This could be un-friggin-real!"

"Sounds like a good start. But this weekend let's just celebrate. And shop. We can get back to work next week."

The slick treatment at IMS, the wad of cash in his pocket, and the abandon with which Mann encouraged him to spend it had the desired effect of crowding out Pavlo's qualms during the rest of the weekend.

He took a quick inventory of his life. He effectively ran Carrier Finance, had finessed the Manatee deal, sold Rapid Advance to Marketing and Sales, and had just received $91,000 of MCI's money that it hadn't a chance in hell of discovering.

That spring evening in 1996, he and Rhoda sat on the pristine beach, holding hands while the warm wavelets lapped at their feet. The engineering classes, the MBA night school, the rat race at MCI—it all now seemed to add up to something. It wasn't the straight-and-narrow path to riches, but for the first time in his life Pavlo felt like he had made it.

Life had never been sweeter, and the future had never looked brighter.

 # This Could Be Ugly

PAVLO'S CAYMAN respite was a bright spot in a darkening landscape. The pressure of running Carrier Finance and traveling almost constantly to chase down MCI's worst customers was taking a toll on his emotions and his health. Adding to the anxiety was the fear that his Orion activities could somehow come undone. He decided that if it did, he would do well to have some ammunition of his own. He began systematically squirreling away at home evidence of MCI's accounting transgressions. If the company ever caught on to his misdeeds, he'd have a story to tell that would make him look like a shoplifter in the company of bank robbers. By his reckoning, he had personally helped MCI hide one hundred million or so in bad debt from regulators, accountants, and investors.

Previously a social drinker, Pavlo had taken to stopping for cocktails every night or working his way through a half-bottle of McClelland's scotch at home. He had gained twenty pounds on his slight frame and was approaching two hundred. The cigarette habit, which he'd picked up at MCI, was up to a pack a day. He started each morning hung over and nauseous, washing down aspirin with multiple cups of strong coffee.

Even Wanserski noticed the change and tried to lighten Pavlo's load by letting him hand off some of the high-risk accounts to James Wilkie. An attack helicopter pilot who had followed his Vietnam-vet father into the service, Wilkie had left the Army after making captain and being told he'd be piloting a desk rather than an Apache.

Pavlo first met Wilkie in 1988 when they both had been working for GEC Avionics. Pavlo had been impressed by the way Wilkie's in-your-face attitude had come in handy when they were rushing out gear for fighter jets during the First Gulf War. Office politics was not Wilkie's forte, however, and he was eventually fired for calling a female co-worker a "blonde bimbo." The bimbo turned out to be the boss's girlfriend.

Pavlo stayed in touch with Wilkie and, in 1995, landed him an interview for an MCI job with McCumber, managing special projects aimed at improving Carrier Finance's billing and order entry. A cowboy at heart, Wilkie had continued flying part-time for the Georgia National Guard. He was assigned to medical evacuations and helping the Drug Enforcement Agency nab pot farmers—usually distinguishable from the air by their desolate trailer homes, late-model Firebirds and watering hoses leading into the woods. The Guard nearly booted Wilkie after he decided to get a first-hand look at a University of Georgia football game and buzzed the stadium so low, the story went, he had turned sideways to get through the goal posts. Seven years Pavlo's senior, and having mellowed a bit, Wilkie seemed the perfect choice for chasing down deadbeats. He began looking after Pavlo's troubled accounts in the Southeast and quickly warmed to the task, enjoying the sense of mission and the frenzied pace.

Even with a ballsy guy like Wilkie helping him, Pavlo had more problems than he could handle and no legitimate ways to fix them. MCI had bowed a bit to reality in April, 1996 by adding $48.6 million to its bad debt allowance.[1] The move reduced the company's reported earnings by an equal amount. But it was still a far cry from the $100 million or so Pavlo had figured was lurking on its books. Hi-Rim alone had burned MCI for $27 million that was yet to be written off.[2]

Pavlo guessed that Sales managers might have been trying to avoid demands that they give back some of their commissions, or getting fired for keeping Hi-Rim connected long enough to do that kind of damage. Or they might have been arguing that holding a promissory note would help MCI get something out of bankruptcy court. Finance might have wanted to avoid digging into its bad debt reserve, which would then have to be topped off again, causing another hit to MCI's profit-and-loss statement. Whatever the reason, it was accounting gimmickry, pure and simple.

But no matter how fast Finance bailed, the ship kept sinking. "We are looking at a complete write-off of over $8 million,"[3] was how Pavlo described in an email to Wanserski and his boss, Jim Folk, the ugly situation that had bubbled up with a customer called ATI. The company was so obstreperous it had already refused Folk's proposal to sign a $7.5 million promissory note.[4]

Pavlo's superiors ordered him to go see the company right away. He had an assistant type up a disconnect notice to have handy just in case, and recruited the six-foot-three Hennessy to go with him as a show of force.

They took a cab from an airport hotel at LaGuardia to the company's offices in a shabby warehouse district in Queens, New York.[5] As usual, Pavlo issued the Zero Tolerance demand and, as usual, the CEO blamed MCI for screwing up the invoices.[6] The guy was red in the face and about as belligerent as any customer Pavlo had encountered.

Fearing the argument risked escalating beyond words, Pavlo excused himself and stepped outside the building with Hennessy. Pavlo called MCI's Revenue VP, Folk, at his office in Arlington, Virginia.

"Cut them off now," Folk ordered.

Pavlo hung up and turned to Hennessy. "You got the disconnect letter?"

"Yeah."

"This could be ugly."

"Are you shitting me? You're giving it to him now? Couldn't we just mail it to the sonofabitch?"

"Folk said hand it to him."

They returned to ATI's office and Pavlo handed over the notice stating ATI would be disconnected in a few weeks if it did not pay up in full. The customer started screaming, slamming his fist on his desk.

Pavlo and Hennessy packed up and left, genuinely fearful that ATI might send goons out to the street after them. Pavlo fumed all the way home. He was pissed at Folk. "Cut them off" was an easy order to give from the distant safety of an executive suite. It was quite another thing to suffer the discomfort and danger of doing it in person. It was something else to hate about MCI.

Pavlo would have felt even more frustrated had he known that while he was crawling the streets of a New York industrial ghetto getting screamed at, MCI's CEO Bert Roberts was planning to unload the company. Roberts had met that Saturday in London with Sir Iain Vallance, chairman of British Telecom, which already owned twenty percent of MCI and was its partner in an international data network.[7]

Roberts had been central to the running of MCI since he became president in 1983. He knew as well as anyone what tumbling long-distance prices were doing to MCI's prospects, to say nothing about the growing hole in Carrier Finance's revenues that Pavlo was trying to fill.

For Pavlo, money was becoming the salve for all his perceived wounds. Shitloads of it. Hilby's TNI was making its $140,000 monthly payments to Orion like clockwork. Ward and Dickson of TM Systems had paid their $175,000 commission to MTC II. As Manatee's first Rapid Advance customer, they would soon hand over control of their company's revenues to Benveniste's firm. Manatee would make sure MCI got paid on time for current network usage, and that Orion got its $22,000 a month for making TM Systems' past debt disappear.

Mann suggested that Orion pay Pavlo and him each $120,000 annual salaries. That was in addition to the money Mann said he would divvy up between their Cayman accounts and that of his CFO, Dave Wickett. Pavlo didn't like the idea of reporting two telecom salaries on his tax returns, so he arranged for his share to go to Rhoda. She'd gone back to work full-time doing office work for a small shipping company and went along with his argument that it would look better if he wasn't being paid by an MCI customer.

With so much money coming in, Mann encouraged Pavlo to live it up. He ordered a Eurocard linked to Pavlo's Parnell account and hauled him off to Bespoke Apparel in Atlanta, a men's tailoring shop that catered to the rich and famous. Pavlo felt reckless picking out a $2,000 suit and a few pairs of pants. Mann scoffed. "C'mon, Wally. You can do better'n that!" He began rifling through wool swatches, tossing aside candidates. By the time they walked out, the value of Pavlo's wardrobe had increased by $15,000.

The pot lid of a miserable, humid summer settled on Atlanta. Mann escaped for his annual summer *intermezzo* at his lakeside cottage near Toronto. Pavlo headed off to San Francisco in mid-June for an industry conference.[8] Each morning, he left the luxurious sanctuary of his room at the Westin St. Francis to spend a humiliating and soul-draining day chasing down delinquent carriers on the convention floor. By the last night he was ready to let loose. He got plastered at the open bars hosted by the various convention sponsors. Then, in hallowed tradition, he headed off with a pack of MCI managers and other conventioneers to Mitchell Brothers O'Farrell Theatre, a legendary strip club. For a few hours he was in an adult Disneyland, far away from the pressures of his job, his crimes, and his failings as a father and husband.

He finally staggered onto O'Farrell Street at two o'clock in the morning, tipsy and feeling in need of a good hot shower. He started walking back to the St. Francis and was a block away when a homeless woman in greasy, dusty rags blocked the sidewalk, her hand outstretched. Pavlo sized her up for a second and then an irresistible urge overcame him. He reached in his pocket and pulled out a wad of Orion money, about five hundred dollars, and handed it to her. Without a word, the woman slipped it into a pocket and lumbered off into the darkness.

Pavlo slept better that night than he had in months.

|||

In late June, he got a call directly from Jim Folk, Wanserski's boss. Sharp, in his late forties, with a math degree and MBA, Folk had been with MCI since 1990.[9] He was a company man, having done stints in government sales, consumer and wireless.[10] A vice president of revenue operations from November, 1995,[11] he had quickly zeroed in on Carrier Finance's serious "ramp-up" problem, in which resellers were running up big bills and disappearing.[12]

"I need you to put together a presentation that'll bring senior Finance people up to speed on the carrier problem," Folk said. "I don't want this mess pinned on us."

"Us" was a good start. "Glad to do it," Pavlo said, "but it's not going to be pretty. We could write off, I don't know, a hundred or a hundred-fifty million right now and still have plenty of doubtful accounts on our plate."

"Christ! A number like that would bust the damn budget. It's gotta be done carefully."

"Do you want me to break out Caribbean Tel, since everyone's calling it a watershed?"

"Hell no!" Folk blurted. "The last thing we need to do is play up our biggest disaster."

Pavlo prepared a draft of the presentation. With Wanserski on vacation and a pressing deadline, he flew to Virginia to meet with Folk and review the first draft. Pavlo explained that marginal small carriers stiffing MCI were only part of the problem. Three of its biggest accounts, WorldCom, Cable & Wireless, and Frontier, were also financial black holes.

Together, the three used more than $90 million a month in MCI long-distance, representing just over half of Carrier Finance's revenues.[13] One of the problems was that Business Development, MCI's contract negotiators, had locked MCI into long-term deals with the three that turned out to be money losers. MCI Finance tried to wriggle out of them by unilaterally tacking on $16 million a month in "surcharges."[14] All three customers balked.[15]

Pavlo was caught in the crossfire. The disputes pushed his total accounts 90 days or more past due to nearly $50 million, $24 million of it owed by the three big customers.[16] Accounting knew about the surcharge ploy, but Pavlo was feeling increased pressure anyway.

Folk was specific with Pavlo about how he wanted Carrier Finance's problems presented: state the issues clearly but do not make them look like a hopeless cause. "Work these changes into the presentation and I'll get the audience together for the meeting," Folk instructed Pavlo.

|||

The following week Pavlo traveled to Chicago to meet with Pete Cassidy, a local Sales vice president, and to present Rapid Advance to his reps. Neither Folk nor Wanserski, who were in town on other business, seemed to have caught wind of the Manatee program and Pavlo preferred to keep it that way. After meeting with them, Pavlo sneaked off to meet with Cassidy, feeling like a kid slipping out the bedroom window in the middle of the night for some mischief.

When Pavlo walked into the room, Cassidy's reps broke into applause. He thought they were psyched about Rapid Advance but it turned out they were cheering his Bespoke Apparel suit. Jesus, he thought. I may as well wear a sign saying "Embezzler." He decided to go back to wearing the cheap suits he'd worn before Mann redressed him.

The reps ate up his Rapid Advance presentation, and then Cassidy took him to dinner at Morton's Steak House.

"There's a client called Tel-Central Communications that could be really big for us this year," Cassidy told him. "It's ramping up like crazy, but I've got doubts about its owner. A guy named Denny McLain. You know him?"

"Not the pitcher who won thirty games?"

"Thirty-one," corrected Cassidy. "For the Detroit Tigers in 1968."

"Tel-Central's on our watch list, but I had no idea Denny McLain was involved," Pavlo said. "I've been dealing with some finance guy but haven't gotten anywhere."

"Denny calls the shots. He's a real piece of work, too. Flies his own plane around. He's had some serious brushes with the law too. Did time for trafficking coke some years back.[17] He also got indicted this May for helping himself to some company's pension fund."[18]

"Can you get McLain to come down to Atlanta for a little powwow?" Pavlo asked.

"I'll see what I can do. Watch him, Walt. I mean it."

A few days later, McLain flew to Atlanta. Pavlo was shocked to see how the Cy Young award winner had turned into a swollen middle ager. He was wearing an untucked tropical shirt, blowsy pants, and deck shoes with no socks. Instead of a briefcase, he was carrying a small Converse gym bag like Pavlo had used in high school.

What did impress him about McLain was his gift of gab. A radio personality in Detroit, he regaled Pavlo with accounts of his athletic derring-do in the 1968 World Series, and against Mickey Mantle.

"They say I served up a home run to Mantle, but the son-of-a-bitch could hit anything a mile. He favored my fastball though," McLain said with a wink.[19]

"I don't even want to know what that means," Pavlo said holding up his hand. "Listen, I need a commitment from you to start paying on time. They pay me to make sure you play by the rules."

"Good Lord, of course I'm gonna play by the rules! Promise! Our problems were temporary. You got any kids, Walt?"

McLain was a manipulator, like most of the people Pavlo had to put up with. He wondered where this manipulation was going.

"Two sons."

"What're their names?"

"Bubby and Howie."

The former superstar pulled a pen and two baseballs out of his gym bag. "Is that B-U-B-B-Y?"

"Yeah. And H-O-W-I-E." McLain signed the balls and set them on Pavlo's desk. His sons would be ecstatic.

The baseballs were about all he could get from McLain beyond a promise to pay. Pavlo had no time to babysit his account. He'd just have to hope McLain came through.

 **A Good Back Waxing**

WHILE ATLANTA prepared to play host to the 1996 Summer Olympics, Pavlo headed off on August 1 to Chateau Elan, a French-style hotel and winery about forty miles north of the city that doubled as a conference center. His destination was the meeting he had been preparing for over the previous weeks with Folk and Wanserski.

MCI's senior executives had retreated to Chateau Elan ostensibly to talk business but in actuality to plan which Olympic events and galas to attend while enjoying a round of golf and spoiling themselves with manicures and back waxes. Underlings like Pavlo were summoned to attend a handful of meetings that could have taken place in a Dunkin' Donuts but added an air of legitimacy to the extravagant use of corporate assets.

Pavlo was acutely aware now that he was wearing two hats. Under the white one, he was galloping after the bad guys to collect MCI's debts. Under the black one, he was robbing his employer blind. He and Mann had been in business together for four months. They had banked $940,000 in their Cayman accounts and had another $162,000 a month in installment payments coming in. Hennessy had done his part, making $11.5 million dollars disappear from MCI's bad debt total to hide the theft.

Pavlo kept telling himself that the amounts he was swindling *from* MCI were chump change compared to the amounts he was swindling *for* MCI by papering over the true condition of Carrier Finance.

Even as bad debt escalated, the department had posted write-offs of just $10 million in 1995, or $2 million less than the year before.[1]

Now, eight months into 1996, Carrier Finance revenues were forecast to nearly double for the year to $2.1 billion.[2] Under an honest accounting of the most recent figures, bad debt would jump fourteen-fold to $142 million, eight percent of total revenues, and a four-fold increase over the old benchmark. The total included $64 million in "actuals," meaning debt already recognized as uncollectible; $51 million in "exposure," representing zombie companies that were dead or dying but not officially delinquent; and Hi-Rim's $27 million that MCI still carried on its books even though it had been off MCI's network for five months,[3] had filed a breach of contract claim against MCI, and was owned by Teletek, a company under grand jury and SEC investigation.[4]

Also on the Chateau Elan agenda was the disputed surcharge issue with WorldCom, Cable & Wireless, and Frontier. That had added $20 million or so to Pavlo's headache, not to mention countless hours he had to spend in meetings with company lawyers who were handling the legal end of the pissing matches.[5]

Elsewhere in telecom, the story was similar. AT&T would end up taking a $200 million charge in 1996 for carrier accounts,[6] attributing the problem to "increased bankruptcies, delinquencies and fraud."[7] WorldCom was on the way to getting burned for nearly a quarter-billion dollars by Cherry Communications,[8] the guys with the free panties. Owner James Elliott would later blame Cherry's mismanagement on finance chief Jerry Slovinski for "coming in late and leaving early, sneaking out to work out, and 'chasing p---- all day.'"[9] Slovinski ended up suing Elliott, winning $2 million in punitive damages for emotional distress.[10] WorldCom would lose another $100 million on Communications Network Corporation, known as Conetco, which was also on its way to the corporate graveyard.[11]

MCI senior management had been informed about Carrier Finance's problems from the start. McCumber had been tight with CFO Doug Maine and spoke his mind. Pavlo had been sending monthly "High Risk" reports up the chain of command for months. With a sell-out on their minds, his bosses had fiddled over a strategy to win the war, leaving Pavlo to do his best at financial triage.

Adopting tricks already in wide use at MCI, and coming up with flourishes of his own, Pavlo had written bogus promissory notes and gotten accounting codes approved to credit MCI for payments not yet received, re-dated invoices so ancient debts appeared new, posted credits from potential customers who hadn't yet signed contracts, and delayed credits to customers who had. He had turned millions in monthly "unapplied cash" into a slush fund to bury accounts that risked going over 90 days past due. When even those ploys had fallen short, he had come through with Rapid Advance. Pavlo had been a clutch player in enabling MCI to stick to The Plan.

Folk, Wanserski, Pavlo, and Wilkie had spent much of July trying to strike the right balance in their upcoming presentation between explaining the scope of the looming disaster and why it wasn't their fault. Folk, the obvious person to speak for Carrier Finance, shifted that task on to Wanserski and Pavlo.[12] "Spare them the details," he told Pavlo.

A who's-who of MCI Finance directors and VPs was gathering in the Swan Room at Chateau Elan as Pavlo arrived. Among the leading lights were Folk; Jim Schneider, finance chief for Pavlo's entire division (and future chief financial officer of Dell Computer); Business Development VP Suleiman Hessami; Business Markets VP John McGuire; and a dozen or so rank-and-file Finance execs.[13] Wanserski, Wilkie and Pavlo were the only ones in suits.

The rest were dressed in golfing costumes—khakis and polo shirts. In the middle of the conference table a speakerphone patched in Don Lynch,[14] a senior vice president of Finance with a reputation as a bully.

Wanserski passed out the documents they'd prepared and took a seat at the table. Unlike every other MCI presentation Pavlo had ever attended, this one had no leader. Nobody, it seemed, wanted ownership of the content.

Wanserski began by covering his own ass. "Although I've only been in charge of Carrier Finance a few months, I've put together information to detail the significant issues the department faces."

"And a number of initiatives we've put in place to address these issues," Folk chimed in.

Wanserski continued, "Since the issues go back before I took control earlier this year, I've asked Walt to give us a little background."

"The situation is this," Pavlo began. "Over the past two years, Sales has proven extremely successful in expanding our carrier business. That includes long-distance resellers, debit card vendors and 900 information providers. Unfortunately, this has created a serious collections issue. Through 1994, defaults among wholesale clients never topped $12 million or so a year and carriers were never a significant credit risk.

"Unfortunately, the previous assumptions no longer hold. The clients' high growth and cash-based operations have dramatically worsened the credit profile. In fact, given the large amounts of cash the calling card vendors can collect, many of them appear to have launched with the specific intention of ramping up and defaulting on their debts to us.

"Since they weren't planning to pay us anyway, many have discounted their retail rates well below their contracted cost. We found one carrier advertising 20 cents a minute to India for which it's supposed to be paying us 80 cents."

"This is a new trend we're monitoring," Wanserski broke in. "Some carriers tell us they're low-balling on price to get better rates on new contracts or earn some other incentives. It's a gamble most of them lose."

Pavlo resumed, "Such competition has forced clients who intended to build legitimate operations to lower their rates to compete. That, in turn, renders them unable, or unwilling, to comply with the terms of their contracts."

The speakerphone crackled to life. "In other words, the bastards are stiffin' us?" Don Lynch's voice barked.

"That's correct," Pavlo said.

"What percentage we talkin'?" asked McGuire. His group had negotiated the sketchy contracts, so he stood to get some of the blame when they soured.

"I don't think we have a single prepaid card customer that's current," Pavlo said.

"Who tops your problem list?" McGuire pressed.

"The biggest losses so far are from Hi-Rim at $27 million and ICCO at $15 million." Pavlo stuck to the script that excluded Caribbean Tel, which was yesterday's story anyway. "A lot of the action lately's moved to South Florida."

"Who else?"

"Denny McLain of Tel-Central. He's ramped up quickly and looks like he's going to be trouble."

"The ball player?" asked Tom Schilling of financial planning.

"Former ball player and convicted felon," Pavlo replied. "Tel-Central owes us $5 million. We're concerned about its usage to countries where it doesn't have particularly good rates, like China. We think it's selling way below cost, but we can't prove it."

"Is Sales helping with this guy?" asked McGuire.

"They're aiding and abetting," Pavlo said. The room burst into laughter.

"Who in Sales is handling McLain?" came the voice of Don Lynch.

"The account reports up to Pete Cassidy," Pavlo said, fingering the vice president in charge of McLain's region.

"What's the contribution?" Lynch asked. "Contribution" was MCI-speak for a client's profit percentage.

"Fifty," said Schilling. "If that bastard McLain walks on his bill, that's $2.5 million pre-tax lost."

"We just can't let this happen. We gotta get that money," Lynch said. "Cash is king."

"We're on it," Folk said. Pavlo's heart sank. Another mission impossible. Wanserski madly scribbled notes as if receiving the word of God.

"What's the deal with Hi-Rim?"

"It's parent company, TeleTek, is under criminal and SEC investigations over stock manipulation," Pavlo said. "I'm not expecting a happy ending."

"Are these guys going to jail?"

"Michael Swan, the president, is at the center of the investigation and he's stepped aside. We're dealing with others now. McCumber told me one of their guys laid a gun on the table when they met."

"They're crazy if they think they're going to fuck with McCumber," Lynch said, drawing laughs.

"Whose region is it?"

"Terry Neal's."

"Maybe Neal will challenge the Hi-Rim guy to a duel and we'll get rid of two problems." More guffaws.

"It says here they owe us $27 million," said Schilling, perusing the sheet passed around at the beginning of the presentation.

"That's the number. They were disconnected back in March but we haven't written it off yet.[15] We're waiting on Accounting."

"Next," Lynch barked.

"ATI out of Queens. We gave them a disconnect notice in June and pulled the plug a few days ago. There were major issues with billing and–"

"Hold it," Lynch barked. "What's the deal with these billing problems? These guys have their own equipment to time calls and bill customers. They're just making excuses. You guys need to do whatever you gotta do to make these guys pay. Is there a way to get hold of their bank accounts or something? What assets do they have?"

"Other than the bags of cash, none."

"Can you get that?"

"You mean collect millions in cash?" Pavlo asked.

"Why not?"

"I don't know. What would we do with it?"

"Take it to the goddamn bank!" Lynch said.

Pavlo imagined himself touring the country in a Brinks truck outfitted like an RV. That would simplify things for Orion, he thought. He could just scoop some of the cash off the top.

"We don't have the ability to take cash deposits of that size, Don," Ed Smith of Accounting said.

"Look into it," Lynch said. "Next."

The meeting went on the same way for another half hour, moving from one client disaster to the next. The discussion of the disputed international surcharges was equally inconclusive and ended with the same exhortations: Keep up the pressure. Get the money. Cash is king.

Folk and Wanserski put their best spin on efforts to maximize collections. Their intentions were good but only a full-scale retreat from the wholesale market would staunch the flow of red ink.

"We need to consider The Plan in all our actions," Lynch declared as the session wound to a close. "That means getting with these bastards and squeezing the cash out of them."

The meeting broke up and Pavlo made a bee-line for the door.

Folk caught up with him in the hallway. "Good job. It's a presentation you only make once."

"Thanks," Pavlo said. He decided Folk either meant that he had adequately off-loaded the problem or that he'd be fired before it troubled such an exalted group again. Either way, he was stunned that none of MCI's executives had been willing to take decisive action, or own any responsibility for the mess they had created. He had prepared for the meeting expecting direction and commands that would help him solve Carrier Finance's spiraling problems.

Instead, they'd given him the same old line: squeeze blood out of stones. And do it without breaking any. The meeting had been a farce. An exercise in ass-covering. MCI would continue hiding its financial cancer. It helped assuage his guilty conscience some to see firsthand that nobody cared about reality, and that he was not the only one for whom the end justified any means.

|||

Pavlo returned to the office to face yet another crisis. MetroLink Communications was a local and long-distance reseller headquartered in luxury offices fifty-five stories above Chicago's West Madison Street. The company touted itself as "the only vendor able to provide customers with a full-service telecommunications package."[16] To Pavlo, it was just another client with a bad credit history and more *braggadocio* than brains. Hackers had gotten into the company's phone switch and run up an extra $7 million in stolen calls to Mexico and South America.

Pavlo called John Paulsen, MetroLink's thirty-something president, to inform him that he needed to start paying down his tab right away or risk disconnection.

"You've got to help us out," Paulsen pleaded. "Do it for MCI. We're on the verge of totally breaking through. I swear."

"Gee, John. You sound a lot like my last call," Pavlo said wearily. "I'd like to help, but we're not the ones who let the hackers in."

"Listen, I'm not supposed to tell you this," Paulsen said lowering his voice, "but we're bidding on Advantis. Lehman Brothers is backing us and we've raised about $130 million in commitments for the deal. I've got it on good authority that we've got the inside track."

Advantis was a phone network MCI had developed for IBM. Now IBM had decided to take advantage of the giddy telecom market by putting it on the block. Still, Pavlo was skeptical that a small regional outfit like MetroLink would be a frontrunner for a major deal like that. He doubted that Lehman Brothers would back it. But then again, Salomon Brothers had thrown its muscle behind Bernie Ebbers and was turning the former basketball coach into one of America's most powerful businessmen.

"When's the sale supposed to be announced?"

"Soon," Paulsen whispered. "We've pre sold most of the capacity already. I swear, Walt, in a couple months we'll be throwing off cash like you wouldn't believe, if you'll just hold off."

"I'm gonna have to get back with you," Pavlo said. The wheels started spinning. If MetroLink really was the front-runner for Advantis, it would need bridge financing to pay its delinquent MCI bills. Paulsen was desperate. MCI had him by the balls. It sounded like a job for Harold Mann and Orion.

First, Pavlo needed to check Paulsen's story. He knew some Finance people involved in Advantis, but they were pretty tight-lipped about anything that might affect MCI's stock price. Besides, Pavlo didn't want to cause any gossip about MetroLink around Finance. He decided to ring up his Sales buddies instead. They always knew what was going on and loved gabbing about it. He was surprised to hear confirmation that MetroLink had presented a bid and, with Lehman behind him, Paulsen was a legitimate contender for Advantis.

Pavlo called Mann at his summer cottage in Canada.

"Put the cat on the roof, Wally."

"How?"

"Call Paulsen. Tell him you know an investor who might be interested in MetroLink."

"Then you call and put the cat on the road?"

"Meow."

Paulsen not only took Mann's bait but agreed to run his future invoices through the MCI-Manatee Rapid Advance program. It was all so easy. Pavlo set up a meeting at Manatee's Atlanta office between Paulsen, Mann, Benveniste, Hennessy, and himself. Mann, cocky and anxious to get out of the Atlanta heat to resume his Canadian vacation, began with a bang.

"Gentlemen, let's not fuck around, eh? I've got the money to swing this deal." Mann plowed on, acting like a Wall Street master of the universe. Pavlo and Hennessy rolled their eyes at each other.

Then Paulsen launched into a long spiel about lit fiber utilization rates, net margins under various market scenarios and how bandwidth demand was doubling every hundred days.

"Hold it, hold it," Mann finally interrupted. "You guys need to leave John and me alone for a few minutes, eh?"

Pavlo, Benveniste, and Hennessy shared glances with arched eyebrows, but they'd had their fill of Paulsen's geek-speak and Mann's bluster. They headed to the parking lot for a smoke. By the time they finished, Mann had sealed the deal.

In mid-August, Paulsen signed an agreement under which MetroLink agreed to pay $500,000 up front and $92,592 a month to Orion's newest Cayman affiliate, Hightower Investments.[17] Mann took its name from the street where his horse farm was located. In exchange for MetroLink's payments, Orion took responsibility for its past-due $5 million MCI tab.[18] That meant Hennessy would make MetroLink's debt vanish from MCI's books. Paulsen also signed an agreement for Manatee to control MetroLink's revenue via Rapid Advance. Manatee then advanced MetroLink $754,573 to pay Orion, MCI, and its other bills.[19]

As amazed as he'd been by Mann before, Pavlo was now awestruck. Thanks to MCI's carelessness and the deviousness of Pavlo and

Hennessy, Mann effectively controlled whether MetroLink lived or died.

A few days later, Pavlo received a call from Suleiman Hessami, the Business Development VP who'd been at the Chateau Elan meeting.

"I need some information on a carrier named MetroLink," he said, trying to assess whether the carrier, a front runner to take over Advantis, would be a good fit for MCI's client list.

"Sounds familiar, Sulei. What do you need?"

"Usage. Whether they're paying on time. General stuff."

"Lemme see..." Pavlo said, pretending to look up MetroLink. "Seems like they're doing pretty well. Pre-paid through the end of the month. Usage is ramping up nicely. Why you asking?"

"They're bidding on Advantis," Hessami said. "Let's just say it's not looking bad for them and we might end up getting a little business out of it."

"You don't say?"

|||

With the Orion payments pouring into the Caymans, one of Pavlo's and Mann's biggest problems was how to get the avalanche of cash into the U.S. where they could spend it. Pavlo had put $75,000 into a mutual fund, wired $15,000 to a contractor for work on his basement, and burned through tens of thousands more with his Eurocard. Still, the money was piling up in the islands. Mann, as always, kept coming up with new ways to spend it.

"You're gonna like this one, Wally," he said one day with childlike glee. "It's something we can really sink our teeth into."

"I'm already cringing."

"You know Jeremy Duffy, eh?"

"The Meat Man?"

"Yeah. The guy's got the best steaks and seafood in Atlanta. Delivers right to my freezer, too. Anyway, Jeremy's got his eye on a $200,000 house in Alpharetta. He's doing well, but not $200,000 well. So I was thinking. The house would be a great investment. What if Orion helped Jeremy buy it and he paid us the rent in surf-and-turf?"

"Tell me that's a joke."

"Hear me out. We buy the house together. The Meat Man makes

his mortgage payments to us in meat and in two or three years we sell the place and split the profits. I'm talking damn good meat, Wally. Not the gristle you get at Kroger's."

There was no debating with Mann once he got an idea. A few days later, the Meat Man arrived at the Pavlos' home in St. Marlo and began off-loading the month's rent. From then on, the truck arrived weekly and the delivery man stuffed their freezer with the best prime rib, shrimp, and scallops money could buy. Nervous as he was about his double life, Pavlo couldn't help being amused by the absurdity of it all.

Dead On Arrival

NOT LONG AFTER he returned from Chateau Elan, Pavlo fielded a call from one of MCI's sales reps in Ohio, Fred Johnson*, about a carrier customer named Communications Options, Inc.—COI. "It's having a tough time," Johnson said. "They need financing."

Pavlo thought that was an odd way to phrase it. He punched up its account—$600,000 in arrears.

Johnson sounded desperate. "I was wondering if you could work out something for them like you did for TM System. You know, with Orion."

Orion? Alarm bells went off in Pavlo's head. Where the hell did Johnson catch wind of Orion? Rapid Advance was an openly promoted, MCI-sanctioned program, if you ignored Pavlo's unauthorized signing of an MCI loan guarantee. Orion, a pure scam, was supposed to be top secret.

"What have you heard about Orion, Fred?" Pavlo felt a trickle of sweat running down his side.

"Not much, really. Just that my client was at a conference in Palm Springs and heard Doug Dickson, with TM Systems, talking about an investor named Harold Mann. His company's Orion something-or-other."

"I don't think there's much I can do for you." Pavlo didn't want to get drawn into a discussion of what he did or didn't know about Orion.

"Pleeease," Johnson pleaded. "I wouldn't push but this is my biggest account. I lose them and I'm out on the street. You must know this guy, Mann."

* Pseudonym

"I'll see what I can do."

Pavlo called Mann, who calmed him down with his usual bravado. "You worry too much, Wally!" Then he called COI to set up the usual deal. COI agreed to pay Orion $100,000 up front and $3,846 a week to the Cayman account of yet another entity—Brookhaven Investments, named for a station on Atlanta's subway system. Mann also extracted an option to buy 30 percent of COI for a dollar. It was a small deal by Orion's standards, but only took Mann a couple days to throw together.

Pavlo found he couldn't push Johnson's comment out of his head. It kept repeating on him, "Orion something-or-other." If a low-level sales rep from Ohio had heard about Orion, how much more gossip was floating around the industry about these squirrely financings? How long before those rumors made their way up the grapevine to the ears of someone important?

Pavlo realized he shouldn't be surprised. Orion Management Services had in five short months done deals with TNI, TM Systems, MetroLink, and now COI. Its offshore affiliates had banked $1.7 million and were receiving monthly payments of $271,000. It was turning out to be a life-changing summer.

Back at MCI, the bottomless pit of deadbeat accounts kept Pavlo on the road, but instead of being directed to go see certain clients, he now could fashion his own itinerary. Under Wanserski, like under McCumber before him, Pavlo was the Target Man and there were plenty of targets to choose from. He had become enamored with the exotic atmosphere of Los Angeles and decided to visit a delinquent long-distance reseller named Host Communications in the heart of Beverly Hills.

Host had been struggling to stay afloat in the fiercely competitive international market until an enterprising MCI rep figured out a way to boost its usage by taking advantage of "Power Rates," a promotion intended for small new business accounts. The rep had collaborated with Host to sign it up under multiple contracts, each using a different company name that was a variation on Host but would show up as new business—HOST Communications, Inc., Host Comm., HCI, Host-CI and HC, Inc.[1]

The Host ploy was part of a broader bending of the rules by MCI's General Business Sales division—which wasn't even supposed to be marketing to other carriers—that ended up generating ever greater confusion and more angry customers who refused to pay their bills. The mess ended up in Pavlo's lap and had gotten so bad that he put together a list of these accounts and distributed it under the heading "DOA Report"—Dead on Arrival.

One of Pavlo's young billing managers uncovered the Host ploy a few months after it was hatched. Pavlo alerted his bosses, who declared the multiple contracts invalid. That left Pavlo to collect $4 million from Host, an amount that had been revised upward to reverse the lower promotional Power Rates the company had improperly been offered but wasn't entitled to.

To Pavlo, Host would have been just another customer on its way to bankruptcy except that it was an early, and legitimate, Rapid Advance customer.[2] It had signed a factoring deal in which it received $197,000 from Manatee in exchange for allowing the finance firm to collect a larger sum directly from Host's customers.

Pavlo took Hennessy with him to visit the company. They had become buddies as well as cronies in crime, and Pavlo thought it was a good idea to have a witness when dealing with miscreant carriers. On this mission, he found himself in a new and uncomfortable spot. MCI had sent him to collect its $4 million. But if he pushed Host too hard and it croaked, the bogus MCI guarantee Pavlo had signed might well float to the surface, like a ripe body. If it did, Orion's undoing could follow.

Pavlo expected the usual stalling tactic from Steve Salek, Host's owner, but instead he coughed up a check for $500,000. It wasn't $4 million, but by DOA Report standards it was a home run.

Pavlo and Hennessy headed back to the Sheraton on the Avenue of the Stars to celebrate their triumph and kill time before a conference call Pavlo had scheduled with another reseller. They downed a few beers and tried out the $1,500 worth of cigars they'd picked up at the Davidoff shop on Rodeo Drive.

Between puffs of his Anniversario, Pavlo told Hennessy that Mann was setting up an account for him in the Caymans. "I need a name for it."

"I don't care," Hennessy said. "How did you pick Parnell?"

"It's the road I grew up on in a poor section of Savannah. I'm not going back. I picked it to piss on the system."

"Exeter," Hennessy said. "E-X-E-T-E-R."

"What's that?"

"The street I grew up on. It wasn't poor. Just a regular road in Lowell, Massachusetts."

"Okay. Exeter Investments. You'll get a charge card and live like a king." Pavlo stepped over to the mini-bar fridge to pull out another beer. He popped the tab and chugged a long swallow.

He caught Hennessy staring at him. "You alright?" Hennessy asked.

"Hell yeah." Pavlo said. "Un-fuckin'-believable!"

"Me too, I guess. But do you ever…you know…feel bad about this shit? I know there's some seriously screwed-up stuff going on at MCI but–"

"Don't even go there. If it's okay for everyone else to cheat the system, why shouldn't we get our share?"

"I'm just talking, Pavlo." Hennessy fell silent, stood and shuffled to the window, gazing out at the LA skyline and the Hollywood Hills. Pavlo stared at his back for a long boozy moment, then plopped down on the sofa, his head fuzzy from drinking on an empty stomach.

In the awkward silence, he had one of his many, and increasingly frequent, spasms of guilt and self-hatred. In addition to his own sins, he had lured young Sean out of any idealism he may have had and into Pavlo's hellish world of disorganized crime. Setting up Hennessy's Cayman account was the final step in his complete corruption.

Pavlo felt bad, but they were too far down the road to change destinations now. Besides, he wanted the company. He didn't completely trust Mann, but Hennessy was like having a cool little brother to teach things to. Some goddamned lesson, he thought.

He took another sip of beer and pulled himself together enough to put on a cheerful tone. "Hey! Let's get that friggin' phone call out of the way and go have some fun. We're in Hollywood and the big boys're payin' for it."

The scheduled call was to North American Telephone's president, Hans Kasper. In response to demands for payment of a $150,000 balance, Kasper was challenging the accuracy of his monthly invoices, the usual carrier stalling tactic.

Pavlo dialed, hit the speakerphone button, and a gruff voice answered on the first ring. "Kasper."

"Hi. This is Walt…"

"I know who it is! You guys have screwed up our billing like I can't believe. You're charging for private lines you should've disconnected. Your switch timer's a joke. You're overcharging me and you damn well know it!"

Pavlo opened another beer and admired the long, silky ash on his Anniversario. He looked over at Hennessy. "You ready to go?"

"Yeah, but…" Hennessy trailed off. He pointed at the speakerphone and gave Pavlo a puzzled look.

"Who the hell you talking to?" Kasper growled through the speaker.

Pavlo picked up *USA Today* from the sofa and rattled it. "Mr. Kasper, I have in my hand a disconnect letter I'm going to overnight you this evening. It results from your failure to make timely payments as required in your contract."

"You slimy sonofabitch!"

Pavlo set his beer down on the coffee table and stood, hunched over the speakerphone with his hands on his hips, like a parent about to berate a misbehaving child. He felt a rush of alcohol mixed with adrenaline exploding in his brain.

"Mister Kasper, sir. Go fffff-uck yourself! You're a filthy, fucking thief. Fuck you! Fuck every fucking one of you!" Then he mashed the disconnect button to end the call.

Hennessy looked up at him with wide eyes and a slack jaw. Pavlo fell back on the couch, staring numbly ahead like he'd just shot someone and was waiting for the police to come and arrest him. In the hundreds of heated discussions he'd had with MCI clients, he'd never once raised his voice, much less cursed anyone.

"Pavlo, man, you gotta chill!" Hennessy said. "I mean, screw this. It's not worth it."

"Aw, I'm fine. I'm just pissed at these guys. Sick of 'em!"

"These guys? There was only one guy on the phone, dude, and you just shat all over him. Yanked his balls off."

"He deserved it. Fuck 'im! C'mon, let's get outta here and go spend some of the money we stole from the crooks."

Hennessy looked startled, confused, even a little scared. "Sure man. Whatever you say. I could use some fresh air."

They walked down Rodeo Drive, Pavlo in his Bespoke Apparel pants, shirt, and sport coat, with Hennessy, a head taller, in a T-shirt, shorts, and sneakers. They entered George Hamilton's cigar bar on Little Santa Monica Boulevard, but were intercepted by the *maitre d'*.

He gave Hennessy the top-to-bottom once-over with a look like he'd just swallowed a bad oyster. "I'm sorry sir, but we have a strict dress code."

"Can't you give him a coat?" Pavlo asked.

"Yes sir. But we have no pants," he said casting a disdainful look toward Hennessy's woolly legs.

"Okay. We can fix that. We'll be back." Pavlo marched Hennessy across Rodeo Drive to Saks Fifth Avenue. They found the men's department and Pavlo told a sales clerk, "My buddy here looks like shit. How 'bout making him look like a thousand bucks or so? Fast."

"Yes sir."

The salesman called over an assistant and set about giving Hennessy an instant makeover–Ralph Lauren sport coat and slacks, Hugo Boss shirt, Cole Haan shoes. Pavlo added a few ties for himself to the tab. Then he whipped out his Eurocard and paid the $1,200 bill.

Hennessy was happy for the new duds, thanked Pavlo, and played the pliant sidekick for the rest of the evening, which included returning triumphantly to Hamilton's and blowing $300 on scotch. The next morning, Pavlo couldn't remember what they'd discussed, or anything else about the evening. But he had the $500,000 check from Host, so his trip to L.A. must have been a success.

 **Scamming the Scammers**

EFORE PAVLO HAD BEEN bewitched by Mann, he and Rhoda had been habitual and proud penny-pinchers, managing to run a household with no credit card debt and savings that grew steadily each month. They'd nursed a high-mileage Honda for years to do it and even bunked with Pavlo's parents while saving up a down payment for their St. Marlo home.

Now, only months into their new life, Pavlo couldn't imagine going back to clipping supermarket coupons. He was the sort of junkie who got hooked on his first high. Now he needed ever stronger doses to get the same buzz. He had moments of recklessness that would have been idle fantasies before, but now he had the resources to act on them.

One day he and Rhoda were headed home in the new car after a gourmet lunch when they noticed a musical instrument store. On the spot, the couple bought a $25,000 Yamaha baby grand piano, with a digital player since no one in the family knew how to play it.

Rhoda had hired an interior designer who took her on wine-sipping shopping junkets. In one two-hour session, she blew $30,000. Pavlo dropped $2,500 on a climate-controlled humidor for the hideously expensive Cuban cigars he had smuggled through customs from the Caymans. They rarely ate at home anymore, frequenting Carbo's Café, a high-end eatery in fashionable Buckhead.

The Pavlos lavished designer clothes on their sons, even though they were happier in tattered jeans. The boys were more excited by the profusion of video games, computers and grand vacations that suddenly filled their lives and were the envy of their school-yard chums.

Pavlo and Rhoda had an unstated "don't ask, don't tell" policy about the source of their sudden prosperity. At most, Pavlo spoke of his "consulting" work and how well it was going. This shared secret, shameful to each in different ways, began to poison the rest of their lives. An emotional fault line was slowly widening into a chasm.

Aside from Hennessy and Mann, Pavlo had no one to talk to about his secret life. Hennessy was a kid, and Mann was a shark. His only real buddy was Jim Wilkie, the former chopper pilot who had worked with Pavlo before MCI and whom Pavlo had recruited to work in Carrier Finance. Wilkie was responsible for keeping the cash flowing from the company's customers in South Florida. As it was for many other industries, the area was a hothouse for fraud in telecom. Or, as Wilkie and others had come to refer to it, the tele-con business.

Wilkie was a striver, but he wasn't making much progress. He lived like Pavlo had before Mann arrived in his life. He also had two boys, and even with the extra pay from Wilkie's weekend National Guard duty, and his wife Becky's full-time job as an airline reservations agent, they were sinking into a suburban quagmire of mortgage, auto, and credit card debt. It didn't help that the Wilkies had bought a house in upscale Alpharetta a few years earlier and were forever stretching to keep apace of their wealthy neighbors' lifestyles.

Pavlo and Wilkie used to pass comments to each other, or share complaints, about how great it would be to have a little extra money, get a better job, win the lottery. They were work-weary subdivision dads and even though they were suffering, they were suffering together and they could share all the inside jokes about the company and the incompetents who ran it.

That had changed abruptly the first Sunday Pavlo arrived back with Rhoda at Hartsfield airport, refreshed by the first-class service and a weekend in the Caymans, a roll of hundreds smoking in his pocket. He could no longer respond with an honest, "Yeah, I know what you mean," when Wilkie griped about how a dead washing machine was going to blow his monthly budget and how his life would be so much better if only he had a bit more money.

Pavlo decided the decent thing to do was spread the wealth. Wilkie, like Hennessy, knew how the accounting game was played at MCI, and he had a barrel full of fish down there in South Fraud-ida. You could throw a dart at his aging report and have a solid chance of hitting a crook with a pocket waiting to be picked by Mann and Orion.

Pavlo invited Wilkie out for drinks one evening and, once again, worked off the script he'd first heard from Mann, and had repeated to Hennessy.

"How's it going in Florida?"

"Good, man. You warned me about the resellers down there, but dealing with them in person's still a trip. I sometimes wonder if any of 'em are running real businesses."

Pavlo nodded and blew out a cloud of cigarette smoke. The tobacco, mixed with the smooth, oakey scotch, gave him that "Big Time" glow.

> *I'll be a big noise with all the big boys*
> *There's so much stuff I will own*

"Yeah," Pavlo said. "I swear, this shit's more out of control every day."

Wilkie drained his tumbler and shook the ice to see if he'd missed any. "No new word on stabilizing the situation?"

"Not since the Chateau Elan farce. We've gotta be sitting on close to $200 million in bad debt and getting zero guidance on Zero Tolerance. I've thought this whole thing was a setup, ever since McCumber bailed."

Wilkie reacted as Pavlo had hoped. It had been a deliberately provocative statement.

"Gimme a friggin break," Wilkie said. "A setup by who? Why? It's just raw fuckin' greed and incompetence. End of story."

"Think about it. When things really started to head south, McCumber takes off. He sees the shit coming and knows enough to get out of the way of the splatter. Plus, he's a stand-up guy. He got tired of fighting. Now we've got Wanserski. He's never around. So when the shit does finally hit the fan, who's the one left standing in front of it? Me."

Pavlo saw a light flicker on in Wilkie's eyes. The story was so plausible Pavlo half-believed it himself. Even though he knew Wilkie was right, and that greed and incompetence were the root of MCI's problems, someone would have to take the fall.

"Jim, they're setting me up. So the way I see it, the thing to do is beat these bastards at their own game. Start looking out for yourself." He sipped a fresh Scotch and looked at Wilkie over the rim of the glass. "If you know what I mean."

Wilkie leaned back against the booth and crossed his arms. "I don't."

"You know," Pavlo said with a coy shrug. "Get your fair share."

Wilkie uncrossed his arms and leaned toward Pavlo, smirking. "What, precisely, is my old pal and esteemed colleague proposing?"

Pavlo grinned. "Did I propose something?" He was enjoying the tease, and feeling vastly benevolent knowing he had the power to help solve all his friends financial problems.

Wilkie shook a finger at Pavlo. "Like I haven't seen all the whispering between you and Hennessy lately. You better be up to something or I'm gonna start thinking you're a couple of queers."

Pavlo loved Wilkie's jaded sense of humor, and his warrior instincts.

"Okay, Jim. You can relax. We've been up to something, working on a way to make some cash on the side. We thought you'd fit in nicely."

Wilkie beamed. "You're getting me wet. Go on."

"I've gotta warn ya. I've thought it through pretty well, but there're still risks."

Wilkie waved a hand. "Yeah, yeah. Just tell me what the deal is. If I like it I'm in. If not, we just had a couple drinks. We're adults here."

Pavlo described the scheme and diagrammed the money flow on a bar napkin.

"I'm in," Wilkie declared. "South Florida's a target-rich environment. This could be great." He was already planning his attack.

"Think you could push your targets to use Manatee?" Pavlo asked. "That way we make sure we get paid."

"I could, but I thought Manatee was legit."

"Yes and no," Pavlo said. "Benveniste and I cooked it up to legitimately improve MCI's collections. It has. But nobody knows I committed MCI to guarantee Manatee's bank loans."

"Why didn't you just go to Wanserski?" Wilkie asked.

"You know, the only kick you get out of this job is when you do something creative and actually win a round. Sitting there with Manatee's bankers, I was in the zone. I just thought 'they're paying me to make my numbers, so fuck it.' After all this work, I wasn't gonna let some corporate chimp kill this deal. You know he would've. It just so happens that since Manatee got up and running, we've used it to get Orion paid as well as MCI."

"Without Manatee knowing that Orion's a scam?" Wilkie asked.

"I don't think Benveniste or his boss Jack Hammer know it is," Pavlo said. "They just collect the money and send it on."

Wilkie shook his head. "That's friggin' hilarious. Everyone's hot on this Manatee and Rapid Advance shit. MCI's customers. Its sales reps. Management. I think it's great too. It's the only thing that's making any of these bastards pay their bills."

"It took on a life of its own. Accounting thinks Marketing started it and Marketing thinks Accounting did. I'm not sure Wanserski even knows it exists."

"I gotta hand it to you, pal. You worked this out like Sun Tzu in *Art of War*. Divide and conquer." Wilkie shook his head, chuckling. "You're one seriously sick dude. You shoulda been in the Army."

"It was easy once I figured out how to play on everyone's weakness."

"Which is?"

"Greed. Flash enough dollar signs in people's eyes and it blinds them to the stupidity of what they're doing."

"Except us, right Walt?"

"When rats are fighting over the cheese, you need to think like a cat," Pavlo said. "From the Book of Harold Mann."

Wilkie held up his drink. "To Harold Mann."

|||

The following Saturday, Pavlo dropped by Wilkie's house with $3,000 in cash from the fireproof box he kept under the bed. He told Wilkie it was a down payment. Pavlo was glad to give his friend a taste of the sweet life that lay ahead.

Meanwhile, he still had his day job. He had about 450 problem customers to deal with by late August, and ignored most of the requests he was getting to visit them. He made an exception when Denny McLain, the old ball player, offered to meet him in New York City. McLain's Tel-Central tab had ballooned to $9.3 million since he had become an MCI customer nearly a year earlier.[1] And that didn't even count the most recent month's usage, which was yet to be billed. The larger-than-life, celebrity personality and the gesture of signing baseballs for his kids had left Pavlo the impression that the guy was a harmless old has-been. Clearly, Pavlo had underestimated him and felt he had a score to settle.

They met in the lobby lounge of the Marriott World Trade Center, in lower Manhattan near Wall Street. McLain brought an associate, Irwin Schneider. Pavlo had no way of knowing it, but Schneider was a disbarred securities lawyer[2] who'd specialized in manipulating stock prices for an associate of the Bonanno and Genovese crime families. Nor did Pavlo know that Schneider himself was already on the FBI's radar.[3]

Schneider seized the agenda right off the bat, pitching Pavlo on a stock deal that would solve everyone's problems and make a lot of money. McLain's privately-held Tel-Central would buy a small publicly-listed company, and then use its access to the stock market to raise a pile of money from investors. This scheme, known as a reverse merger, is a favorite of penny-stock scamsters seeking to raise money from outside investors while avoiding regulators' scrutiny.

Tel-Central was just another incompetently-run cash machine being looted by its owners, one of hundreds across the country. But by the summer of 1996, any stock with "tel" in its name could find friends on Wall Street. Tel-Central claimed to be doing $7 million in monthly billings, more than $80 million a year. That would be small for a public company, but big enough to attract some of the investment money that was chasing this hot new trend.

As he listened to Schneider, Pavlo had a fantastic brainstorm. Why not roll up all the companies Orion was scamming and do one big reverse merger? He calculated that Orion's customers together were generating revenues of about $150 million a year. MetroLink could provide the network backbone, TNI toll-free and caller-pays services, COI conventional long-distance, TM Systems local calls and faxes, and Tel-Central debit cards. It would be Ma Bell's slutty little sister.

Orion would own, or have rights to buy, a piece of each company. That meant Pavlo and Mann could cash out their stakes in Orion's "clients." Pavlo could repay all the debt owed to MCI, and still walk away a rich man. If he was going to lure Schneider into helping put such a deal together, he would have to keep Tel-Central breathing and on MCI's network.

"A reverse merger might have potential," he said. "But first MCI needs Tel-Central to make a payment. If not, my bosses are going to insist on drastic action."

"C'mon. Give an old right-hander a break. I'm good for it. I swear." McLain held his hand up, Boy Scout style.

"You gotta do better."

"I can't right now. But you heard Irwin. The cash is gonna be coming in large chunks pretty soon."

"Pretty soon isn't good enough, Denny. What Tel-Central needs is interim financing."

McLain grimaced. "Yeah, right. I'll just call Bank of America and they'll send over a truckload of cash this afternoon."

Pavlo reached in his pocket, extracted one of Mann's Orion business cards, and handed it to McLain.

"Call this guy," Pavlo said, winking.

He enjoyed the startled look on McLain's face. "You think he can do something?"

Like a cat feigning indifference to its prey, Pavlo paused to look into his glass and swirl the ice. "I think you'll find him receptive. Call and find out."

|||

Pavlo's cell phone rang as soon as he got to the south parking deck at Hartsfield International Airport.

"Where you been?" Mann barked. "Off with some babe making good use of our hard-earned money, I hope."

"New York. On business."

"Business with Denny McLain, by any chance?"

"He called you already?"

"The question is, can you make $15 million go bye-bye from MCI's books."

Pavlo assumed that in addition to $9.3 million already due, Mann's $15 million included McLain's most recent usage, which hadn't appeared on MCI invoices yet. "Fifteen million? That's three times what we did with MetroLink, Harold. I was thinking we'd only do part of what Denny owes. I need to check with Hennessy."

"No rush. Tomorrow's fine. Just sleep on the idea of how a $750,000 commission and $25,000 a week could enhance your lifestyle. Oh, yeah. I was also talking with this guy Irwin Schneider about some reverse merger shit. Let's meet tomorrow for breakfast. Eleven at Olde Towne Athletic Club," he said, referring to the upscale but under used swim and tennis venue around the corner from Mann's Marietta office. "By the way, I already told Denny I'd get this done. Don't make me look bad now. *Ciao*."

Pavlo, nursing a hangover that was worse than usual, called Hennessy into his office the following morning to tell him about the Tel-Central deal.

"Fifteen million? Have you lost your fuckin' mind?" Hennessy waved his arms, agitated. "That's a huge number. I'm running out of places to hide this stuff!"

"I know it's a lot, but look how much you hid already and nobody's said a damn word." He wasn't in the mood for a debate.

"Let me think about it."

"How 'bout thinking about a hundred grand in your pocket?"

"Fuck the money!" Hennessy was on the verge of shouting. Pavlo put a finger to his lips. Hennessy hissed, "This shit could land us in jail."

"C'mon Sean. Nobody said anything about getting caught. And if you were gonna puss out, you shoulda done it before we got so deep into this shit." Pavlo hated putting the screws to Sean. He liked the kid, but they really were way past the point of no return.

"It probably woulda been a good move," Hennessy growled.

"Look. I gotta go," Pavlo said. "You think about it. Everything's gonna be cool, okay?"

"Yeah, sure. I'll just bet."

Hennessy had been loyal, a good soldier, but he told Pavlo he'd had enough. He wanted out. The pressure was getting to Pavlo too, but he persuaded Hennessy to do Tel-Central by promising to make it the last Orion deal for both of them. Hennessy would have to stick around MCI for a few months to tidy up the accounts but then could walk away with his $100,000, more than triple his annual salary.

When Pavlo had been chasing Denny McLain for MCI's money, it had been impossible to keep him on the phone for more than thirty seconds before he begged off with some lame excuse and a vow to make a return call that never came. Now that McLain was hot to do his Orion deal, he had left a flurry of phone messages for Pavlo. It was time to call him back and put the cat in the road.

"Harold's a great businessman," McLain gushed. "He's gonna take Tel-Central to a whole 'nother level."

"Not unless you start paying on time, Denny."

"Christ, Walt! You know nobody's tried harder than me to make this work out. I'll keep up. You've got my word as a gentleman." Pavlo had to stifle a laugh. He knew McLain's word was worthless, but now it didn't matter.

Pavlo and Hennessy rode over to Orion at the end of the day to brief Mann.

"Damn, I'm good!" Mann bragged.

"Good at what? Scamming dumb shits like McLain?" Hennessy spat. Hennessy was the guy putting his neck on the line, and his contempt for Mann had reached critical mass. Mann was the lazy, rich hunter sitting on his ass while the beaters and the dogs flushed the game to him. All he had to do was raise the gun and pull the trigger.

"Hey, Sean. I'm good at seeing the big picture," Mann said, unfazed by Hennessy's caustic tone. "All these companies together could be worth a fortune. Let's take 'em public, eh?"

"First of all, that was Pavlo's idea," Hennessy said, fists clenched and his face flushed. "Second, the only thing keeping any of 'em alive is that they're using MCI's network without paying. What do we put in their stock prospectus where it says 'Business Description?' Scam artists?"

"Tell you what," Mann said. "I know this forensic accountant kid named Ian Ratner. I'll ask him to give us the skinny on fat-fuck McLain, eh?"

Hennessy folded his arms and sulked.

"Sounds good," Pavlo said as brightly as he could. "How about a name for the Cayman company that's gonna handle his money."

Mann looked out the door of his office and yelled to the janitor who was making his afternoon rounds. "Hey buddy!"

"Yes sir."

"What's your name?"

"Jake Simpson."

"Thanks, Jake. Keep up the good work." Mann grinned as he dialed the phone and got Michael Howard of IMS in the Caymans on the line.

"I need you to set up a new company for us, eh Michael? Jake Investments, Inc. Yes, J-A-K-E."

Hennessy looked at Pavlo and shrugged, flashing a weak smile. They broke out the Chivas Regal, and celebrated another score.

Jim Wilkie, meanwhile, was raring to do his first deal with Mann but it was taking some time. To keep him motivated, Pavlo had advanced him a few thousand dollars more in cash, and took him to Bespoke Apparel for a wardrobe upgrade. They were both getting fitted when Pavlo's cell phone rang. The caller ID showed it was Hennessy.

"What's up?" Pavlo answered.

"The jig is friggin' up!" Hennessy sounded frantic. "I just got a call from Accounting. They're asking about a 900 account they said 'looks suspicious.'"

"Hold on, Sean. Just tell me what happened." Pavlo's heart began to hammer. Wilkie shot Pavlo a questioning look.

"It was Mylinda Greenwell," Hennessy raced on. "She was asking about Christian News Network.[4] Christian-fucking-News. Can you believe it?"

"What's that?"

"Where I buried a couple million from Tel-Central and MetroLink. We're fucking fucked."

"What did you tell her?" Pavlo had to gulp for air.

"Nothing. She left me a voice mail. She's coming over to Concourse for some other meeting. She wants to stop by."

"Okay, get your ass outta there right now," Pavlo said. "Act sick or something. I'll call Mylinda and see what the deal is."

"*Act* sick? My friggin' gonads are in my throat. I swear I'm gonna puke."

"Relax. I'll take care of it and call you later. Everything's gonna be alright."

Shit! Pavlo thought. Hennessy had used unapplied cash to fill a dormant account called Christian News with millions of dollars in credits. Then he had shifted the bogus Christian News credits to MetroLink and Tel-Central, to make their debts disappear. He had logged onto the database using the name of ex-employees and destroyed the paper trail. It had seemed foolproof. But now Accounting had picked up the scent.

Pavlo spent a restless night, catching snatches of sleep interrupted by dark, feverish dreams. He had to prepare himself mentally to place the call to Greenwell, and sound like whatever she was interested in was a routine matter easily disposed of. But when he got her on the phone, she didn't even mention Christian News. Was her earlier call to Hennessy just a weird coincidence? Had she been poking around old accounts as part of a push Pavlo initiated to cut down on *innocent* accounting errors, and by some fluke picked out Christian News?

A few days later Pavlo spotted Greenwell in the hallway, headed in the direction of Hennessy's cubicle. He picked up some papers and positioned himself within earshot in the corridor. She was reading off a list of former employees whose log-ons Hennessy had used to cover their tracks.

Hennessy's voice said, "That one, she was some temp loser we had to let go. Did she screw up Christian News?"

"She seems to have moved $250,000 there," Greenwell said. "I can't figure out why. The account's dead."

Pavlo breathed a small sigh of relief. Maybe the other $3 million

Hennessy had shifted to Christian News was still buried.

"I'll fix it," Hennessy said enthusiastically. "Damn it's hard to find good help these days."

Hennessy could in fact fix the Christian News problem, temporarily. But if Accounting pried further, Pavlo and Hennessy would be facing the task of trying to "fix" a series of linked transactions, and do it ahead of any probing. There were only so many pockets to hide them in. Eventually, they'd run out.

The Christian News incident forced Pavlo to consider further how he might protect himself if Orion blew up. In just five months, they had erased $28 million in debt from MCI's books to cover their tracks as they had stolen $2.5 million in cash and had deposited it in Cayman Islands accounts. Mann alone had spent $620,000 of his share on boats, planes, and home improvements.

Pavlo sensed the walls beginning to close in. He focused his energy on finding an escape hatch. Rolling up Orion's "clients" into one entity and taking them public via a reverse merger was an attractive strategy but he couldn't do it from his office at MCI. He had to get Mann to take it seriously and make it happen.

Assuming MetroLink bought Advantis, the revenues of the "Orion Group" could exceed $300 million. The way Wall Street was valuing telecom stocks, that could make it worth $1 billion as a public company.

Given its ownership rights, Orion would get seventeen percent of its constituent companies' pre-IPO shares. If they went public, and the value was a billion, they stood to make $170 million. With that much sloshing around, it would be easy to convince Mann to part with enough money that Hennessy could slip it back into MCI to cover what they had taken and reverse the transactions. They'd still have over $140 million to divvy up. It was a brilliant idea, on paper.

As fall approached, Pavlo and Mann took their wives to the Cayman Islands for a weekend of R&R and to pick up some walk-around money. Mann invited Mark Benveniste of Manatee and his wife Jennifer. They all stayed at the Coral Stone Club and invited Michael Howard of IMS to join them Saturday evening for dinner.

Mann ordered bottles of Cristal champagne at $400 each, and before long everyone was enjoying a relaxing buzz. Pavlo noticed that Rhoda had drunk more than usual and was acting tipsy. Mann was holding forth about how much money Orion was making and how he was spending it, addressing Pavlo and Benveniste as if the wives were invisible.

As dessert was being cleared, Rhoda turned to Jennifer Benveniste and declared loudly, "I have no idea what they do, but they must be damn good at it. Right, Harold?"

Mann laughed. The rest of the table joined in, except for Pavlo.

"I think we should go," he whispered in Rhoda's ear.

"Why?" she asked in a belligerent tone. "I'm just starting to have fun."

"C'mon Wally," Mann said. "I'll get the bill. We can all walk the beach home."

"You're so much fun, Harold," Rhoda said. "Walt's no fun anymore. Always working. Always so serious, like something's not right with this great life of ours."

Pavlo was mortified. He could tell Rhoda was cranked up and ready for a fight.

"Let's go," he said. Pavlo got up to leave but Rhoda remained in her chair staring straight ahead.

"We're all tired from the trip down," Pavlo said, addressing Michael Howard.

"Of course," Howard smiled.

"Should we get a Cristal to go, Wally?" Mann asked as he settled the $2,300 dinner bill.

"No."

Howard, the British gent, rose and excused himself. "Let me know if you need anything, Walter. My job is to make sure you all can do your jobs better."

"No," Rhoda said, struggling to her feet and taking Howard's hand. "Your job is to keep them out of jail."

Pavlo felt a hot flush of shame rise up his neck. He nudged his wife out the door and onto Seven Mile Beach.

"Goddamnit, Rhoda! What are you trying to do? These are important people. This is how we make our money, okay?"

"The stuff seems to be falling off the trees these days, but nothing changes. You're always working and never home." She began to cry. "When do we just get to be happy?"

"What are you talking about? Isn't this what we've been working for all along? The trips? The house and cars? I've busted my ass for all this. I'm happy! Why can't you be?" But he was lying to her and to himself. He was miserable, brimming with self-hatred. He had worked so hard, risked so much, and now that the money was rolling in, every day was hell.

"I know you're cheating at something, and for all I know you're cheating on me," Rhoda sniffled. "But one thing I know for sure. You don't love me anymore." She stopped, fell to the sand, a sobbing heap.

A hundred yards or so behind them in the dim light Pavlo could hear Harold, Karen, Mark and Jennifer laughing at another one of Mann's jokes. He knew he should comfort Rhoda, but he was too angry with her. He was confused and drunk and left her on the beach to walk back to the Coral Stone Club and climb into bed. Rhoda was a few minutes behind him. They both fell into an alcohol-induced sleep without another word.

The next morning was awkward as they packed to return to Atlanta. Pavlo finally broke the ice. "I'm sorry, Rhoda."

"No, I'm sorry. No more champagne. Let's just forget it."

"I love you," Pavlo said.

"I love you, too. Maybe we can go somewhere, just the two of us."

"Where?"

"I don't care. We just have to go somewhere. Do something. Just us." There was a note of desperation in her voice.

"I'll think of a place and let you know." Pavlo smiled at her

Rhoda nodded, laid her head on his shoulder, and began crying again.

 **The Mac Daddy Card**

JIM WILKIE was eager to get going with Orion but South Florida had become such a beehive of telecom fraud that his first couple of targets went bust even before he could lure them in. Then he came up with a new angle that he pitched to Pavlo during a cigarette break outside the Concourse office.

The company he identified as the target was Champion Communications, a good MCI customer that paid its bills. Not like Orion's other marks. "What kind of deal?" Pavlo asked.

"Suppose I have Mann call Champion's owner, Eric Cherry, and offer him a discount for paying early?"

"How much of a discount?"

"However much Mann can negotiate."

"I gather Champion's 'discount' payment goes to the Caymans instead of MCI?"

"Exactly. Mann'll tell Champion that he's a big MCI customer and has tons of long-distance credits with it from some settlement. Whaddya think?"

"I think it's insane," Pavlo said. "The other companies we're scamming weren't gonna pay MCI anyway so we could kind of, you know, justify it."

"Who cares about justifying it?" Wilkie said. "This is beautiful for two reasons. First, Champion has lots of money and pays its bills. And second, nobody gives a shit how we do this job as long as the money is coming in, or looks like it's coming in, if you know what I mean," Wilkie said, eyebrows raised.

"Let me think about it."

"That sounds like a Wanserski line."

"I'll talk with Harold, okay?" Pavlo flicked his butt into the bushes.

"I already did," Wilkie said. "He loves it."

That was a jolt. What was Wilkie doing freelancing with Mann? Why hadn't Mann told him about it? Pavlo's plan was to personally control everything connecting Orion to MCI. Wilkie was a good friend but he was turning into a loose cannon.

"How much you looking to do?"

"Champion owes $690,000 for three months' usage. Hennessy erases it. When Wanserski looks at the aging report it'll look great, and that's all anyone gives a shit about anyway. Maybe he'll even promote me," Wilkie said, grinning.

"It's too risky. It feels like us chasing customers," Pavlo said. "I like when they're desperate and come to us. If we're not careful, this whole thing could spin out of control."

Wilkie threw his arm around Pavlo's shoulders. "C'mon, my man. Let's go steal some serious fucking money. Not the chump change you've been scrambling for. If we're gonna take these kinds of risks, let's go for home runs. I'm telling you, this one's a grand slam."

Pavlo chuckled. Wilkie had turned into an even bigger junkie than Pavlo. As they walked back inside, Pavlo figured he still had veto power. Hennessy was the key to making any of this happen and he was set to bail after Tel-Central. Pavlo would use Hennessy's departure to kill Wilkie's idea, then walk Wilkie through a deal like the others.

Before Pavlo could put a stick in the spokes, Mann called Champion's owner, Eric Cherry, in Delray, Florida, claiming he had millions in MCI long-distance credits he was looking to sell at a discount. If Champion would pay Orion $600,000, Mann would use his credits against Cherry's $690,000 MCI bill. The only catch was that Mann said Champion had to pay him via a Cayman account.

The Champion boss was interested but suspicious. He called Carrier Finance to check out the story. Yes, Mann's credits were legit, Senior Manager Jim Wilkie assured him. To make doubly sure, Cherry called his MCI sales reps. They confirmed that Wilkie spoke for Carrier Finance and had authority to negotiate with Champion any terms he wanted. Cherry still wanted a letter from MCI approving the deal.

He got his letter, on MCI stationery, dated October 21, 1996. It assured him that Champion's $690,000 balance with MCI would be retired "pursuant to the agreement negotiated between Champion and its financing partner."[1] The signer on behalf of MCI: Jim Wilkie, Senior Manager, Carrier Financial Services.[2]

Mann called Pavlo to crow. "Never doubt me Wally."

"About what?"

"Champion. It's done," Mann said.

"It can't be. Not without Hennessy."

"We put fifteen grand into his account today. All of a sudden, Hennessy's gung-ho again. Gotta love capitalism, eh?"

"You're shitting me, right?"

"I shit you not. Check it out. *Ciao.*"

Pavlo hated "*ciao*" even more than "Wally." He was angry and scared. Orion was out of his control now. He strolled over to Hennessy's cubicle. Sure enough, he was tapping out Champion's journal vouchers using a long-departed temporary employee's log-in. Wilkie would then approve them and pass them on to Miss J., who would key in the entries along with a thousand others that day. Then she would hand them over to Hennessy to file, but he would destroy them instead.

"We're swimming in the soup, Pavlo," Hennessy said.

He smiled, but he didn't like it.

The next day Champion transferred $600,000 to ACC Telemedia Corp.,[3] the same entity that handled TNI, at Barclays Bank in Grand Cayman. Mann parceled out the money, including $50,000 to Pavlo's Parnell Investments account.

To celebrate his first Orion score, Wilkie flew to the Caymans with his wife Becky. With Harold Mann's good name as entree, he opened an account through Michael Howard's IMS with $100,000 from the Champion transaction and named it J Four Investments, Ltd., after James Wilkie, IV. Howard handed him the customary $11,000 cash. The Wilkies had never seen, let alone held, so much money in their lives.

Becky thought Jim's story about earning the windfall off MCI commissions didn't quite add up but, like so many others, she chose to believe what she wanted, and ignored her doubts. Howard issued the Wilkies each a Eurocard. Soon they were out of debt and had a beautifully refinished basement, replete with a Bose home theater system and 53-inch Sony television. Wilkie quit his grueling weekend National Guard routine and with it went the chance to earn a military pension. His sons got so used to Wilkie whipping out the Barclays plastic they nicknamed it the "mac daddy card," after the rap lingo celebrating the blingest of bling-bling.

Pavlo got his next big scare on November 1, 1996, when Wanserski called him into his office and asked him to shut the door. Pavlo removed a stack of papers from a chair and sat, his heart thumping. He hadn't spotted any cops or MCI security people lurking around, but he was prepared for anything.

"British Telecom is buying MCI," Wanserski said. "Our stock's going through the roof."

"That's great," Pavlo said, letting out a trembling sigh. He had been hearing takeover rumors for months. He tried to divine what this meant for Orion. Maybe this was the exit strategy. Big mergers had a way of papering over all kinds of problems.

"Do you know what this means?" Wanserski asked.

"Our bosses will have British accents?"

"Stock options. No more waiting for them to vest. They're fully exercisable the day this goes through. Add the jump in the stock price and…you can do the math. It's welcome news for all of us. We've worked hard for this."

Pavlo had a few hundred thousand dollars worth of options, though it paled next to his $700,000 Orion stash. MCI vice presidents would walk away with millions. Chairman Bert Roberts would be able to cash in $23 million and chief executive Gerald Taylor $18 million in restricted compensation.[4]

"That's great news," Pavlo said, trying to sound enthusiastic.

"Potentially great. A deal this big could take a year to close. Maybe more."

"That long?" A year of nail-biting, he thought.

"Sure. And Walt," Wanserski said, lowering his voice. "We've got to hang in there until it's complete. MCI has a plan to get through this takeover and we all need to stick to it."

Suddenly everything that had happened at MCI over the preceding year or so started to make sense. The Plan, the one MCI's senior execs used to sweep so many problems under the rug, had been to sell the damn company and get rich off their stock options. They needed to keep the patient alive long enough to get through the wedding.

The company had tried everything from buying into Belize Telecom[5] to pushing a big Internet initiative to getting into TV. But with the long-distance sector going to hell, MCI's stock was still lower than it had been three years earlier.[6] Until, that is, word of the BT buyout pushed it up 20 percent in a single day, to $30.25.[7]

"Can I tell my people?" Pavlo asked.

"Sure. It's all over the news. I've got calls to make myself."

Pavlo tracked down Hennessy and Wilkie and headed to the Concourse pond. Everyone lit up.

"BT's buying MCI," Pavlo said.

"No shit!" Wilkie blurted. "We oughta be able to hose them limey fuckers for a bundle." Pavlo realized he'd created a monster in Wilkie.

"It's the American fuckers I'm thinking about," Pavlo said. "The buyout's why Hi-Rim hasn't been written off and why we have so many other disconnected accounts wasting away on MCI's books."

"Meaning what?" Hennessy asked.

"Meaning they've been pumping up the carrier business to pretty the company for a sale. The day this thing goes through they're all gonna get filthy rich." Pavlo felt vaguely vindicated for his misdeeds.

"Those greedy bastards," Wilkie laughed.

"This could be great for us greedy bastards too," Hennessy said. "Our accounts are so screwed up, if we merge our books with BT's, nobody's ever gonna untangle the mess. We're in the clear."

"Not necessarily," Pavlo said. "This deal's gonna take awhile to go down. God knows what kinda scrutiny we'll be under in the meantime."

"Then we need to hit Champion again while the hitting's good," Wilkie said.

"You just finished hitting them a few weeks ago," Pavlo said.

"Eric Cherry called. He wants to play again." Wilkie and Hennessy exchanged a knowing look.

"I get the impression I'm hearing the tail end of this conversation," Pavlo said. "You guys do what you want."

"We all want the same damn thing," Wilkie said. "To get filthy fucking rich. I'm telling you, the way to do it isn't to chase assholes like Denny McLain. You gotta go for the big bucks, and that's what my Champion deal's all about."

"I told you before. Champion's different."

"Yeah it's different. They've got a real business and can keep paying us."

"What I'm telling you, Jim, is I'm out. Period." Pavlo had lost control and what he couldn't control he wanted no part of. He felt bad enough about what he had turned himself into, and worse about what it had done to Hennessy and Wilkie. Now he couldn't even stop them.

"Sure, Walt, you're out," Wilkie said, shrugging.

"Seriously. Do what you want. What am I gonna do? Rat on

you?"

They all laughed. It wasn't funny. It was just true. They were all going to escape together, or go down together.

|||

Pavlo had lost control over Orion and now became preoccupied with covering his tracks. He sent Mann a letter on MCI stationery dated November 6, 1996 demanding that Orion affiliate ACC Telemedia pay MCI $125,000 pursuant to its financing agreement with Bob Hilby's Telemedia Networks Inc.[8]

As Pavlo expected, Mann called fuming and accused Pavlo of trying to frame him. But then he admitted it wasn't a bad idea to give the dealings a patina of legitimacy. He sent in the money. It was the first and last payment Orion or any of its affiliates would ever make to MCI. When the payment came in from the Cayman Islands,[9] nobody at the company said a word.

A week after Pavlo made his request, Dave Wickett, Orion's finance chief and Mann's all-around money guru, resigned.[10] He quit not only Orion but Denmark Dial and the score or so of other Mann companies in Europe, Canada, and the Cayman Islands—wherever he held corporate titles. The rats were jumping ship.

Wilkie, not content to wait three months for Champion to run up another quarter's worth of usage so he could "discount" its next bill, cut a deal with owner Eric Cherry granting a rate cut on *future* bills. His letter went out just before Thanksgiving, confirming that MCI would grant credits on Champion invoices over the next two months. In exchange, Champion paid $600,000 to the Cayman Islands.[11]

Hennessy used unapplied cash from Champion's own account to bury the debt. Then, after a little urging from Pavlo, Hennessy quit MCI for Orion. Pavlo felt like a heel seeing what leading the double life was doing to the guy. He'd evolved into a beefy, callous boozer.

Even so, Pavlo's feelings were mixed. With Hennessy leaving MCI, he was losing his key confidant. The upside was that Hennessy would be able to keep an eye on Mann. Inside MCI, Pavlo would also be able to blame "errors" on Hennessy's absence, just as Hennessy had done with the department's former temps.

The two kept in close touch, and what Hennessy had to say gave Pavlo no consolation. Mann was lazy and careless. He spent no more than a couple hours a day in the office while burning through Orion's cash at a frightening clip. He was negotiating to hire attorney Harvey Linder at $180,000 a year in addition to carrying Hennessy at $80,000—three times his MCI salary—and various other hangers-on.[12] One employee babysat the Manns' kids, washed their cars, and ran personal errands.

Mann was also sending what he called "our money" to his brother and father-in-law at Denmark Dial, the Toronto phone-sex business that was barely operating. Mann was making other mysterious bank transfers to companies and people familiar only to him in various parts of the world.[13] Given these transactions, and Mann's complex dealings with Michael Howard in the Caymans, there was no way to know where all the money was going.

Pavlo, exhausted and paranoid, had traded in his Prozac prescription for a more potent anti-anxiety medication—Xanax—which was dispensed by Harold Mann in the hope that it would steady his partner's nerves through a few more deals. Pavlo had no intention of pulling off any more Orion transactions, but with Hennessy gone he needed someone who could manipulate the books to keep accounts like Christian News under wraps. It had to be someone who knew the ins and outs of carrier accounting and could be trusted.

Hennessy suggested Tina Lincoln*, a young analyst with long blonde hair, blue eyes, and an icy demeanor honed over years of staring down her many male admirers. Pavlo and Hennessy invited Lincoln for a chat to Park Place, the same *bistro* near Concourse where Pavlo had recruited Wilkie.

"I left MCI for a startup named Orion where we're doing exciting things in telecom finance," Hennessy said. "We wanted to see if you might be interested in playing a role in its development."

"You wouldn't have to quit your job at MCI," Pavlo piped in.

"What kind of role?" Lincoln asked.

"Oversight," Hennessy said. "It might not require you to do anything but be available."

"For what?"

"Account reconciliation."

Lincoln took a puff of her cigarette and blew smoke slowly over the middle of the table. "I knew you guys were up to something."

"What does that mean?" Pavlo put on his best 'Who, me?'

* Pseudonym

expression.

"Before Sean here left MCI, he was practically soiling himself any time someone came near him and his precious computer," she said, then batted her blue eyes and in a low sexy voice added, "Not that being up to something is necessarily a bad thing."

"This something would pay very well," Pavlo said.

"What exactly, and I mean exactly, would you want me to do?"

"There's no exactly yet," Pavlo said. "But there might be a time when we need you to finagle some accounts receivable to make 'em disappear."

"That doesn't sound like anything new. How much accounts receivable are you talking and how much you gonna pay?"

"I don't know yet," Pavlo said, surprised that Lincoln had gotten to hard numbers so quickly.

"I can't say you guys are making this easy dancing around the details like a couple of sissies, but if you can make it worth my while I'll see what I can do." Lincoln was in.

Now, Pavlo's goal was to get out of MCI without getting caught. Meanwhile, he had to muster the will to continue the receivables fight. By Thanksgiving week, Carrier Finance had written off $72 million for the year.[14] The original budget had been $15 million.

Even so, the company had decided to roll over another $13 million into 1997 for several other carriers who had already been unplugged, plus $27 million for the Hi-Rim debacle. Thus Carrier Finance would begin the new year with $40 million in bad debt on its books, which was already more than the entire $32 million annual budget.[15] Pavlo figured $75 million would be a realistic starting point.

He delivered the bad news to Wanserski. "I'm just letting you know what's out there so when the time comes to clean up, nobody can say I didn't warn them."

"It's not all gonna be this year,"[16] Wanserski declared. "Get with Alex Harriman to work out the details, okay?"

Pavlo called Harriman and told him, "I got my marching orders."

"Me too," Harriman replied. "Can you have your numbers together for the next meeting?"

"I think so, but this shit gets more ridiculous by the minute. I have no idea anymore what we're being measured on."

Harriman chuckled. "We're measured on our level of complicity."

"Then we should both be up for raises."

"Yeah, right. By the way, we're trying to reconcile some weird stuff that's popped up in your 900 accounts."

"Really?" Pavlo's scalp crinkled.

"Mylinda Greenwell's looking into it. She was working with Sean Hennessy. Since he left, who should she get in touch with?"

"Tina Lincoln," Pavlo blurted out. "But those accounts are such a mess. There's no telling what you might find."

"I hear ya," Harriman said. "It's probably nothing."

Pavlo hung up with his stomach churning. Accounting had found another rogue transaction and Hennessy wasn't around to clean it up. He disposed of a few small chores and was about to head out to the pond outside the building for a smoke when Tina entered his office.

"Let me guess," he said. "You just got a call from Mylinda Greenwell."

"No, but Tel-Central's usage is going through the roof," she said. "They did a million last week."[17]

Pavlo slammed his fist on his desk so hard that Tina flinched. "That motherFUCKER McLain! Get me a breakdown of his usage. I bet it's all international, and he doesn't have the rates to be doing anything but selling below cost. Let me know which countries."

Lincoln nodded and left. Shortly before he had bolted MCI, Hennessy made it look like Tel-Central had paid $7.5 million of its debt to provide cover as Orion embezzled some of it. If Tel-Central suddenly welshed on an even larger sum, MCI's Accounting sleuths would swarm to it like flies to shit. Pavlo picked up the phone and dialed Mann.

"Harold Mann, please," he said brusquely to an unfamiliar voice that answered. "It's Walt...Walt Pavlo...with MCI." Christ, he thought, Mann's hired so many goddamn people nobody knows who he is anymore.

Mann answered singing, to the tune of "Hello, Dolly," "Well hell-o, Wally!"

"Harold, McLain's usage is off the fucking charts. What the hell's going on?"

"I'm not surprised." Mann sounded unperturbed.

"What does that mean?"

"It means I got back the forensic accounting report from that kid Ian Ratner I told you about. Good guy, Ian. Anyway, Denny's selling way below cost. I've asked him to slow it down."

"*Asked* him? Harold, if his usage skyrockets and he doesn't pay up we're in a world of shit. We told everyone here he just paid MCI seven and a half million bucks. Nobody's gonna believe he's suddenly broke!"

"Denny claims his prices reflect excessive market competition," Mann said. "Maybe you should bring it up with your bosses. It sounds like a customer service issue to me."

Pavlo was hyperventilating. "Of course there's excessive competition! They're all cheating! Denny told me the majority of his traffic was domestic. If he's sending minutes to India or the Caribbean we're fucked. He can never pay us that kind of money."

"I'm going to take a wild guess–it's all international," Mann said calmly. "That's what I'd do if I was Denny. A man's gotta eat."

"Tell him to stop Harold. I mean it."

"I'll see what I can do. *Ciao*."

Pavlo grabbed his cigarettes and headed for the elevators. Lately he felt like he spent half his days circling the Concourse pond, a cigarette in one hand and his cell phone in the other. Even the ducks had started recognizing him and paddling away.

McLain had to be running a bust-out scam pure and simple, Pavlo decided. It was a classic swan dive used by sleazy calling card outfits. Flood the market with cheap international calling cards–selling minutes below what they were supposed to be paying MCI, collect the cash, go bust and disappear before MCI's creaky billing system could catch up.

"Pakistan and China!" Tina yelled as she approached the pond with the information Pavlo had requested.

"What's the rate?"

"Ninety-nine and a half cents a minute to China and a buck twenty-four to Pakistan.[18] They're expensive minutes."

"I bet McLain's printed like 40,000 cards and is selling them for fifty bucks a pop to every Chinese and Pakistani between here and San Francisco. Then he'll pack the cash into his plane and fly off with it. We're screwed."

"What do you want to do? Can't we disconnect?"

"No," Pavlo said sternly. Disconnecting Tel-Central would only speed the discovery of his own fraud. The infamous Denny McLain had him in a corner. "Give me a few minutes."

Tina headed back upstairs.

Pavlo returned to his office, dialed McLain, and let him have it.

McLain assured Pavlo all his October calls had been domestic and the traffic report "must be a mistake." He swore he'd send MCI a $1 million check immediately but Pavlo knew he was lying.

He couldn't take the issue to Wanserski. Pavlo had falsified Tel-Central's account statement[19] to make it look like MCI was dealing with a $7.5 million dollar problem—not the $15 million one he had made disappear so Orion could embezzle $800,000. Now McLain was running up $500,000 a day in traffic that he'd never be able to pay for. At that rate, he'd be into MCI for another $15 million in a month.

 **It's All a Lie**

WITH HIS WORLD closing in on him, the one place Pavlo still felt safe was the Cayman Islands. To celebrate the Thanksgiving weekend, he took Rhoda, the boys, and Rhoda's parents to the Coral Stone Club. Pavlo swung by Barclay's Bank for the ritual pickup of $11,000 in hundreds. He spent the weekend chauffeuring the family around and, without Mann around, enjoying being the big shot for a change.

The weekend they returned to Atlanta, Mann threw a holiday party for Orion by renting out the Robinson Atrium of the High Museum of Art in Midtown Atlanta for a private showing of a Matisse exhibit, followed by a black-tie dinner and dancing to a ten-piece orchestra.

Pavlo took Rhoda and his father, Walt Sr. His mother said she'd feel out of place so she stayed home.

"Whatever happened to just giving workers and customers smoked sausages and fruit cakes?" the elder Pavlo asked, looking around the lavishly appointed atrium with a mix of wonder and disgust.

"Have a drink dad. It'll make all the luxury easier to swallow," Pavlo teased.

Jim Wilkie was there, with Becky sporting a Kokichi Mikimoto pearl necklace, courtesy of her Cayman mac daddy card. Sean Hennessy, with his fiancé Brenda, was there as well. As the party got rolling, Pavlo, Wilkie, and Hennessy stepped aside for a chat.

"Who are all these people?" Wilkie asked.

"Mostly Mann's riding club pals, I think," Pavlo said.

"Plus as-yet unscrewed neighbors and business associates," Hennessy said, munching on a jumbo shrimp.

"I bet a lot of 'em would choke on their roast duck if we told them where the money for this thing came from," Wilkie said.

"Oh shit! The king's coming to address his courtesans," Hennessy said.

Mann approached in tuxedoed, inebriated splendor. "Gentlemen."

"This is quite a bash Harold."

"Nothing makes money happier than being around other money. You guys check out the Matisse exhibit? That little lady over there will give you a private tour if you want. Maybe some special service too, if you find an empty gallery."

Pavlo grabbed his umpteenth glass of champagne from a passing waiter. "This is wild. How much is it costing us?"

"Nothing. It's an investment. Can't you smell it?"

"The food?" Wilkie asked.

"No. The money. It's all around us. Our job is to get everyone to part with some of it."

"You're not hitting up people to invest in Orion, are you?" Pavlo asked.

"Hell no. That's our deal and too complicated for these simple fucks. But it's never too early to plan for the next one."

The evening was surreal. All that wretched excess paid for with money stolen from MCI, all made possible by Pavlo.

As the New Year approached, Pavlo was intent on sticking around MCI just long enough to make sure his Orion deals remained buried, and to keep Wilkie from running amuck and exposing him. Wilkie was concocting ideas for new scams–starting a rogue telecom company; running a calling card ruse; and even stealing MCI checks that he would deposit in a Cayman account with a similar name: M.C.I.

Orion needed Pavlo's attention, too. Between Mann's lavish parties, mysterious bank transfers, and bulging payroll, he was burning through cash almost as fast as Orion could take it in. Pavlo was supposed to have an equal financial interest in Orion, but Mann controlled everything–how the money came in, how it went out, and how it moved between accounts.

Pavlo needed to get some of his money out of Mann's hands. He'd been speaking with his father about helping him buy a business–Valley Steel, a small metal-fabrication shop in Sistersville, West Virginia.

Walt Sr. had been doing some consulting work for the company, and with its owner terminally ill, it was up for sale. He had always dreamed of owning his own business and his son believed his father had the instincts and work ethic to make a go of it. What Walt Sr. needed to make it happen was $800,000.

Shortly before Christmas, Pavlo and his father put together a plan for a January, 1997 closing and persuaded Mann to go see the plant with an eye to putting up the money. Mann chartered a plane to whisk himself, Pavlo, Hennessy, and attorney Harvey Linder off to West Virginia. The entourage switched from the plane to a limo for the ride to Valley Steel, a run-down little factory. As they toured the modest facility, Mann spoke of telling his rich pals he owned a "steel plant," conjuring images of glowing blast furnaces tended by thousands of salt-of-the-earth hardhatters. Valley Steel employed 30 and made heat exchangers and water towers. But Mann agreed to sign off on the deal.

Back at MCI, Accounting's Mylinda Greenwell was trying to figure out for the year-end closing how much of the millions of dollars MCI had collected from regional phone companies it was supposed to pass on to 900 providers. She had noticed that more than $5 million had been moved from Christian News to Denny McLain's Tel-Central.[1]

Greenwell wanted to talk to Pavlo about the strange accounting entries but she was swamped with work and he managed to keep putting her off, hoping the problem would somehow go away.

She wasn't alone in her curiosity. Jamie Dollinger, Bob Hilby's caustic accountant at TNI, called Tina Lincoln the same week. Dollinger, a former MCI employee whom Pavlo had laid off earlier that year during a reorganization, said Hilby wanted immediate written confirmation that Orion had in fact paid off TNI's $2 million debt to MCI.

Lincoln went straight to Pavlo, who found Hilby's sudden interest uncanny. And unsettling. Pavlo guessed that Dave Wickett, Mann's finance chief who had suddenly quit, and who knew Hilby from back when Mann was his partner at TNI, may have tipped Hilby off that Mann was on the make.

Hilby despised Mann, and Pavlo figured he himself was also high on Hilby's shit list, given how he'd brushed off Hilby's Simple Access job offer in San Francisco. His skin crawled at the thought of how Hilby would react if he learned the reason Pavlo stayed in his old job was to bilk TNI.

Later the same day he answered his phone and Hilby's voice, dripping with sarcasm, began, "Mr. Pavlo. Bob Hilby. Remember me?"

Pavlo gulped for air. "Hello Bob. What can I do for you?"

"You've done just about enough. I know you're in with Harold on a few things. And they're sure as hell not the kinda things that'll earn you a merit raise."

"I... I don't know what you're talking about."

"I should have known," Hilby went on. "Your turning down my generous offer. Your love-fest with Harold. Orion insisting on getting paid in the Cayman Islands. Your little brother Chris even worked for Orion last summer. Maybe he's in on this too."

A wave of self-righteous rage welled up inside Pavlo's brain. It was true that his college-age brother had done odd jobs for Mann during his break from Georgia Tech, but he had nothing to do with Orion's scams. "Listen you sonofabitch. You leave my family out of this or I'll break your fucking neck!"

"Slow down there, Walt," Hilby taunted. "You wouldn't want threats of bodily harm added to your crimes."

Shit! Pavlo thought. I'll bet Hilby's recording the call. "Fuck you Hilby! Fuck you!" He slammed down the phone. His hands were trembling.

The terror that had kept him awake nights was MCI Accounting or Legal nabbing him. But not Orion's clients. He had figured if any of them got suspicious, they'd just stop paying and move on, as long as MCI didn't come after them for money. This Hilby thing was out of left field, and potentially disastrous. He called Orion.

"Harold? I just got off with Hilby. He knows a lot."

"A lot of what, Wally? What's to know?"

"That MCI hasn't been paid. Did you tell him Orion was actually going to pay MCI $2 million?"

"I don't remember. But you know Bob. He's all bluster. Blubber too. You busy this weekend?"

"The dude is fucking pissed, Harold. It might get under your skin too if you'd just found out you were sending a couple guys a hundred-forty grand a month for dick-all."

"It's not dick-all. We're providing a valuable service here," Mann said, calling out to his secretary for coffee.

"You think MCI Legal's gonna see it that way if Hilby phones them?"

"C'mon, Wally. Lighten up."

"C'mon, Harold. What would you do? Laugh it off?"

"He's got nothing. Nothing. I'm telling ya. Listen, I've made reservations at Carbo's Café. They've got an oyster special going on. You in?"

"No, I'm not in. This is serious, Harold. You better hope Hilby doesn't start calling around MCI 'cause your ass is riding on it too."

"I'll leave the worrying to you, Wally. You're so good at it. Listen, I gotta go."

Pavlo was shaking with rage. How could Mann treat all this with such carelessness, as if it were just Pavlo's over-active imagination or paranoia? But then a funny thing happened: Mann turned out to be on target.

After his testy chat with Pavlo, Hilby had phoned Anne Jarvis, in MCI Sales, where Hilby was known for erratic mood swings and talking about all the psychiatric drugs he was taking. Now he came to Jarvis with a fantastic tale of angel investors turned devils, Cayman accounts, and a conspiracy run straight out of Carrier Financial Services by Senior Manager Walt Pavlo, whom Jarvis had tried to recruit to leave Finance and go to work in Sales.

Hilby's rant fell on deaf ears. Orion dodged one more bullet.

|||

Manatee's Mark Benveniste called Pavlo over the New Year holiday and insisted the two of them meet with Harold Mann the first day back at work. Pavlo was puzzled. Rapid Advance was about the only thing working for MCI Carrier Finance. Under the program, Manatee had loaned MCI's legitimate clients $7.7 million through December, 1996, and about half had already been paid to MCI.[2] Carrier Network Services was also in contract negotiations to put another twenty or so "switchless" resellers on the Rapid Advance factoring program.[3]

All that was separate from the money Manatee was collecting from MetroLink and TM Systems as "clients" of Orion—a company that Benveniste had up to that point seemed to want to know little about. Now Benveniste was urgently requesting that he and Pavlo have a sit-down with Mann at the Olde Towne Athletic Club. Pavlo expected trouble, and found it.

"I don't have a lot of time so I'll give it to you straight," Benveniste said with uncharacteristic bluntness. "Harold here borrowed $5 million from Manatee last year, which he personally guaranteed, and he hasn't paid it back. It's about to come due, and if he doesn't pay up,

Manatee is going to default on our $20 million credit line with National Bank of Canada and NationsBank."

"What's the deal, Harold?" Pavlo asked.

"Remember Nordiska Tele8? The guys who were doing billing and collections for Denmark Dial? The pricks ran off with the money I was counting on to pay Manatee back."

"But you signed a personal guarantee with Mark. That's your problem."

"Hey, Wally boy. Remember what I told you? If it flies, fucks or floats, I lease it." He turned to Benveniste and shrugged. "So sue me. I own nothing. And what I have is in the name of one of my companies. I've got plenty of 'em." Mann snatched a handful of peanuts from a bowl on the table and popped them into his mouth.

"You've got a dog in this fight too, Harold," Pavlo said. "Manatee is collecting money for two of Orion's customers, TM Systems and MetroLink. If Manatee goes, those deals are toast. Who's gonna collect for you?"

"You mean for us. That's an excellent question," Mann said. "But I still ain't payin'."

"Harold and I have been 'round this racetrack," Benveniste said.

"So what's it got to do with me?" Pavlo asked.

"The burgers here are great." Mann said.

"I've got a solution but it requires your help," Benveniste said, fiddling with a fat legal folder.

"I think I'll start with the French onion soup. Au gratin," Mann said to the waitress. "Can I get some bread with that? You got a boyfriend?"

"I'm listening," Pavlo said to Benveniste.

"Your client MetroLink owes Orion $5 million," Benveniste said. "Harold has agreed to sign over to Manatee MetroLink's obligation but I still need some kind of backstop to assure our banks we'll get repaid."

"Like what?" Pavlo asked.

"Like a guarantee that if it ever became necessary, MCI would step in and make good on the MetroLink debt."

"You've gotta be kidding. You want MCI to guarantee MetroLink's debt to Orion?"

"The point is, MetroLink owes Orion $5 million," Benveniste explained. "We can use that $5 million obligation as collateral until

Harold can come up with the money."

"He said he wasn't going to pay," Pavlo said.

"That's right," Mann said smiling. "I'm not paying Manatee. But I will work with it to get our money back by suing those Tele-8 bastards who screwed both of us over."

"Harold's right, Walt," Benveniste said. "We'll win in court eventually. More important, MetroLink is also about to get funding from Lehman Brothers to buy Advantis. As soon as it does, it'll pay off the note and our problems will be over."

"Is that so?" Pavlo asked warily. It sounded like more finagling and he was sick of finagling. He could hardly keep straight all the lies and phony accounting entries they'd made at MCI.

Benveniste leaned in. "Walt, the only ones who're ever going to see this guarantee are you, me, and the banks. I swear."

Mann was sucking up his soup, fighting long strings of melted cheese. He shrugged as if to say it was up to Pavlo. Pavlo was boxed in. If he didn't sign and Manatee went under, Orion would go with it. He was living in a house of cards he'd created himself.

"I'll sign, Mark, but I'm telling you now. MetroLink better come through or we're all in very deep shit. This guarantee isn't worth the paper it's printed on, and you know it."

"Relax. MetroLink's gonna come through," Benveniste said, sliding the guarantee letter he'd prepared across the table to Pavlo.

"Just the banks will see this, right?"

"Just the banks."

"Waitress! A bottle of champagne here, please," Mann said. "Good deals always go down better with a little bubbly and this is one good deal."

Pavlo shook his head and shakily scribbled his name. "It better be."

|||

The following Tuesday, January 7, 1997, Pavlo returned from lunch to find an email in his inbox from Alex Harriman reporting that Mylinda Greenwell had found "suspicious transactions" in the Tel-Central account. Wanserski had left a handwritten note on his desk saying Harriman had called him, too, and that Pavlo needed to look into the Tel-Central problem right away.

Below Wanserski's note Pavlo found a pink "While you were out" memo from Tina Lincoln. Denny McLain's latest check, for $800,000, had bounced.[4] Clipped to her note was a report showing Tel-Central's China and Pakistan marketing campaigns had been frighteningly successful. His December usage had shot up to $6.5 million.[5] That was in addition to the $15 million or so of Tel-Central debt Pavlo calculated he'd already hidden from MCI.

Pavlo reached into his desk fishing for the plastic bottle of Xanax. He would have washed the pills down with a few cocktails, but holding the line and not drinking on the job was one of the few shreds of self-respect he had left. He downed two Xanax with a glass of water that did little to wet his cottony mouth. Then he called Harriman, saying he would put $5.5 million back on Tel-Central's MCI tab and figure out where the cash had gone.

Pavlo was at most buying himself a day at a time. For what he didn't know. He'd just signed another fraudulent bank guarantee. Wanserski and Accounting were sniffing around his crooked transactions. He'd stolen nearly $4 million from his employer and shunted it off to the Cayman Islands. His co-conspirator, Harold Mann, was either siphoning off most of the money for himself or pissing it away. His buddy Wilkie was totally out of control. Even Hennessy seemed to have a renewed passion.

Pavlo kept himself medicated and the next day he and Wilkie drove to the Olde Towne Athletic Club to have lunch with Hennessy and Mann. He was done with Orion, but he needed to stop McLain from running up even more traffic before MCI cut him off, exposing the Orion scheme from another angle. McLain was still paying Orion, so Pavlo hoped to persuade Mann that it was in his best interest to play the heavy.

But first he told his buddies that Accounting was closing in and his days at MCI were numbered.

"What you need to do, Wally, is chill out, eh?" said Mann. "Everything's going according to plan."

"We're even expanding the MCI franchise," Wilkie said.

"Huh?" Pavlo managed.

"Success breeds success," Mann said. "We have a few other MCI guys wantin'ta deal with us. You've got some competition there, Wally." Wilkie and Hennessy erupted in laughter.

"You know JD Services? The guys who owe MCI $900,000?" Wilkie asked.

"Yeah."

"Let's just say they've agreed to pay $600,000 to a new Cayman account beneficially owned by Orion," Mann said. "One of your under-lings is making the necessary adjustments to MCI's books and records to ensure the money isn't missed."

"I don't wanna hear about it."

"No problem. We're hearin' plenty," Hennessy said to more yacks.

Pavlo couldn't take any more. The wheels were coming off. McLain's Tel-Central would have to wait. "I'm not feeling well. I gotta go. You guys do what you want."

Showing up at MCI each day now felt like running a gauntlet. He kept playing the scene from Oliver Stone's film "Wall Street" in his mind, the one where Bud Fox arrives at work to find SEC investigators in his office and a cop with a pair of handcuffs.

The day after Pavlo's lunch with Mann and the boys, Wanser-ski ordered him to call Denny McLain and to tell him MCI was on the verge of cutting off Tel-Central. McLain demanded a conference call with Wanserski the following day. Pavlo guessed that McLain had been comparing notes with Bob Hilby, or that his criminal experience had helped him sniff out Orion. Nobody hates being robbed more than a thief. It's a matter of pride.

Pavlo got no sleep that night, practicing what to say if McLain made any outrageous but true claims. He arrived at work recovering from his scotch intake during the wee hours, powered by multiple cups of strong coffee and a few doses of tranquilizers. When he saw Wanser-ski arrive, he felt a wave of nausea and rushed to the bathroom. But nothing came up. He headed to the pond for a cigarette. His hands were trembling so much it was a struggle to light up.

"Walt Pavlo! How you doing?" It was Ralph McCumber, his old boss, catching a smoke. "Jesus, Walt. You look kinda green around the gills. What the hell's wrong?"

The sight of McCumber suddenly unleashed a wave of intense emotion. "Nobody understands this job. I can't do it any more. It's a lie. The whole thing's a lie," he babbled. Tears filled his eyes and ran down his cheeks.

McCumber put his arm around his former protégé. "What is it Walt? What the hell's wrong with you?"

"They did this to me. Those fuckers did this to me."

"I have no idea what you're talking about but you need to get out of here. Do you have your car keys?"

"I don't know."

McCumber patted his pockets. "Here. Let's get you home." McCumber led Pavlo to the parking garage, put him in his BMW and told him to call as soon as he got home. Pavlo sat in the car for an hour until he thought he was calm enough to drive.

He tried not to think of Wanserski upstairs getting the goods from McLain. He called Rhoda at work and asked her to meet him at the tennis courts near their house. They used to meet there for romantic talks when they wanted to be alone. He was exhausted and afraid for his family. As soon as Pavlo saw Rhoda he started crying again.

"You're not going back to MCI," she said. "The job's killing you."

Pavlo nodded. The notion of never going back to Concourse was a relief. They passed a pond near their house. Pavlo unhooked the pager he'd turned off earlier to stop the incessant buzzing. He tossed it into the water. They broke into laughter. It was a sound they hadn't shared for months.

 **Everyone's Nasdaqable**

HEIR SONS were still in school when the couple arrived home. Pavlo headed straight for the refrigerator and poured himself a tall glass of chardonnay. He went into the living room, slumped into his favorite leather chair and took a long slurp. It was 10 o'clock in the morning.

Rhoda rushed between the kitchen and office looking for the directory of services available under MCI's medical plan. She was hoping to get her husband an immediate appointment with a doctor, preferably a psychiatrist, to evaluate his mental instability.

Pavlo sat quietly, gazing at a photo of the family vacationing in the Cayman Islands, the baby grand piano that had sat silent for months and pieces of expensive new furniture he barely recognized. They were the trappings he had once seen as marks of success but that now left him feeling empty and ashamed.

Pavlo made a single call, to check in with Hennessy at Orion. Pavlo reported that he had left MCI and was afraid of what McLain had told Wanserski. Hennessy replied that McLain called Mann right after talking to Wanserski. Pavlo braced himself.

"You're gonna get a good laugh out of this, Pavlo," Hennessy chortled. "All McLain did was bitch to Wanserski about the usual crap. Messed-up bills and call records, and how he was being over-charged. That sorta shit." Pavlo exhaled. The bullets were getting closer but just how close he did not know.

Sensing Pavlo was on the edge, Hennessy had not mentioned that he had been getting reports from Lincoln all day that MCI Accounting had been calling with more questions.

Later that day Pavlo sat down with Rhoda. She had secured him a doctor's appointment, where he got more tranquilizers. She also convinced him not to return to MCI. She wanted him out of the company and fully focused on nursing himself back into mental shape, preferably with professional help. He agreed.

III

To avoid running into anyone, Pavlo and Rhoda visited his 10th floor office at Concourse that Saturday evening. Together they filled three boxes with family photos and other personal items. On the way to the elevator, Pavlo stopped outside Wanserski's office. He had his letter of resignation, but he couldn't bring himself to go in. Rhoda, who had to guide him around like a lobotomized mental patient, took the letter dated for the following Monday from his hand and put it on Wanserski's leather chair.

Dear Jim,
> *I am submitting this letter of resignation effective today, January 13, 1997. I have decided to pursue other opportunities outside MCI.*
> *I appreciated the opportunity to work for MCI and wish the company well in the years to come.*
> *Sincerely,*
> *Walt Pavlo Jr.*

Pavlo spent the rest of the weekend playing video games with his sons in the family room and basketball in the driveway. Bubby, who was six, and five year-old Howie were ecstatic to have dad home for two days.

Hennessy, meanwhile had set off Sunday morning with Mann for Chicago without saying a word to Pavlo. Their mission was to meet with Orion's "customers" in an attempt at taking the conglomerate of misfits public through a reverse merger.

Pavlo had been pushing Mann to do it for weeks. It was a long shot, but if it worked, it could solve a lot of problems and he might walk away rich after all. To pull it off, however, they needed leadership, which meant Mann had to perform.

On a frigid January evening in Chicago, Mann gathered his Orion clients in a suite at the Hotel Intercontinental. After a brief introduction, Mann grabbed a vodka and orange juice and headed to the back of the conference room.

Irwin Schneider, the disbarred securities lawyer, rambled for an hour about how a "reverse merger into a public shell" could convert their terminally ill companies into hundreds of millions in stock valuations. Anticipating questions about whether it was possible to put enough lipstick on these pigs to get them past the stock-market regulators, Schneider had assured them that "Every one of you guys is Nasdaqable." It was hardly a stretch, given that Federal Reserve Chairman Alan Greenspan had a month earlier warned investors about "irrational exuberance."

Hennessy was standing with Mann at the back of the room, observing the reactions. "Let's get out of here before one of these losers wants to go to dinner with us," Mann whispered as the meeting broke up. They slouched off to the hotel bar and treated themselves to a $1,000 dinner.

When Mann failed to show up for the scheduled morning session, Hennessy went up to his room and found him laying on the bed in his boxer shorts watching a John Wayne movie.

"C'mon, Harold! I've got a bunch of people waiting on you downstairs."

"I bet Capone stayed here," Mann said, surveying the room. "You gotta love these 1920s furnishings. They're so...historic."

"Fuck the furnishings! People are just sitting around. It's embarrassing."

"Let 'em talk to Schneider. My head's killing me after all the cognac and champagne we drank. Tell 'em I'm sick, okay? Then c'mon back and we'll order some lunch. You like truffles?" Mann turned up the TV volume.

Hennessy was mortified. He told the group that Mann had been called away to an urgent meeting. They would have to soldier on without him. The only way this group would have any chance of becoming Nasdaqable was to get Pavlo to run the show.

By 9:30 Monday morning, the Pavlo home phone was ringing nonstop with calls from Finance, Sales, Accounting, California, Texas, New York. Pavlo let them all go to his answering machine. He didn't even take one from the Meat Man, who was still paying off his Orion mortgage in frozen food. Tuesday he took a call from Wanserski, who insisted Pavlo come in to talk. Over Rhoda's objections, he decided the smart move was to go in and at least find out what MCI knew.

Pavlo felt nauseous as he entered the Concourse building and made his way directly to Wanserski's office. He felt the eyes of his staff on him but nobody said a word. The rumors were already flying.

Once again, Pavlo was surprised to find no G-men with cuffs at the ready. No perp walk today, he thought.

Pavlo read Wanserski's expression as worried rather than suspicious or angry.[1] "I know you've been under a lot of pressure. Heck I've entertained thoughts of quitting myself. But the merger is just around the corner."

"Jim, I..."

Wanserski held up his hand. "No, wait! Don't say a word. I've got your resignation letter, but I don't buy it. No sir. Walt Pavlo is no quitter. It's just a rough patch. We'll scale back your duties."

Pavlo's head was spinning. He just wanted out.

"Look, I've made up my mind. I think I'd like to try working with my father. He's buying a small metal shop and ... " He shrugged.

"Do me a favor. Take the week off. You've earned it. Then come in next Monday and we'll talk. If you still feel that way, I'll accept the letter. No questions. Until then, just take it easy."

"Okay," Pavlo said. He jumped up and strode out as fast as he could manage without appearing to run. He waved to a few people casting bewildered looks his way and quickly made for the elevator. On the drive home he wondered if it was all a ruse, to get him to relax and confess. Or to trap him into saying something. He thought Wanserski was on to him.[2]

As soon as he walked in the house, his cell phone rang. Pavlo recognized the caller ID as Alex Harriman's number in Accounting. He wanted to know more but he dreaded having to talk to Harriman.

"Walt? Christ, are you alright?"

"I'm getting better Alex."

"What happened?"

"A total fucking meltdown."

"I heard you're leaving. I know it's tough over there. Is something special bugging you?"

"It's everything. I can't take it anymore," Pavlo said. He imagined the fraudulent Tel-Central records sitting on Harriman's desk in front of him.

"Listen, I called Folk. He wants to talk with you. He knows about your relationship with Wanserski. Talk with him. You'll get somewhere."

"I don't know. I just got back from talking with Wanserski."

"Forget him. You need to talk with Folk."

"Wanserski was fine. I said I'd think about my future until next week."

"Do that. But talk with Folk, too. He's gonna buzz you in a few. Do it for me, okay?"

"Sure, Alex." Of course Harriman wanted him to stay. Pavlo was Harriman's Mr. Fixit. Bad debt a problem? Not anymore. Over-nineties out of control? He could fix that too. Walt Pavlo could even get deadbeats like TNI, MetroLink, and Tel-Central to pay their bills. As long as nobody asked how.

Folk's pitch went much like the previous two, with exhortations for Pavlo to "hang in there" and a promise that his future with the company was bright once the merger went through. When he told Folk he'd agreed to meet with Wanserski again the following Monday, the senior VP sounded only slightly relieved. He made Pavlo promise to call him right afterward, to "make sure Wanserski didn't fuck it up."

Pavlo was more confused than ever. They had to know he was up to something. But maybe they didn't. He knew things could never go back to normal, but he hoped to get back in the door long enough to fix things before he resigned for good. He just had to get himself together to pull it off.

Later that morning, Mann called as well. "Hey Wally. I hear you had a bad day at the office."

"You could say that. Got any openings at Orion?"

"For you? Absolutely. But what you really need is a break."

"That's what they tell me."

"I'm the only son of a bitch who's gonna do something about it."

"Like what?"

"I've got a private jet lined up at Briscoe Field. What say you, Rhoda, Karen and me hop down to the Caymans for a few days of R&R? I'll even bring my chiropractor, in case you need some skeletal adjustments."

"I'll need to check on a babysitter."

"Eleven grand'll buy you a shitload of babysitter."

"How's the weather this time of year?"

"Beautiful. As always. Make it a Thursday departure, eh?"

"I'll talk with Rhoda."

Mann could be repulsive at times, but he had the touch–he knew how to make Pavlo feel like a big shot. He had a college prank-ster's approach to crime. No big deal. We're just having some good clean fun.

Pavlo felt the jig must be just about up, so he figured it wouldn't hurt to get out of town, pick up some cash, and maybe get a sense from Mann about how things might play out. Rhoda was reluctant but he convinced her it would be good for them both.

The morning after they arrived in George Town on a chartered Lear jet, the women went to sun themselves on the beach and Pavlo and Mann eased into the day with Bloody Marys on the balcony overlooking the turquoise Caribbean. Mann brought the phone from the table and set it on the ottoman in front of his patio chair. He punched the speakerphone and began dialing.

"Guess who I'm calling?"

"Who?"

"Jim Wanserski. I'm supposed to talk with him about Tel-Central. I thought you'd get a kick out of listening in. Wanna say hello? Tell him how much fun you're having?"

"Are you crazy?"

"Relax. It's a favor for Denny. Remember, he gave me an option to buy a piece of his company and thinks it'd be good for me to get involved."

"You're out of your mind." Pavlo was mesmerized by Mann's gall and guile.

Mann chatted up Wanserski with breathless talk about what a managerial genius McLain was and how his own deep-pocketed commitment to Tel-Central would ensure MCI got paid.[3] Wanserski took it all in, but he'd have been shocked had he known Mann was calling from the penthouse balcony of the Coral Stone Club, or that Pavlo was eavesdropping. It was just another illusion brought to everyone by the telecom industry. The call ended inconclusively.

Pavlo kept his appointment with Wanserski that Monday, feeling self-conscious about his mid-winter tan. But his boss seemed oblivious. He spent an hour trying to convince Pavlo to stay. Pavlo eventually agreed to stick around through February.[4] He knew he would catch hell from Rhoda over the decision, but he figured it would give him a chance to bury some of the evidence of his crimes.

Soon after he discovered that there weren't many holes left and the evidence was getting too big. Accounting had figured out that $5.5 million of the money Tel-Central had "paid" hadn't come from the company at all but from a mysterious little 900 account. It reversed the entry to increase the balance Tel-Central owed by $5.5 million once again.

Pavlo needed to pull the money from somewhere else before Accounting figured out the real reason for the deficit was that the money had been stolen.[5]

It was a big number to finagle with so many people watching, and with Wanserski personally supervising Tel-Central and Denny McLain. Nor did it help that Hennessy, his master manipulator, was out of MCI. Pavlo needed a miracle, and he got one.

MCI and WorldCom were negotiating a contract renewal of a network cross-connect, known as an SS7, that WorldCom needed to continue offering long-distance service. The existing agreement was set to expire on January 16.[6] During the talks, MCI set the condition that WorldCom pay $41.5 million in international surcharges it had been disputing for the past half year.

The day the SS7 contract expired, MCI sent a delegation of lawyers to WorldCom's Mississippi headquarters to force the issue.[7] Negotiations broke down and MCI "busied out" WorldCom's SS7 service, leaving millions of its customers without long-distance service.[8] WorldCom had a quick change of heart, and wired $41.5 million to MCI's lockbox on January 23.[9]

Pavlo needed $5.5 million to backfill Tel-Central's outstanding balance. Wilkie happened to be the senior manager on the WorldCom account. They took a walk around the Concourse pond and set the scheme in motion.

Wilkie told Debra Rader, a manager involved in handling Tel-Central, that the company needed more time to come up with its payment. Meanwhile, he directed her to make a journal entry crediting Tel-Central with $5.5 million from the WorldCom payment, assuring her that the credit would be reversed when Tel-Central's money came in.[10] It was a huge number, but Rader knew such "covering of agings" was a routine way departments competed inside MCI to look good on the monthly aging tally.[11] WorldCom was credited for the remaining $36.1 million. It was a risky ploy, but Pavlo was out of options.

Besides, it seemed to work. On February 10, Pavlo received a letter from Jim Folk saying "as a special recognition for your outstanding work and contributions" he was being granted 300 additional MCI shares. That was on top of 2,450 options exercisable at $36.25 each, a bonus of $7,500 for 1996 and a hike in his 1997 target bonus to $10,000. "Be bold and aggressive," Folk wrote. "Remember that I, and the rest of the management team, are completely behind you."[12]

Like a zombie, Pavlo attended another industry conference, in

Palm Springs, California, tracking down money from delinquent customers. He took along Wilkie, his presumed successor, to introduce him
to sales reps and clients. Working the conference floor, they came away
with over $3 million in checks.

While they were there, Wanserski learned that only $36 million
of WorldCom's $41.5 million payment had been applied to the correct
account, and the rest ended up in Denny McLain's Tel-Central. The first
time money was misappropriated to Tel-Central it had been discounted
as a mistake. For it to happen a second time was more than funky.
Wanserski called Wilkie, WorldCom's nanny at MCI, in Palm Springs
wanting an explanation. Wilkie immediately found Pavlo.

"How did they find it?" Pavlo asked. He was such the cornered
rat that he couldn't see the obvious.

"I guess a lot of people were watching to make sure it got
applied correctly," Wilkie said. "What should we do?"

Pavlo sighed loudly and sank into a chair. "You can try to fix it
if you want. I'm done."

"Don't go defeatist on me now. Let's go have a few drinks. We'll
think of something."

"I'm up for drinks, but I'm out of answers. I should never have
come back."

MCI threw a big bash the second night of the conference with
music by the 1970s pop band America. The duo made numerous trips
to the open bar. But as things wound down, they were no closer to
coming up with a fix for their problems. When Pavlo got back to his
room, he had sober-sounding voice mail and urgent email messages
from Wanserski. He was to call his boss at 7:30 a.m. Atlanta time, 4:30 in
the morning in Palm Springs.[13] Pavlo couldn't sleep anyway, so he sat
and watched the clock until it was time to call.

At the appointed hour he dialed, and Wanserski picked up on
the first ring.

"Hi Jim," Pavlo started. "I got your email. How much do you
know?"

"How much do I know?[14] Walt, what in tarnation is going on?
We've got five and a half million dollars of WorldCom's money bouncing around like jumping beans and nobody seems to know why."

"I moved it," Pavlo said. "I don't want anyone else to get in
trouble. I've done too much already."[15]

"Moved it? Why?"

"I worked on my own. It was me."

"Look. We need to talk about this in person. I need some answers. Accounting has a real bee in its bonnet this time."

"I bet."

"When are you flying back?"

"Tomorrow." Pavlo stared out the dark window.

"Good. Let's talk the following day at, um, 3 o'clock."[16]

"Fine."

"You okay?"

"Nah. But it doesn't matter anymore." Pavlo hung up.

Late that night, when he was sure his boss wouldn't be around, Pavlo sent Wanserski a one-sentence email resigning from the company for good.

He would never set foot in MCI's offices again.

# Die Like an Aviator!

WHEN PAVLO didn't show up for his meeting with Wanserski on February 20, his home phone was silent. Wanserski sat down instead with Jim Wilkie and Deb Rader to ask why cash had been bouncing between the WorldCom and Tel-Central accounts. They told him that Pavlo had said he needed the money until the end of the month.[1]

Suspicious, Wanserski met the following day with Edward McGinty, a senior investigator with MCI System Integrity, the in-house cops. McGinty immediately opened a file on the Atlanta Carrier Finance unit stating that the Tel-Central account appeared to have been manipulated.[2]

McGinty, Wanserski, and others started interviewing Carrier Finance employees.[3] Cocky as ever, Wilkie came out of his grilling, called Pavlo and boasted "They got nothin'!" Then he flew off to New York as the guest of Melaleuca, a nutritional supplement marketing company[4] that had decided to apply its multi-level marketing scheme to selling long-distance service on MCI's network. Wilkie was treated to a night at the Grammy Awards, where he watched Celine Dion win album of the year for "Falling Into You," while his hosts tried to get him to go easy on their mounting debt.

Wanserski called his boss, vice president Jim Folk, to report that the Tel-Central account misstatements involved more than one transaction. Folk emailed his Finance bosses that "moving money among accounts has taken a very bad turn,"[5] then flew to Atlanta with some of his staff and spent the weekend trying to unravel the mess.[6]

When Wilkie returned to MCI's Concourse Six office from New

York the following Monday, he got the modified Bud Fox ("Wall Street") treatment, escorted from the building by security, without any of his belongings. He'd left behind a day planner on which the former English Lit major had recorded lunch menus, tennis matches—and trips to the Cayman Islands with inscriptions like "Great day. Picked up eleven grand," and "Can't wait to show these accounts to Harold. Payday!"

The shit was beginning to splatter but it had not yet reached NationsBank and National Bank of Canada. Even as MCI was getting its first full-bodied whiff, the banks increased Manatee's credit line by 50 percent, to $30 million.[7]

Investigator McGinty was appointed to work MCI's internal investigation with Folk and David King, a Baltimore attorney.[8] McGinty filed a report the following day stating that Pavlo and Wilkie had made numerous calls to the Cayman Islands from their offices.[9] Hennessy's old Carrier Finance buddies passed him word that Pavlo's and Wilkie's offices had been searched, the locks changed,[10] their computers seized[11] and their former employees questioned at length. Many were shown the door, including Tina Lincoln.

Three days later, MCI filed a proxy with the Securities and Exchange Commission, recommending that shareholders approve British Telecom's $20 billion offer.[12] The statement made no reference to the bodies now floating to the surface in Carrier Finance.

By the following weekend, the investigators were bringing the scam into focus. Folk sent an email Sunday, March 9 to Nate Davis, who was monitoring the situation in MCI's corporate offices. It stated "at least two collections Sr. Mgrs, Walt Pavlo and Jim Wilkie, were manipulating Tel-Central's A/R (accounts receivable) records for personal gain…It's especially painful because a number of people told me that they always suspected something was wrong, and others had observed questionable entries and let them pass. The environment where basic financial functions completely broke down and remain [sic] undetected for so long is unacceptable."[13]

Folk acknowledged that Pavlo, Wilkie, and Carrier Finance were not the only ones at fault, writing "I believe the groundwork was laid a long time ago. The competition among business divisions for the best aging results stimulated the posting of memo entries (credits to MCI) in advance of the actuals (cash in hand)… Over time this practice became more the rule than the exception."[14]

Folk said the surge in bad debt from the second half of 1995 was due to "big growth in the carrier segment which brought in unethical and shady companies. Their business motivations combined with the manual intensity of A/R management is, in my opinion, the root problem for this event and all other carrier account failures. It allowed people in positions of trust with inordinate powers to cover up illegal activity for their personal gain."[15]

Folk recommended firing several Carrier Finance employees and disbanding the department to separate its accounting from its billing and collections. MCI quickly complied. Folk also laid blame at one other pair of feet: Jim Wanserski's. "My conclusion is that his judgment of people and processes were not acute enough to detect a serious problem. His weakness was singular reliance on loyalty with his directs (direct subordinates), not sufficiently checking on their performance details. He understands that flaw and how he was taken."[16]

As bad as things looked, Pavlo was comforted by Jim Wilkie's stoicism. The former helicopter jockey told him that when an aircraft is dropping out of the sky, the honorable thing is for the pilot to "Shut-up and die like an aviator!" In a variation on the theme, they figured if they were going to go down as criminals they might as well go in style.

Pavlo and Wilkie spent $40,000 on a 25-foot Mariah Bow Rider speed boat with an ocean-blue hull, a 300-hp Volvo engine, and cream-colored naugahyde seats. She wasn't as grand as WorldCom chief Bernie Ebbers' yacht, the *Aquasition*, but Pavlo and Wilkie figured they had outdone him in christening her the *Miss Deeds*. To Pavlo's fear, paranoia, and guilt he now added the giddiness of a child incapable of keeping a straight face while being scolded — a kind of nervous hysteria. Away from the office, the customers, the secrets, and the opportunity, Pavlo, Hennessy and Wilkie regressed to become college buddies who'd bungled a prank and were waiting to find out if they'd just get suspended, or expelled. In the back of their minds the knowledge that the consequences of this prank were enormous for them and their families was as inescapable as the way forward was uncertain.

With little else to do besides worry, they spent much of their time, when the weather was warm enough, cruising and water skiing with their families on Lake Sidney Lanier, a sprawling man-made lake system about fifty miles northeast of Atlanta.

Stripped of his all-consuming career and a job reference, Pavlo went to work at Orion along with Mann and Hennessy. Orion had taken in about $5.5 million, but by March, 1997 its "customers" had received disturbing phone calls from MCI indicating that they may have been duped and stopped sending in their checks. Mann, ever resourceful, conjured up a local phone service reseller to generate some cash, naming it Corvus.[17] He liked the mythological sound, but might have made a different choice if he'd bothered to learn the legend behind the name. Corvus was a white bird that lied to Apollo, who condemned it to eternal thirst and turned it into a black crow.

Throughout the recent emotional roller coaster, Pavlo consoled himself with the knowledge that he had $620,000 in his Parnell account and hardly gave a thought to the source of funds that he constantly spent with his Eurocard. Once at Orion, he got a look at the books and discovered that it was operating much the way Pavlo and company had been keeping MCI's accounts. Mann had put large sums of their shared loot into sketchy ventures that went south. He was constantly shuffling money between a couple dozen or so entities in the U.S., Canada, the Cayman Islands, and Europe.

Pavlo knew that if he didn't do something fast, Mann would end up spending or stealing every last cent. He pushed Mann to quickly finance the Valley Steel buyout for Walt Sr. Mann pulled the money together from Wilkie's third and final Champion Communications deal, which in February had brought in $821,611, purportedly to pay for $1.1 million worth of MCI usage through the coming July.[18]

Pavlo and Hennessy flew up to Sistersville, West Virginia to help Walt Sr. with the Valley Steel financing. It was a bittersweet experience. Pavlo was helping his father's dream come true, but with stolen money. The March morning after they arrived in West Virginia, Rhoda called in a panic. MCI investigator McGinty had been to the house. He'd left a phone number and said the matter was "urgent."

That spooked Pavlo and Hennessy. They imagined themselves being greeted as they came off the plane by badges and handcuffs. So they rented a car and drove ten hours overnight back to Atlanta. Every time they saw a cop car, Hennessy called out in his New England accent, "Look out for the *lawr* man!" Anything to cut the tension.

The chase was on, but it was still taking place off-stage. Pavlo told Mann that he wanted a lawyer. Mann insisted he was overreacting but reluctantly flipped through a long list of candidates from his many legal run-ins. He recommended Donald Loft, a civil litigator with Morris, Manning & Martin in Atlanta. Pavlo visited Loft in his Buckhead offices, and told the attorney that he'd been hiding bad debt to make his budget numbers and to avoid getting fired. It was a grain of truth wrapped in layers of falsehoods, but Pavlo wasn't sure whom he could trust.

Loft called MCI to let his former employer know Pavlo had a lawyer and it was to conduct no more drive-bys of his home. His next mission was to feel out MCI on what it knew and what it intended to do about it. Pavlo figured he'd whip out his purloined evidence of MCI's accounting games and let Loft negotiate a settlement.

Hennessy's moles reported that MCI's Orion investigation had led it to the contract with Manatee Capital. On that one MCI faced a tough call. Despite the murky origins of the deal, Manatee had provided about $19 million in financing to MCI's clients.[19] If MCI pulled the plug on the Rapid Advance partnership, the money would stop flowing and it could end up stuck for a lot more. Folk and other MCI Finance executives held several meetings with Manatee's Mark Benveniste and Jack Hammer trying to untangle the convoluted relationship.[20]

On March 25, 1997, one year to the day after Pavlo had signed the original agreements between MCI and Manatee, Benveniste showed the MCI executives the loan guarantee Pavlo had signed putting MCI on the hook for Manatee's debts.[21] Wanserski and Benveniste were equally surprised that Pavlo's boss hadn't known about it earlier.

As dicey as things started getting between MCI and Manatee, neither told the banks financing the entire mess that there were any problems.[22] Instead, MCI tried to have its cake and eat it too by continuing to accept payments from Manatee under Rapid Advance while arguing that doing so in no way constituted recognition that the contract between them was valid or binding.[23]

Meanwhile, Denny McLain, whose Tel-Central was having its own problems, was sentenced to eight years in prison and ordered to pay $2.5 million in restitution for looting the pension fund of the meat packing company he had taken over and run into the ground. It would be McLain's second trip to the slammer.[24]

While Rome proceeded to burn, Manatee's banks remained ignorant of the developing dispute over the legitimacy of the loan guarantee Pavlo had signed. In fact, through bankers' eyes the prospect of making loans with MCI guaranteeing repayment was so appealing that a third institution, CIT Group/Business Credit, joined National Bank of Canada and NationsBank in the financing syndicate on May 12, increasing Manatee's line of credit from $35 million to $45 million.[25]

MCI, possibly under pressure from a separate federal investigation of McLain underway in New York,[26] finally took its internal investigation to the U.S. Attorney in Atlanta.[27] Sensing where things were going, Pavlo hired a criminal attorney, Bruce Morris, a partner at Finestone & Morris. Considered one of the top white-collar defenders in Atlanta, Morris attained minor celebrity status as the attorney for

Hustler magazine founder Larry Flynt in a pornography case in Law-renceville, Georgia. Morris was a diligent lawyer and, during the trial, he'd stayed behind in the courthouse to do research while Flynt and his entourage went out to lunch. On their way down the courthouse steps, Flynt and Morris' colleague were badly wounded by an assas-sin's bullets.[28] Morris had dodged a real bullet, and he got the charges dropped.

Pavlo repeated the fiction-by-omission that he was a hard-working mid-level manager who'd tried to appease the greedy bosses and cling to his job in a corrupt corporation. He paid Morris' $50,000 retainer from a savings account, depleting a major portion of what was left of his life's savings from prior to his dealings with Orion. He felt confident that even at Morris' $260 an hour rate, the entire mess would be wrapped up well before the money was exhausted.

A week later Morris asked him back for another meeting. The attorney's demeanor had been comforting and sympathetic during the first visit. This time he greeted Pavlo with a face like a fist, and a formal tone in his voice.

"You want me to help you, right Mr. Pavlo?"

"Absolutely. That's what I'm paying you for."

"Then check the bullshit you told me last time at the door, okay?"

"Excuse me?" Pavlo felt himself blushing hard.

"If you want me help you, you've got to tell me the truth."

"I'm not sure I follow." Pavlo wasn't kidding himself about the truth, but he also wasn't sure how much he should disclose.

Morris glanced at some notes on his desk. "Maybe you could start by telling me about the accounts you and Harold Mann set up in the Cayman Islands."

Pavlo's mouth went dry. "Listen, I'm new at this. I...I need to ask you a question."

"Go ahead." Morris leaned back and the lines in his face relaxed.

"Did O.J. tell Johnnie Cochran he killed Nicole?"

Morris smiled knowingly. "Look, Walt. You've got to start look-ing at me as the one guy who's on your side. Not your wife, your par-ents, or your pals. It's you and me. Get used to it quickly if you want me to help."

"Got it." It was time to come clean, but Pavlo still did it in degrees. He spun Morris a yarn in which MCI's misdeeds were mixed in with his own. It was the truth. Just not the whole truth or anything but the truth. He could see the skepticism on Morris' face. But he wanted Morris to adopt the tactic that Pavlo had enough dirt on MCI—thousands of pages of documents—that could cause a big stink in the middle of a historic merger and it would be better for everyone if all this unpleasantness were settled quietly, out of court. His argument was sound, except that MCI had already spilled the beans to the Justice Department and handed them a juicy white-collar crime case on a silver platter. Whatever its reasons, for Pavlo it amounted to a strategy of killing the messenger before he got a chance to deliver his message.

Meanwhile, MCI continued to finance existing Rapid Advance customers through Manatee into the summer of 1997 while it was assessing the damage. The company even continued to approve Rapid Advance contracts. That included $2.1 million worth of them that the banks claimed Folk gave the go-ahead[29] after Pavlo quit and Wilkie was fired. Folk, who had now taken a personal hand in running Carrier Finance, was finding out what Pavlo had been struggling with for so long—managing the department meant choosing between dicey financing schemes or blowing a hole in the bottom line with huge write-offs.

Mann maintained his jaded, careless, spendthrift attitude. He greeted Pavlo at the office with manic enthusiasm about a new scheme. Communication Systems International, Inc. had run up a $1.5 million bill with MCI and been disconnected.[30] Mann cut a deal in which one of his cronies would represent CSI in negotiating a final settlement. Folk was handling it for MCI. It was a sign of how unglued things had come that vice presidents were involved in such mundane business.

The company was learning the price of not paying attention. With the BT merger breathing down their necks, senior managers had a lot of stock-option money riding on a happy ending. The prettier MCI looked, the bigger the payday. Mann's crony, with some guidance from Pavlo on the sly, got Folk to accept a settlement of $650,000, a sixty percent discount. For arranging the deal, which took about an hour–Orion pocketed a commission of nearly $45,000.[31]

It was a fleeting spot of sunlight on a field of gray. Mann's and Pavlo's legal bills were mounting, Orion's "customers" had quit paying, Mann had continued spending like a drunken sailor and moving money around like a pack rat, and by June they only had $1 million in the bank. Mann had no intention of letting these distractions interfere with his summer vacation. Before heading "back home," he raised Orion some extra capital by pilfering $120,000 from Hennessy's Exeter account and $150,000 from Wilkie's J Four.

Hennessy learned about the withdrawal when he visited an ATM machine. He immediately called Mann, who by then was safely ensconced in his cabin in the Canadian wilds. Hennessy blew his top. Mann tried to calm him down, saying it was just a "loan." Hennessy had no illusions. He'd been robbed, and Wilkie knew he had, too.

The money Mann withdrew as "working capital" went to work in part buying Pavlo a new BMW 740 iL. Pavlo knew the score. Mann needed to keep him around a while longer to do Orion's dirty work.

Pavlo did his best to stop some of the hemorrhaging. He fired the staff, except himself, Mann's longtime secretary and a computer whiz who'd programmed the 900 porn systems. Mann insisted the guy could earn his keep on a new project he assured Pavlo was legal and lucrative, but a scam nonetheless.

Mann, the hawk-eyed opportunist, had come up with the idea of registering a few of Orion's lines as pay phones. Then, he had the computer whiz hook them up to a couple of old computers programmed to dial toll-free numbers 24 hours a day. Pay phone operators earned a 25 cent "bong" charge for each 800 call originating from one of their phones.[32]

Orion ended up earning $80,000—25 cents at a time—dialing toll-free numbers to Delta Airlines, Holiday Inn, and thousands of other companies, and immediately hanging up. The company owed it all to Mann's perverted ingenuity and the Federal Communication Commission's Dial-Around Compensation Program.

If nothing else, Pavlo had to admire Mann's intellectual and creative capacity.

# The Bert and Bernie Show

THE LENGTH IS to which MCI had gone to maintain the fiction that it was still a hot growth company were finally revealed for all the world to see near the end of August, 1997. That's when British Telecom announced it was reducing by $5 billion what it was prepared to pay to acquire the company. The *Wall Street Journal* quoted an industry analyst saying, "There were deeper cracks than MCI was letting on."[1]

Four days after the British Telecom bombshell, Wanserski sent Benveniste and Hammer letters declaring Manatee had "materially breached" its finance agreement.[2] The last straw appeared to be MetroLink. Its Lehman Brothers financing had fallen through and it defaulted on the $5 million it owed Manatee. That, in turn, left MCI in a battle to avoid covering the MetroLink loan guarantee that Pavlo had signed. Even so, Manatee's banks remained blissfully oblivious of the trouble and by their tally lent it another $6.6 million over the next month, $1.4 million of which went directly to MCI's reseller clients.[3]

MCI sent Manatee a second breach notice on September 26.[4] This time, Manatee responded by suing MCI and Jim Wanserski for breach of contract and fraud in a lawsuit that sought $47.25 million in compensation.

MCI finally told Manatee's banks the following day that it did not view itself as bound by its agreements with Manatee.[5] Its notice came eight months after MCI had discovered fraud in Carrier Finance and had begun limiting its Rapid Advance joint venture with Manatee to financing existing customers.[6] The banks immediately seized control of Manatee.

Eclipsing the mess, WorldCom made an unsolicited $30 billion all-stock bid for MCI the same day. Bernie Ebbers, WorldCom's chief executive, explained the offer in a letter to MCI chairman Bert Roberts, dated October 1, 1997:

WorldCom and MCI share similar legacies: pioneering the introduction of competition to the telecommunications marketplace and histories of innovation, agility and growth. Indeed, these two companies are the paradigm of the American entrepreneurial spirit.

Roberts and his MCI managers had good reason to welcome Ebbers' overture. On paper, WorldCom's offer was worth $9 billion more than British Telecom's. WorldCom's stock had returned an average 56 percent a year over the previous eight years, compared to MCI's four percent.[7]

The MCI chief executive and his four top lieutenants personally stood to pocket $71 million from restricted stock, non-vested incentive stock units and options, and retention bonuses the day the deal went through.[8] More than 8,000 other MCI employees would share in the spoils, too.[9] Had Pavlo stuck around, his own share would have been worth more than $500,000.

Analysts' tongues were soon wagging about the "Bert and Bernie show." Two weeks later regional bell GTE jumped in with a $28 billion all-cash bid for MCI[10] that sparked a months-long takeover battle. Hardly anyone noticed when, amid the bidding frenzy, MCI announced on October 23, 1997 "a strategic shift away from carrier [including reseller] sales" and an $83 million charge for "certain uncollectible reseller contracts and litigation matters."[11] Undeterred, WorldCom inflated its original MCI offer by 25 percent and won the bidding, paying with $37 billion in stock.[12]

Meanwhile, the legal wrangling over MCI's esoteric Manatee factoring scandal kicked into high gear. The banks declared their credit facility with Manatee in default and seized what collateral they could find.[13] Then, expressing shock they hadn't been informed of the long-running dispute between MCI and Manatee, the banks charged the two companies, Wanserski, Benveniste, Hammer, Pavlo, Mann, his wife Karen, and just about everyone else involved with civil Racketeer Influenced and Corrupt Organizations (RICO) violations. They demanded damages in excess of $60 million.[14]

MCI fired back with suits against the banks, Pavlo, Wilkie, Benveniste, and Mann for fraud, civil conspiracy, breach of contract, and breach of fiduciary duty.[15] The banks "were extraordinarily negligent in protecting their interests, ignoring the most basic lending procedures...they did not bother to communicate with (MCI) in any way. If any representative of the banks had made but one telephone call, the conspiracy would have been discovered and their losses averted," MCI claimed.[16]

There was a smattering of truth to all the claims and plenty of blame to go around. Pavlo, Mann, Hennessy, and Wilkie had committed egregious fraud at Orion. MCI Carrier Sales had recruited crooked resellers to earn quick commissions. The company's finance bosses had dragged their feet in acknowledging tens of millions of dollars in bad debt as they fattened the pig for sale. Benveniste had abused Manatee's bank credit lines. And the bankers had lent against an MCI loan guarantee that remained too good to be true only so long as they didn't bother to verify it. Sorting all this out would wind up taking two and a half years, millions of dollars in legal fees, and Pavlo's remaining emotional energy.

As the weeks dragged on, Pavlo's legal bills mounted in what felt like an airless bell jar of silence. His meetings with his attorney, Bruce Morris, almost always produced more bad news and more expense. And then his troubles really began.

"Things have started progressing on the federal front," Morris told him in his office in late 1997.

"Meaning?"

"I received what's known as a target letter. It means a grand jury is looking into your case and you're now the focus of an FBI investigation. I'm sorry."

"That's gotta be pretty common?" Pavlo said. "I mean, grand juries and the FBI must look at lots of cases."

"They do. But I have to be honest with you. Once the government's involved it changes everything."

"How?"

"You need to get used to the idea that you're going to be criminally indicted and go to prison. It's the worst-case scenario, but at this point it's a distinct possibility. If you accept that, we can work on building a defense."

Until that moment, prison had been a vague concept to Pavlo. Now, like a patient who'd just been told he has cancer, his life would be defined by the period of hoping against hope that all would be well prior to receiving the news, and the harsh reality that followed. Was he being followed? Were his phones tapped? His mind raced ahead.

"What's it like? Prison, I mean."

"Most white-collar guys end up in a camp. From what I hear it's pretty damn boring. I don't want to sugar-coat it, but people survive and move on with their lives."

"Is there anything else we need to discuss? I've got another meeting."

His only other meeting was with some double vodka martinis. He needed to get away and think. How could he ever tell Rhoda and his sons he was going to prison? How would they survive without him? His crime had seemed victimless. A drop in the bucket for a soulless corporation. It suddenly hit him that the real victims might end up being his wife and young sons.

"I suggest you think about whether you want to cooperate with the government," Morris said. "I know it's early and there are a lot of uncertainties. But pleading guilty and working something out is always possible. It's your case. You call the shots."

"I think this thing might blow over," Pavlo said.

Morris grimaced. "It's a lot to think about. Sleep on it. We'll talk later in the week."

Pavlo left and headed for the Time Out Sports Bar & Grill in Alpharetta, close enough to home that he might make it without getting busted for driving drunk.

As reality sank in, Pavlo became consumed with creating memories of happy times. For Thanksgiving, 1997, he flew the family first class to St. Thomas where they stayed at the Ritz Carlton. Then they boarded the *Meachelle II*, a leased 92-foot yacht, on which they spent a week living like the idle rich, making port calls at Virgin Gorda, the Baths, Bitter End, and other islands while being catered to by a captain, chef, first mate, and personal assistant.

The following month Pavlo chartered a Lear jet to take his family on a surprise Christmas Eve visit to Rhoda's parents in Akron. At the time, the $35,000 expense seemed like money well spent.

Tapped out of cash, Pavlo went to SunTrust Bank on the first business day of 1998 to hit up his Parnell stash. "Account not available" the ATM flashed. He tried another machine. Same result. He drove to Orion and confronted Mann who seemed unconcerned but agreed to call his NationsBank branch to check on a request he'd put in with Michael Howard to have a few hundred thousand dollars wired to Orion's account in Atlanta.

The money hadn't arrived. Howard had never been late before. Mann started making excuses. Pavlo, frustrated and angry, dialed Howard's number and punched the speaker button.

"Good morning. IMS," said a British-sounding woman. Pavlo motioned to Mann to respond.

"Michael Howard please," he said.

"Certainly. May I ask who's calling."

"Harold Mann."

"One moment please." After a long pause the woman was back. "Mr. Mann? Mr. Howard is not available at this time."

"Excuse me," Pavlo interrupted. "This is Walt Pavlo. It's urgent that we speak with Mr. Howard. We won't take up much of his time."

"Let me check," she said curtly.

"Mellow out, Wally," Mann said. "These island folk don't react well to uptight people. I'm sure it's nothing."

"Me? Uptight? I'm about to go into friggin' convulsions. If our money's frozen, we're seriously screwed."

"Mr. Mann," the receptionist said, "Mr. Howard will call you back in five minutes."

"That will be fine," Mann said.

When Howard called back, Mann put him on the speakerphone. "Michael? It's Harold. How're things in paradise?"

"Times could be better," came Howard's monotone response. "What's your question Harold?"

Pavlo and Mann shared a knowing look. Either someone else was on the call with Howard, he was recording it, or both.

"What's wrong Michael? You sound a bit down," Mann said.

"What's your question Harold?"

"It's very simple. I asked you to wire $200,000 to Orion but it hasn't hit our account in the States, eh?"

"I see," Howard said.

"I see? What the fuck does that mean?" Mann demanded. Silence. "You there Michael?"

"We have a rather dark situation here, Harold. Dark indeed."

"I don't care what color it is. Just tell me. What's going on with my money?

"The transaction you requested is...under review."

"It's my goddamn money. Why didn't you send it?"

"On the advice of counsel, who is here with me, I am unable to continue this conversation."

"Who's the lawyer?" Mann asked.

"Ross McDonough. Of Bruce Campbell & Company."

"Fine. I'm going to have my lawyer call Mr. McDonough and let them talk. Is that alright?"

"Oh yes. That would be wonderful," Howard said, sounding relieved. He rattled off the number and hung up.

"Jesus H. Christ. What's the purpose of having offshore accounts if someone can get at 'em?" groused Mann. "Shakes your confidence in the whole system."

Mann called his lawyer, Jack Martin, a local celebrity after helping prove that his client, security guard Richard Jewell, had been wrongly accused of bombing the Atlanta Olympics.

Martin investigated and reported back that three of Orion's twelve Cayman accounts—Hightower, Telephone International and MTC II Financial–were "under investigation."[17] But IMS was freezing all Mann-related accounts, period. That meant $500,000 dollars was stranded, half of everything Orion had and Pavlo's remaining $100,000 personal stash.

Orion's former cash cow, Denny McLain, meanwhile was facing additional troubles of his own. He was indicted in January, 1998 along with mobster John Gotti Jr. over alleged involvement in a telephone calling-card scam.[18] It began to dawn on Pavlo that things were not going to "blow over."

He worried that his father was in danger of being dragged into the mess, too. He figured the best way to avoid that happening was to help him buy out Orion's 90 percent stake in Valley Steel. Pavlo recruited Hennessy and together they drove back to Sistersville, West Virginia and helped Walt Sr. arrange a $400,000 loan, half what Orion had paid for Valley Steel less than a year earlier. Short of capital, Pavlo pulled a page from MCI's playbook and discounted the investment to make the deal work. Mann, desperate for cash, went along. Pavlo and Hennessy were on the road February 4, 1998, driving back to Atlanta—flying was now an unaffordable expense—when Pavlo's cell phone rang.

"Jack called this morning," Mann said, referring to his lawyer. "He said there's something in the paper we should take a look at."

"What is it?" Pavlo's stomach flip-flopped.

"A blurb on all these lawsuits."

"Which paper?"

"The *Wall Street Journal*."

"Are you shittin' me?"

"Would I soil on a buddy, Wally?"

"This isn't funny, Harold. Is my name in that fucking story?" He wondered if there were any Xanax left in his travel bag. He turned to Hennessy. "You hear that Sean? There's a story in the *Wall Street Journal* about us. You better pull off so we can get the paper."

"Mother of Jesus!" Hennessy said.

"Okay Harold," Pavlo said. "What's it say?"

"Nothing really. This is how big companies work. They leak all kinds of crap to their media lapdogs to intimidate people like us. It's harmless. Trust me. Everything's going according to plan."

Mann could fall off a 50-story building and he'd be smiling all the way down, saying, "Everything's going according to plan!"

Pavlo and Hennessy made several futile stops at groceries and convenience stores looking for the *Journal*, joking that at least no one in West Virginia would see the article. They finally found a copy at a bookstore near Charleston and sat in the car to read.

Mann's "blurb" was actually a two-page feature topping the paper's Southeast Journal section, under the headline: "Wrong Number: How Phone Deal Turned Sour." It included a "Dialing for Dollars" diagram of how money flowed between MCI, Manatee, small carriers, and the banks. It quoted Mann's lawyer, Jack Martin, describing Orion as "a consulting type of company." There were mentions of the Cayman accounts. On the jump page there was a quote in a box in large type:

> *"The program fell apart last March, when MCI says it discovered Mr. Pavlo's arrangement with Manatee."*

Pavlo felt sick to his stomach. He had come to accept facing a future of courtrooms and lawyers, but not becoming a public spectacle.

Pavlo and Hennessy stopped at the first bar they could find–a strip joint. A chubby woman sashayed around the grubby stage in an undersized G-string as a handful of truckers washed down their biscuits and gravy lunches with bottles of cheap beer.

"Looks like she's hiding a damn rabbi down there," Hennessy said of the woman's crotch. "She'd need a butt-thong the size of a mess-tent to hide that thing."

"Go ahead. Make me laugh so I don't start crying. Or just ask one of these guys to run over me with his 18-wheeler," Pavlo said. They sipped their drinks and tried to make the best of the brief distraction.

"Where's this all going, Pavlo?"

"Hell if I know. Every time something goes right, something else goes much more wrong. Sometimes I swear I can't stand not knowing any more. Then knowing's even worse. I'm tired of being chased."

"Maybe it'll pass. Mann doesn't seem worried."

"Yeah. That's the problem."

 **Tidying Things Up**

MANN, TRUE TO FORM, had dug up a new cash stream. Rodney Bowles, a black guy partial to gold around his neck, in his teeth, and on his Lexus, had partnered with Mann previously on a "credit rebuilding" scam. Bowles had borrowed about $60,000 from Mann when Orion was rolling in cash. Mann needed it back but was afraid to ask Bowles for it directly.

Bowles started to show up at Orion unannounced, slip into Mann's office, close the door, and dash out minutes later. Their new fraud involved a contact Bowles had inside Dun & Bradstreet, the credit rating agency, who, for $10,000, would slip a pristine credit report into his employer's database for any company Bowles wanted to create.

The partners paid the D&B mole to type up stellar credit reports for a fictitious telecom company named Waltis Enterprises, Inc.[1] Bowles, who could talk like a Harvard graduate, then played the role of corporate executive and recruited a sidekick to play a secondary role at the phone company.

Armed with a company that had Dun & Bradstreet's seal of approval, Mann worked his contacts at AT&T, WorldCom, and Business Telecom, Inc. to sign contracts allowing them to charge up to $120,000 a month to each in long-distance usage. Given Waltis' glowing D&B report, and the big telecom carriers' lax standards and ravenous appetite for new business, no site visits were required. Within weeks, Waltis had run up a $600,000 tab selling capacity to other shady telecom outfits and then vanished.[2]

Meanwhile, ever since Sean Hennessy discovered that Mann had looted his Cayman account, he had been looking for another job and a way to move on with his life.

Pavlo made a date and met him at a bar. Pavlo handed Hennessy a Publix paper grocery bag containing $35,000. Hennessy peered inside and gave Pavlo a look of astonishment. Pavlo had elicited a similar response when the same day he'd handed a shopping bag containing $10,000 to Tina Lincoln, who had been one of the victims of MCI's Carrier Finance purge.

"Spend it wisely," Pavlo said. "It's likely the last money you'll get out of Orion."

"No shit. Harold's so low he rips off his own friends. I can't believe you're staying with that guy."

"Where else can I go, Sean? Besides, the game's almost over. You need to be ready."

"For what?"

"For the damn cops. People are gonna get busted. Get yourself a lawyer, okay?"

"D'you have any idea how much I wish you'd never gotten me into this shit, Pavlo?"

Pavlo felt a flush of shame. Sean had articulated the terrible guilt Pavlo had been feeling for a long time. "About as much as I wish I'd never gotten you into it. Or me, okay?"

Hennessy fell silent. He had looked up to Pavlo, even following his example by getting an MBA while working full-time at MCI. When Pavlo had encouraged him to "take a little on the side," Hennessy had figured his boss, eight years his senior, knew what he was doing. Instead, he'd led Hennessy down a path to ruin. Hennessy wordlessly picked up the grocery sack and walked out.

|||

Mann was away on his annual Canadian vacation in mid-June, 1998 when his lawyer called Orion to report that he'd received a subpoena from the IRS for records of its dealings with telecom companies and Cayman financial institutions.[3] The feds clearly were piecing the puzzle together.

When Pavlo finally got Mann on the phone, he was still in his grin-and-bear-it mode. "I talked with Jack already. It's fine."

"How the hell can a subpoena be 'fine?'"

"They're just fishing, and fish only get caught when they bite the hook. So don't bite, okay?" Mann said. Pavlo could hear Mann munching on something that sounded like potato chips. "You shoulda seen this topless babe I saw sunbathing today."

"I'm not acting, Harold. I'm scared," Pavlo said. "I talked with my lawyer again. He says we could all do serious time for this."

"Don't say that! Christ, you tryin' to curse us? Nobody's going to jail, okay? The government'll take a look at some Orion records, see they're legit and move on. End of story."

"What about the Cayman stuff?"

"Of course we don't give them that shit. We don't even keep it in the office."

"There was a file cabinet full last I checked."

"Work with me, Wally. We're consultants to those companies, okay? We don't keep that stuff around the office."

"You mean the companies whose assets the Cayman government froze?"

"Froze is one thing. It's still the Caymans. They're not gonna hand that shit over. It'd be bad for their reputation. So just settle down. Let me talk with Jack again, okay?"

"You coming back to Atlanta or not?"

"If I have to. But I'm telling you. This isn't a big deal. Besides, the trout are biting up here like you wouldn't believe. Why don't you, Rhoda, and the boys come visit?"

"I've got work to do."

Pavlo started sifting through reams of Orion documents. Mann was right. A lot of the collections paperwork, carrier payment schedules and the like actually looked legit. Handing over some of the other stuff would be like giving the feds a flow chart of how nearly $6 million of MCI's money had poured into the Cayman Islands.

Pavlo would have to tidy things up. Since the fate of Wilkie and Hennessy also rested on how well they sanitized Orion, Pavlo called them up for help. Before they arrived, he stashed away some of the most incriminating evidence in case he needed bargaining chips to use with prosecutors. He had no intention of saving himself by throwing his pals under the bus, but he wanted to be prepared in case they tried to throw him there first.

Hennessy and Wilkie had found new jobs in Atlanta but were, like Pavlo, haunted. Hennessy was drinking profusely and waking up nights shaking. Wilkie had brief stretches each day when he felt normal, but he'd wake at night from fitful sleep, head down to the basement he'd fixed up with Cayman money, watch movies, and stew. The only one enjoying the summer was Mann, whose conscience never seemed to bother him. Pavlo doubted he had one.

Hennessy arrived first. Pavlo was alone in the conference room getting down to business.

"What the fuck's that? A wood chipper?"

"No. It's a paper shredder," Pavlo said. "The thing's big and old but it cuts everything into tiny little pieces."

"I'd love to see the shit Mann's put through that thing over the years." Hennessy said. "But you gotta hand it to him. He's got the tools for the job."

Wilkie arrived and over the next four hours the trio made confetti out of thousands of pages relating to Orion transactions, Cayman corporations, and personal bank accounts. When they were done, they loaded five garbage bags into the trunk of Pavlo's BMW 740 iL—bought with the money Mann had looted from Hennessy's and Wilkie's accounts—and tossed them in a dumpster at a construction site. Just like in the movies, Pavlo thought.

Mann remained in Canada while his lawyer continued to stall the IRS as best he could. Pavlo, meanwhile, was spending a lot of time at an Internet startup Mann had invested $50,000 in when times were flush. It didn't pay anything, but Pavlo hoped to cash in on a public offering. Then on a July morning Hennessy called in a panic.

"The FBI and IRS just showed up at Tina's apartment."

"What did she say?"

"Nothing. She was in the bedroom. Her roommates covered for her. But they'll be back."

"How's she doing?"

"How the hell do you think she's doing? She's apo-fucking-plectic."

"Tell her not to talk without a lawyer. I just gave her ten grand. Does she have any of it left?"

"I don't know," Hennessy said.

"Either way, tell Tina to get a lawyer and tell the truth."

"Okay."

"And Sean? You need to do the same. Tell the truth. You'll be helping both of us."

"What the fuck's the truth? I sure as shit don't know anymore."

"The truth is we both need to take a deep breath and calm down. Things'll work out."

"What're you gonna do?"

"Stick to Mann."

"Why?"

"You know, the *'Art of War'* thing," Pavlo said. "'Hold your friends close and your enemies closer.'"

"Take care of yourself, Pavlo."

A week or so later, Pavlo called to check in with Hennessy at his new job and got his voice mail. Hennessy never returned the call. When Hennessy's lawyer spurned an offer to meet with attorneys for Pavlo, Mann, and Wilkie later that week, the message was clear: Hennessy had rolled over on them. Pavlo expected a knock on his door any day. It didn't come. The only ones making noise were Manatee's banks and they were making lots of it.

As part of their scorched-earth legal strategy, NationsBank, National Bank of Canada, and CIT Group hired Wilmer "Buddy" Parker, a former Assistant U.S. Attorney who'd specialized in criminal Racketeer Influenced and Corrupt Organization cases. Having filed a civil RICO case against MCI, Pavlo, and numerous others, he began taking depositions. Jim Wanserski topped the list. Pavlo, as a defendant, was entitled to attend and chose to do so. He wanted to see how Wanserski handled himself.

The first installment took place in the conference room of Kilpatrick Stockton LLP, an Atlanta law firm representing MCI.

Carrier Finance had been dismantled and its collections operation moved to St. Louis and Arlington, Virginia.[4] Wanserski had stepped down and was given a one-year contract in October, 1997 with the title, "Director, Special Assignment." Working out of his house, he would receive his full pay through June 1, 1998 even if he took a job elsewhere. Wanserski's main duty was to assist in MCI's legal defense.[5] He also agreed that for over a decade he would "not make any statement or criticism, nor take any action that is adverse to the interests of MCI."[6]

The lawyer for the banks elicited the information that, at $138,700, Wanserski had been earning twice what MCI paid Pavlo. Yet Wanserski seemed only vaguely clued in on Carrier Finance's affairs. He answered a string of questions with the customary cover-your-ass "I don't recall" response.

Wanserski didn't recall specific discussions in 1996 about fraud at Hi-Rim,[7] the client that was bounced in March of that year and burned MCI for $27 million. He only recalled "generally" that its debt was carried on MCI's books into 1997.[8] He didn't recall what was discussed at the crucial Chateau Elan meeting about the department's largest debtor,

Caribbean Tel,[9] which had since gone bankrupt and stuck MCI for $55 million. And he didn't recall what year he first heard of Rapid Advance or how he heard of it.[10]

When Jim Folk's turn came two months later, he carried himself more ably. But when asked why workers in numerous divisions competed to credit MCI for money it hadn't actually received, he said "they get to keep their job [sic]."[11] He said MCI had not investigated TNI owner Bob Hilby's accusations as early as October 1996 of potential fraud in Carrier Finance because the MCI customer "had made a lot of claims and taken a lot of positions that were imaginative."[12]

Pavlo, Mann, and Wilkie all exercised their Fifth Amendment rights against self-incrimination and refused to testify at their depositions. However, federal officials had other ways of getting suspects to cooperate.

William L. McKinnon, Jr., Assistant U.S. Attorney for the Northern District of Georgia, offered Wilkie a deal he felt he couldn't refuse: plead guilty to negotiated charges or face the possibility that his wife, Becky, would also be indicted, for multiple counts of money laundering for using her Cayman-issued credit card.[13]

Wilkie copped a plea to one count of wire fraud involving his three Champion deals, worth $2.1 million, and carrying a maximum of five years in prison. He also agreed to help build cases and testify against Pavlo, Mann, and Benveniste.[14] Since Wilkie's admission included the shredding incident, and Hennessy was already cooperating with the feds, Pavlo now stood alone facing an obstruction of justice charge on top of his other legal woes.

Wilkie ignored the admonition of the prosecutor and his own attorney and stayed in contact with Pavlo, who took it as a sign of Wilkie's loyalty as a soldier under fire. Their friendship went beyond their crimes, which they had agreed not to discuss. They met in crowded bars, and drank heavily. Wilkie raged against Mann. Pavlo raged against MCI.

"You remember the part in *Exodus* about Pharaoh and the Jews?" Pavlo asked.

"Vaguely."

"We studied it in Catholic school," Pavlo said, sipping his scotch. "Pharaoh's heart so hardened with hatred toward Moses and his people that the logic of releasing them eluded him. The more Pharaoh hated, the more his heart hardened and the more destructive he became."

"The moral of this story is?"

"The more I hated MCI the more destructive I became," Pavlo said. "I'm just sorry I dragged you guys down with me."

"No need to apologize," Wilkie said. "Bottom line, we're a bunch of greedy fucks getting what we deserve. We had our eyes wide open. Our only real regret is that we got caught. Case closed."

"It's sure looking that way."

Bring a Bazooka

S EAN HENNESSY had been leading a double life in the seven months since he left Orion, building a new career as a financial analyst at a big consulting firm and telling everything he knew to federal investigators.

It had started shortly after he left Orion in April, 1998. Hennessy had taken up Pavlo's suggestion and hired attorney Bruce Malloy to defend him. Malloy laid out a strong case in a meeting with Assistant U.S. Attorney McKinnon that Hennessy, the only one talking deal at the time, could unravel the entire caper for the government and deliver damning evidence about his co-conspirators.

Hennessy walked out of the meeting with the impression the tall, thin prosecutor with the penetrating stare was still intent on putting him away for a long time. He retreated to the Russell Federal Building's parking lot and fought back tears. Malloy emerged having won him "transactional immunity." Hennessy still faced the threat of prison time, but might manage to stay out if he detailed for FBI Agent Raymond Kyle and IRS Agent Patricia Bergstrom every illegal transaction he'd been involved in—and the role his pals had played. He had to meet with the feds before work a few days a week, and to cooperate with MCI investigator Robert Avey at night to help the company put its Carrier Finance accounts back together. It was a grueling routine, but his only shot at beating the rap. Then, one day shortly before Thanksgiving, 1998, his office phone rang. He picked it up and heard a jarringly familiar voice.

"How ya doin', my boy?"

"Harold?" Hennessy was stunned.

"Where the fuck you been?" Mann asked, as if Hennessy were late returning from a beer run. "Wally'n me were wondering if you went to the dark side or something. You okay?"

"Sure. I've got a new job. Things're fine," Hennessy said nervously. "How 'bout you guys?"

"Swimming in deals. Want your old job back?"

"We had a run, Harold. No question. Look, I'm in the middle of something. Give me your number."

"Same as ever. I was just calling to see if we can get together for a few beers. You, me, maybe Wally. Just to catch up."

"Let me look at my schedule, okay? I'll call you back."

Hennessy, his hands shaking, dialed his attorney, Bruce Malloy.

"What did he want?" Malloy asked.

"To meet," Hennessy said. "Weirdest damn thing I've ever heard."

"Weird but possibly very good for our side. Stay where you are. I gotta make a call."

Malloy called Hennessy back and said he'd just spoken with Assistant U.S. Attorney McKinnon. Hennessy's chance to earn full immunity had arrived.

Pavlo, meanwhile, had stuck with Orion to keep an eye on Mann—the only person left whom he might rat on, or who might rat on him. He was also utterly lacking in motivation to find another job, given that every day he expected the FBI to show up at his door with handcuffs.

"Hey, Wally. I've got a surprise for you," Mann said, sticking his head into Pavlo's office. "A little party to talk about the good old days."

"Yeah, great," Pavlo said, staring at his computer screen. Pavlo was still trying to work the Internet venture to earn Orion some legitimate cash. Mann was forever interrupting.

"Hennessy's coming over for drinks."

Pavlo froze. "You're kidding."

"I figured we'd better offer a sympathetic ear or risk him talking to someone we don't like, eh?"

"C'mon Harold. He's already singing like a canary and you know it."

"There you go, always looking at the dark side. He's just a kid, Wally. Let's meet with him. It'll be okay."

"There's no way in hell," Pavlo said. "What if he's wearing a wire?"

"You've been watching too many damn cop shows. They don't give a crap about pee-wees like us with MCI and the banks pissing all over each other. Besides, they don't got dick on us. I'm telling ya. This is perfect!"

"Why risk it?"

"Fuck it. I'll meet the guy myself. He'll be here at seven."

"Tonight?"

"There's no night like it. I stocked the fridge with cold ones. You know those Irish boys, eh?"

Pavlo packed up his things and took a long look around before getting in his car and driving off. He felt certain he was being watched.

Hennessy pulled into the parking lot of Mount Bethel United Methodist Church a mile from the Orion office at 6 o'clock. Two police cars and a van with eight federal agents inside were waiting. Agents Kyle and Bergstrom, who had been debriefing him on his MCI activities, were there to prep him.

Hennessy was both pumped and exhausted. The night before he had been overcome with such a case of the shakes that the bed had banged against the wall and woken his wife. Mann could burn in hell, but Hennessy was praying his pal Pavlo wouldn't show. Looking him in the eye while betraying him was more than Hennessy could take.

The agents handed Hennessy a cell phone. It contained a transmitter that would be picked up live by the agents' earpieces and recorded on tape in the van.

"Remember, if things go bad or you feel threatened say 'code red' and we'll be there," agent Bergstrom said.

"You better bring a bazooka or I'll kill that fucker," Hennessy said. The agents had a good laugh.

"Ask him about the deals," Bergstrom instructed. "The Caymans. Just keep him talking."

"That's never a problem with Mann," Hennessy assured them.

He drove to Orion with the agents following in a second car. The van stopped around a corner, and federal agents positioned themselves behind the tall bushes surrounding the courtyard entrance to Orion's ground-floor office.

Hennessy entered. "I hope you got some fucking beer in this shit hole," he yelled.

Mann came into the lobby. Hennessy put out his hand to shake.

"Fuck that," Mann said, opening his arms for a bear hug. As they embraced, Mann yanked Hennessy's shirttails out of his pants.

"Just makin' sure you're not wired for sound, old friend."

"Fuck you." Hennessy said laughing nervously. "You think I'm a snitch?"

"A snatch is more like it. Speaking of snatches, Wally's being a paranoid pussy as usual."

"He's not here?"

"Nope. Wanna beer?"

"Like fifty of 'em," Hennessy said, relieved.

"Come on in." Mann led Hennessy into his office. "How's Brenda?"

"Fine. Me too. I like the new job. Not as hard as the shit we did here."

Mann grabbed two Heinekens from his office refrigerator and sat down behind his pristine desk. Hennessy settled into his chair and put his car keys and the cell phone the FBI had supplied on the corner of the desk. Mann was intent on catching up and instructing Hennessy what to do if the cops ever knocked on his door. That included walking Hennessy through a cover story for each of Orion's clients and Cayman accounts. It was a discussion that sealed different fates for Mann and Hennessy.

|||

Shortly after Wilkie cut a deal with prosecutors, Pavlo told Bruce Morris he wanted to do the same. The Cayman money was no longer a secret. Hennessy and Wilkie were talking to the government about everything from destroying MCI journal vouchers to puffing Cuban stogies on Seven Mile Beach. It was either go in now, Pavlo figured, or risk being the last one in the pool.

Morris suggested Pavlo first clear up the matter of $620,476 in payments that had gone to his Parnell account in Grand Cayman but he hadn't paid taxes on. Mann had previously told him there were no tax consequences on money held in the Caymans, as long as he didn't receive it personally. Pavlo now realized the IRS was unlikely to agree with Mann's liberal interpretation of tax-exempt income.

Pavlo was glad he'd had the presence of mind to file his taxes separately from Rhoda's, so she wouldn't be implicated in his misdeeds.

He visited an accountant his wife recommended, Wendell R.

Veal, and met with him to go over the details. Veal, tall and overweight, worked out of an office with papers piled from floor to ceiling, tucked into an aging little complex. It reminded Pavlo of a visit to Wanserski's office, only worse.

"I need to make some adjustments to my returns for 1996 and 1997," Pavlo began.

"Sure. Just tell me where the problem is and what backup you have."

"The problem is with 'Other Income,'" Pavlo said. "I don't have any backup."

Veal smiled. Pavlo imagined Veal thought he'd maybe squirreled away a little extra money from a moonlighting job, or poker winnings. "We'll categorize it as 'Omitted Payments' on Schedule C," Veal said. "How much are we talking for 1996?"

Pavlo pulled a slip of paper out of his back pocket. "Three hundred seventy-one thousand three hundred and twenty-two dollars. And zero cents.[1] It's a bit less for 1997."

Veal's jaw dropped. "You're serious?"

"'Fraid so," Pavlo said.

"You do realize accountants do not enjoy the attorney-client privilege, right? I mean, if asked to do so by government authorities, I must disclose what I know." Veal shifted in his chair.

"Then it'll make both our lives easier if you don't know too much. Got a calculator?" Pavlo read him a breakdown from a Parnell statement of the amounts he'd wired to himself from the Cayman Islands. He offered no paperwork and Veal didn't request any. After a few minutes of number-crunching Veal looked up.

"I don't imagine you've taken the $400 annual deduction for charitable contributions."

Pavlo laughed. "Do what you think is right. Let's just get this thing filed as soon as possible."

"Sure. But do you plan on paying this? I mean at one time? It's gonna come to about $150,000, plus penalties and interest."

"No problem. I'll just hit up a couple more banks on my way home," Pavlo said. Silence. "That's a joke, Wendell. Naturally I'd like installment terms. Gimme terms!"

"Of course."

Pavlo's final tab was a total of $153,455 for both years.[2] He started making $15,000 monthly payments to the IRS, burning through what savings he had left, including $200,000 he'd managed to put away in an Individual Retirement Account.

The visit to Veal marked the start of his new mission: make things right in his life, even if that meant going broke and to prison. Both were distinct possibilities.

Morris contacted Assistant U.S. Attorney McKinnon the following month and was told that Pavlo's deal would require him to plead guilty to one count of money laundering, and to cooperate in government investigations of Mann and Benveniste. The government, it turned out, had doubts about whether the former Manatee boss had used its credit lines for the intended purposes and was investigating him for possible bank fraud.

The charge Pavlo faced, money laundering, was a particularly nasty white-collar crime, carrying a potential sentence of seven years. Pavlo knew that the sooner he went in, the better off he'd be. But he couldn't bear to think of leaving Rhoda alone to raise Bubby and Howie, then ages eight and ten, and that they would be teenagers when he got out. Nor, in the end, could he bring himself to volunteer for such a harsh fate. He rejected the deal and went back to his old life at Orion, secretly continuing to gather what evidence he could against Mann and Benveniste on the outside chance it would give him leverage later.

By March of 1999, the Pavlos were running low on money. They sold their St. Marlo home, traded in the BMW for a Silverado pickup, and decided to move to Savannah, where Pavlo had grown up and maybe the boys would be protected from embarrassment.

They found a small ranch-style house just off the Wilmington River and Inter-Coastal Waterway east of town. With no money for a down payment, Pavlo asked his father for help. Walt Sr. came through immediately. Pavlo had told his father he was having trouble with some "telecom ventures" but nothing more. Walt Sr. didn't pry.

Meanwhile, the legal machine was grinding away on other fronts. Buddy Parker, the banks' lawyer, called Rhoda in for a deposition. That meant the Pavlos had to hire yet another attorney to accompany her. Rhoda was questioned about her lifestyle, professional activities, and the $120,000 salary she had drawn from Orion.[3] She held her ground, recounting what her husband had told her—she was getting paid for consulting services her husband had performed as a side job. To Parker, the deposition was little help. To the Pavlos, it was one more rip in the family fabric.

Then Pavlo's father called to say IRS agent Bergstrom wanted to meet with him.

"What do you want me to tell her?" he asked.

"The truth," Pavlo said. The IRS had traced the money from Wilkie's Champion deals through the ACC account in the Caymans to Valley Steel. His father's only transgression had been to trust his son, yet there was nothing he could do to prevent Walt Sr. from being tarred with the same brush. But when he showed the IRS that he'd bought out Mann's stake with a bank loan, the Valley Steel piece of the fed's investigation came to a dead end.

|||

Pavlo's civil trial began in Atlanta before U.S. District Court Judge G. Ernest Tidwell on April 10, 2000. The courtroom was packed with lawyers. Six tables had been set up in a space that usually held two in order to accommodate all the plaintiffs and defendants, most of whom were both. MCI and the banks that had lent money to Manatee fielded close to a dozen lawyers. Separate tables held attorneys for Pavlo, Mann, Benveniste, and Manatee.

The gallery held yet more lawyers to ferry documents in and out, agents from the FBI, the IRS and the press. Pavlo had been hoping for a last-minute out-of-court settlement between Manatee, the banks and MCI, even though he knew it would likely leave him, as one of the defendants, owing millions he didn't have. He had already spent almost all his $300,000 in legitimate retirement savings and home-sale proceeds on legal bills. Now he was going to be on the hook to Morris for $3,000 a day to sit through what threatened to be an excruciating, weeks-long trial in which the Justice Department and the IRS could just sit back and get a tutorial on his crimes.

Judge Tidwell had repeatedly urged the litigants to settle, warning that the dispute was so complex no jury would be able to grasp it.

Pavlo and Mann sat next to each other bookended by their respective attorneys. At Pavlo's request Rhoda had stayed in Savannah with their sons. For all he knew Karen Mann, who never seemed too up on her husband's doings, thought Harold was putting in another day at the office.

Pavlo leaned forward with his legal pad and pen at the ready to pass Morris notes should any legal epiphanies strike him. Mann seemed oblivious to his surroundings, offering Pavlo gum and quietly cracking sophomoric jokes.

Now that he had failed to avoid a trial, the judge rushed through jury selection. Morris and Mann's attorney, Jack Martin, wanted the least educated jurors, hoping that confusion would work for Pavlo and Mann. The banks jockeyed for the opposite, striking grandmothers and high school dropouts. Tidwell seated a jury within a couple of hours and called on the banks to present their case.

Parker told the jury, "The evidence will indicate that MCI in 1996 was having trouble...getting the kind of money that was owed to it, the kind of money that Mr. Pavlo was responsible for trying to collect."[4] He went on to argue that Pavlo cracked under the pressure, conspired with Mann to embezzle $5 million and funneled some of it to his wife and father.

He laid out a scenario in which Manatee's Mark Benveniste had used collateral he knew was bogus to keep his banks lending, and how, even after MCI managers realized they had fraud on their hands, they continued doing business with Manatee, deliberately keeping the mess secret from its banks and even denying in court filings they'd known about it.

"The heart of this case is fraud," Parker said. "Fraud, lying, cheating, stealing and attempting to cover it up... It's about people discovering the lying, the cheating and the stealing, and then, it's about people not telling people about what they knew."

Pavlo was angry and embarrassed to have his misdeeds articulated in a courtroom in front of a judge, jury, and the media. He wanted to strangle Parker. Even so, Pavlo had to hand it to the bastard–he had a damn good handle on the story line.

MCI's turn came next. Its attorney portrayed the company not as the racketeer Parker had but as the victim of crimes he said had cost it more than $50 million to the banks' $13 million. "The banks lost money because they made a careless and terribly bad loan," the attorney said. His sharpest barbs were aimed at Pavlo, Mann, Wilkie, and Benveniste, describing a "criminal conspiracy with MCI and the banks both the target."

Mann's lawyer, Jack Martin, told the jury, "We have got two multi-billion dollar corporations here arguing over who should have called who [sic] first." He argued that Mann and Pavlo were guilty of nothing more than coming up with a way "to help MCI to solve its problems in a way that allowed it to clean it [sic] up and move on... My mother used to say no matter how flat the flapjack, it has more than two sides. This case has more than two sides," he concluded. Mann nudged

Pavlo with his elbow and nodded his head as if to say, See, we're gonna be just fine.

Pavlo's attorney, Bruce Morris, began his opening arguments on the second day by saying his client was "under tremendous pressure and was worried about losing his job" at MCI in early 1996,[5] with tens of millions of dollars more in bad debt than his bosses were willing to write off. Management kept telling him "cash is king," so Pavlo committed MCI to guaranteeing Manatee's loans, thinking "This is good for my customers, this is good for Manatee, this is good for Mr. Mann and this is good for MCI." All of which was true, Pavlo knew. So too was Morris' claim that Pavlo had never lied outright or misled Manatee's bankers. What he'd done to MCI and Manatee's Mark Benveniste was another story that Morris avoided mentioning.

The opening statements were hard to listen to, but they were gentle compared to the testimony that followed. Pavlo's best friend, Jim Wilkie, was called first. Having reached an agreement with the government and the banks, Wilkie testified like the cool, credible Army pilot he was. When asked about the $2 million Champion Communications had owed MCI, which he and his cronies had embezzled, Wilkie said simply, "I was in debt and needed the money."

The banks' Buddy Parker called Pavlo next.

"In 1996, Mr. Pavlo, were you employed by MCI?" Parker asked.

Pavlo reached into his coat pocket for the slip of paper Morris had given him and read, "Sir, under my constitutional rights, I assert my rights under the Fifth Amendment and refuse to answer." He was trembling.

He repeated the response to each of Parker's questions, but they kept coming: "Were you and Mr. Sean Hennessy transferring information to Mr. Harold Mann to use in a scheme to defraud MCI resellers?" "Were you aware Sean Hennessy was being paid while an employee of MCI by Mr. Harold Mann?" "Were you aware that Mr. Harold Mann, through a Cayman Island company, purportedly loaned money to pay off a bad debt to MCI?"

Judge Tidwell quickly tired of Parker's showboating and gave him one minute to wrap up.

"Were you, Harold Mann, and Mark Benveniste together discussing creating documents to falsify the books and records of Manatee for a $5.5 million MetroLink loan?" "Did you not know that there was no valid collateral for the so-called $5.5 million that Mark Benveniste caused Manatee to obtain from the National Bank of Canada?" "Did you not benefit directly from that false representation by obtaining monies to purchase Valley Steel, a company in which your father worked?"

"Your time is up," the judge barked. Then to Pavlo: "Step down."

His old boss, Ralph McCumber, was next and described Pavlo as an "excellent employee," in part for "development of a number of ingenious and effective surety devices," meaning ways for MCI to collect its money.

Bob Hilby of TNI, Orion's first victim, next described how Pavlo put the clamps on him to pay the $2 million he owed MCI, which then led him to Harold Mann. Hilby claimed he'd told MCI executives seven months before the banks learned of the scandal that he suspected Pavlo and Mann were involved in a "conspiracy to defraud" him. Pavlo had a hard time stomaching Hilby's self-serving testimony and the admission that he'd been paying himself $500,000 a year even as his company was $3.3 million behind in payments to MCI.

Doug Dickson, the TM Systems finance chief, was even harder to take as the third day of the trial opened. In bankruptcy since 1997,[6] TM Systems had piggy-backed on the banks' litigation and filed its own RICO suit against MCI, Manatee, Pavlo, and Mann. Dickson, holed up at the Atlanta Four Seasons on the banks' dime while he testified, claimed on the stand that MCI's bad billing and failure to honor contract issues were at the root of his disputes with the company.

He was grilled about how MCI had hidden $1.6 million of TM Systems' debt in a promissory note and how his partner, Deb Ward, had collateralized it with her 342-acre ranch in Ventura County, California—a property that was pledged to, and eventually foreclosed on, by another creditor. Pavlo wouldn't have blamed the jury for finding even the witnesses in his trial guilty of something.

Sean Hennessy, like Wilkie, had agreed to testify to avoid getting sued by the banks. Under Parker's questioning, he outlined how, during his four years at MCI, its Carrier Finance unit had grown exponentially to handle around $2 billion a year in revenues. He described how they'd dealt with feverish expansion and burgeoning bad debt by massaging the numbers. "We applied cash to maintain that over-90 (day) balance (of debt) at whatever the goal was at that particular time," Hennessy testified. Then Parker moved on to Orion.

"You were creating false entries in MCI's books?" he asked.

"Correct," Hennessy replied.

"And how did you know about this scheme?" Parker asked.

"I was involved in it from day one through Mr. Pavlo." Hennessy kept his eyes glued on Parker, avoiding Pavlo who sat a few feet away.

Pavlo wasn't mad at Hennessy. He was too numb. It wasn't a bad state to be in, since Hennessy next testified about which resellers Orion had defrauded, how he'd forged documents with Pavlo and Mann to make it look like Orion intended to pay MCI and how he and his family had benefited financially.

Shell-shocked, Pavlo headed to the parking lot alone for a smoke during the break that followed. As he lit up he saw Ralph McCumber. In spite of the probability that it was a violation of some rule or convention to talk to him, Pavlo approached. What was one more crime at this point?

"Mr. Pavlo, how are you holdin' up?" McCumber extended his hand to shake.

"Hanging in there. How about you? I thought you quit smoking?"

"I did, but with all this shit going on..." McCumber laughed.

"I don't know what to say, Ralph. 'Sorry' doesn't cut it. This would never have happened if you'd stayed. It couldn't have. That's a tribute to what you stand for. Not me trying to pass any blame." Pavlo's voice quivered.

The old sailor's eyes welled. "I'm sorry for leaving you. If I'd known how this would end, I'd have taken you with me."

They shook hands. "Permission requested to look you up one day when all this is over, sir," Pavlo said.

"Permission granted."

Pavlo wandered about the lot, noticing dark spots where his tears had fallen onto his bright red tie. When he got back to the courtroom, it was empty. The lawyers were taking another crack at a settlement. He sat quietly until Morris and Jack Martin waved Mann and him over. Mark Benveniste joined the group.

"MCI's saying it'll throw the banks $8 million and Hammer another million to settle, guys,"[7] Martin said, like a quarterback in a huddle. "But you're gonna have to kick in something too."

"Like what?" Mann asked.

"The banks are saying they'll accept $2.5 million if you pay within 45 days. If not, they're gonna ask the Court for a $5.5 million judgment collectively against the three of you."[8]

Benveniste looked stunned.

"Fuck that," Mann said.

"I'll take it," countered Pavlo.

"Like you've got two and a half million bucks," Mann sneered.

"I don't have the money for Bruce to sit through another week of this trial either. This thing's gotta stop."

"You guys have to make a legitimate attempt to pay this," Morris cautioned.

"We'll pay what we can. Or buy lottery tickets," Pavlo said.

"You're crazy," Mann said.

"C'mon Harold, you can do something," Martin said.

"What if I don't?" Mann's tone was childish defiance.

"They'll get a judgment against you."

"Shit Harold, you don't own anything anyway," Pavlo said.

"Our wives aren't responsible for any of this, right?" Mann asked Morris.

"Nope. Just you three guys."

"Fine. Let's settle this, eh?" Mann said it as if he'd discovered a clever out.

Benveniste nodded.

While the paperwork and other mechanics of the settlement were being worked out, Judge Tidwell insisted the trial continue. Parker called back Sean Hennessy. No sooner had he taken the stand than the banks asked for another recess to discuss the settlement. Hennessy stood near the witness stand unsure what to do. He looked at Pavlo apologetically.

Pavlo approached and extended a hand. Hennessy took it. "How you doing?" Pavlo asked.

"Good, man. It's good to see you. Remember how we used to joke about this day?" He cast his eyes to the floor.

"Yup."

"It doesn't seem funny now."

"No, it doesn't." Pavlo felt utterly defeated.

"So what's the deal with these recesses?"

"The lawyers are negotiating a settlement," Pavlo said. "Nobody'll be happier than me when this whole fuckin' thing's over. Whatever that means."

"If I knew something I'd tell you."

"No you wouldn't, but that's okay," Pavlo said smiling. Hennessy's attorney Bruce Malloy signaled to Hennessy to break off. "Take care of yourself," Pavlo said.

"You do the same, Pavlo."

Malloy escorted Hennessy out of the courtroom. Pavlo sat down at his table. Fifteen minutes later the lawyers started trickling back in.

For two and a half years they'd been trying to tear each other's throats out. Now they were joking like old law school chums. The legal factory had produced an agreement. The judge practically cheered. "Bless you, bless you, bless you. I'll let the jury go."

The civil settlement gave Pavlo and Mann 45 days to come up with $2.5 million.

As he made the five-hour drive back to Savannah, Pavlo had no clue how they'd get it together. He worked hard to put it out of his mind. He'd start sweating the money in the morning. But he'd be sweating it alone. Mann had gone home to pack for a week in Bermuda.

 **The End of the World**

PAVLO AND MANN failed to come up with the $2.5 million and the banks entered a judgment collectively against them and Mark Benveniste for $5,474,231,[1] representing the estimated total of the trio's contribution to the banks' losses. The figure was so large Pavlo figured he'd have to live forever to get out from under it—or file for bankruptcy.

But he was facing bigger problems.

The federal criminal investigation dragged into the summer of 2000, when Mann headed off to Canada for his annual vacation. In July, Pavlo's attorney, Bruce Morris, reported that he'd met with the FBI about Mann's latest Waltis Enterprises scam, the one made possible by bribing a Dun & Bradstreet clerk. Pavlo hadn't participated directly, but he'd handled the money at Orion. That made him an accessory.

Worse still, Mann's co-conspirator Rodney Bowles—aka Kevin Thorpe and various other aliases—had already agreed to a plea deal that included 15 months in prison and $603,000 in restitution[2] in exchange for testimony against Pavlo and Mann.

Pavlo couldn't stand being chased any longer. He was nearly broke and emotionally spent. He told Morris he'd accept whatever deal his lawyer could negotiate. Assistant U.S. Attorney McKinnon said that meant pleading guilty to not one but two counts of money laundering, plus two counts of wire fraud, and one for obstruction of justice for the document shredding incident.

Pavlo studied the federal sentencing guidelines. The charges could put him in prison for 30 years, although five-to-seven seemed most likely. It was no worse than what he'd been offered eight months earlier, but this time Pavlo realized he had no choice. Besides, there was still one way he could reduce his time behind bars. If his testimony against Mann and Benveniste offered "substantial assistance" to prosecutors, he could earn a so-called "5k1 reduction." That would allow the judge to depart from the stringent sentencing guidelines. Pavlo took the deal.

Morris met Pavlo just after lunch on August 10, 2000 in front of the Russell Federal Building, where the civil trial had taken place that spring. They headed to the U.S. Attorney's offices on the 18th floor. Morris signed in, giving his affiliation as "The Freedom Fighters." Pavlo smiled and did the same.

Waiting for them in a large conference room were FBI agent Ray Kyle, IRS agent Patty Bergstrom and prosecutor McKinnon. The agents flashed their badges. McKinnon slid a plea agreement proffer across the table toward Morris.

"What about his 5k?" Morris asked of the sentence reduction form.

"That's up to Mr. Pavlo," McKinnon said stone-faced. "If he has what we need then we'll play ball."

Morris looked at Pavlo. He'd have to perform from memory since he'd left his written evidence at home. He figured he would try to get the 5k sentence reduction while keeping the documents in reserve. If nothing else, MCI had taught him to negotiate. Pavlo gave Morris a slight nod.

"I think we have our deal," Morris said, pushing the proffer agreement toward Pavlo. He signed without reading it and slid it back to Morris, who pushed it like a poker chip to McKinnon.

"He's all yours," Morris said.

The questioners readied their note pads. He described his time at MCI from beginning to end, corroborated much of what Hennessy and Wilkie had said, and added events, dates and details they hadn't been privy to.

He also gave them the sweep of the story by weaving in how MCI hid enormous bad debts on its books, the truth from its shareholders, and committed what he considered a far greater fraud than Orion's. He told them about how many small carriers perpetrated the same bust-out scam as Waltis Enterprises, running up big bills and then running off with MCI's money. The feds wrote it all down, but the telecom boom was at its apex. Stories of vast conspiracies would have seemed fanciful even from a witness with no ax to grind. The feds remained intent on closing their embezzlement case by putting Pavlo, Mann, and Benveniste behind bars.

"What do you think?" Morris asked after four hours.

"He seems to be telling the truth and his information's damn accurate," McKinnon said. "I'd say it looks good." The two agents nodded.

"I have documents," Pavlo said. "Lots of 'em."

Bergstrom and Kyle held their pens, paused in mid-air.

"What documents?" McKinnon asked.

"From the Cayman Islands. Wire transfers. Orion accounting records for 1996 and 1997. Every letter written on Orion's computers through 1998."

"We'd be very interested in that," McKinnon deadpanned.

No shit, Pavlo thought. Hennessy and Wilkie thought everything had been destroyed and had told the government as much based on their testimony of the shredding incident. Pavlo agreed to bring the documents to a second meeting in early September. Everyone got up to leave.

"I want to congratulate you on your case against all of us," Pavlo said to Kyle and Bergstrom. "You obviously do your jobs well."

The agents seemed surprised by the compliment but gave him firmer and longer handshakes than the perfunctory ones with which they had greeted him.

At their next meeting, Pavlo handed over tapes from Orion's computer system and hundreds of pages of documents. His 5k was in the bag. All he'd had to do was throw his buddies, Mann and Benveniste, under the bus.

The night he returned from his second meeting with the feds, Pavlo put his sons to bed and wandered with Rhoda out to the Wilmington River dock behind their house.

"I met with the prosecutor today," he started. "I think I've got a good idea how long I'll be going away."

"Okay. I can do this." Rhoda took a deep breath, "For how long?"

"Four years, probably." Then it all hit him at once and he began sobbing. Rhoda took him in her arms. Then she began crying too. The realization that Rhoda, Bubby, and Howie would pay in shame and hardship for his crimes was worse than anything Pavlo had faced. It was the lowest moment of his life and he hadn't even told their sons yet.

"I'm scared," Rhoda said.

"Me too. But you know, I'm also relieved. I can't go on living like this. I swear, even a prison sentence can't be much worse. At least it has an end."

Two weeks to the day after Pavlo's second meeting with the feds, on a late September morning, he was getting Bubby and Howie ready for school when his phone rang. He answered and heard a woman's hysterical voice. It was Mann's wife, Karen.

"My God! They just took Harold!"

Pavlo had been expecting such news, but the terror in Karen's voice stunned him. "Settle down, Karen. Tell me what happened."

"We were eating breakfast. God, the kids were there. The kids were there, Walt! Some guys with 'FBI' in huge letters on their jackets knocked on the door. They took Harold away in handcuffs. What in hell's going on? Tell me!"

"Settle down, Karen. I've got to get Bubby and Howie to school. I'll call you back in ten minutes. I promise."

"Please, Walt. Please help. Please!"

As Pavlo drove his sons to school, he realized that Karen had been living in a world as untethered to reality as her husband's. Pavlo had given Rhoda few details on the source of his money, the federal investigation and the civil trial, but she had long known about the severity of the situation, including the likelihood he'd go to prison.

Mann had kept Karen totally in the dark. She had luxuriated in a huge home, a horse farm, months-long vacations, expensive gifts and other trappings. Now the husband who'd provided so abundantly would be lucky to post bail.

As soon as he'd dropped his sons off, Pavlo called Karen back on his cell phone. "It's Walt. First, where did they take Harold?"

"I don't know," Karen said sniffling.

"Did you call his lawyer? Jack Martin?"

"Yes. He's not in. His brother Jim who works with him knows what happened. Walt, I need to know what's going on. Please tell me."

Karen did need to know but Mann was the one who needed to tell her. Once again, Mann had left the dirty work to Pavlo. He quickly explained to Karen that he and her husband had stolen money from MCI, shunted it off to the Cayman Islands and been declared liable for a $5.5 million settlement. He told her he'd pleaded guilty to three felonies and would soon be going to prison. It was a lot for her to digest. Pavlo hung up after reassuring her as best he could that she'd make it through somehow. It was the last time they ever spoke.

The next morning Pavlo's cell phone rang. "Yo, Wally!" Mann bellowed.

"Harold?"

"*'I get knocked down, but I get up again,'*" Mann sang from the tune by Chumbawumba. "*'You're never going to keep me down…'*"

Pavlo laughed. "Where are you?"

"On my way back down to the bail bond place. Thank God Jack's got some pull in this friggin' town. So what's new?"

"What's new? You just got arrested and you're asking me what's new?"

"Fuck the FBI. I'm fighting this thing. They got nothin' on me. Nothin'!"

"Seems I've heard that before. Did Karen tell you she called me?"

"Yeah, briefly. What did you tell her?"

"Everything."

"Goddamnit Wally."

"What the hell was I supposed to do? Tell her you double parked?"

"Fuck it. I guess the cat's out of the bag."

"Ya think so?"

"They're just trying to scare me but it was actually kinda fun," Mann said gleefully, as if he'd been the butt of a college prank. "The fucking FBI knocks on my door. There was like six or seven of 'em. I answer in my underwear and a sweatshirt with the Bergstrom bitch there and everything. They don't even let me get dressed. Just put on a pair of shoes. They take the laces off and put on the handcuffs. They're just trying to scare me."

"It worked pretty well on Karen."

"Like I was saying, they put me in a holding pen until the judge was ready to set bail. Then they take me into the courtroom in my goddamn underwear. They were just trying to scare me."

"I think you said that already, Harold."

Mann mentioned only in passing that he hadn't been arrested over their Orion activities, money laundering, or tax evasion. They'd nabbed him for the Waltis Enterprises scam, which was the subject of a separate FBI investigation. Pavlo was sure Mann would face more charges in the near future, but he had his own problems to deal with.

A few days after Pavlo officially pleaded guilty in front of Judge Tidwell, Wilkie was sentenced to 21 months for wire fraud.[3] It was less time than Pavlo expected to get, but Wilkie had won the race to the courthouse. He called Pavlo in late October. They discussed their respective fates and carefully steered around the feelings of shame, loss, betrayal, and fear.

"You see the thing on MCI WorldCom?" Wilkie asked.

"Not us again, I hope." Pavlo winced, imagining some retelling of their crimes.

"It just wrote off $685 million in carrier revenue.[4] Get this. They blamed it on a sudden downturn in the telecom industry. Isn't that a fucking hoot?"

"I'll be damned. They waited until the market started to crack and dumped all the shit we hid for them." He had to hand it to MCI. It had managed to keep its bogus bookkeeping under wraps through one blown sale to British Telecom and a successful one to WorldCom. Now, with the telecom industry and stock market imploding, the timing was perfect to blame its losses on "the market."

It wasn't going to affect his life, but Pavlo was angry. He was pleading guilty to his own crimes while MCI WorldCom was burying its. He'd told his corporate corruption yarn to lawyers, the IRS, the FBI, and a federal prosecutor. Nobody had taken him seriously. He thought of calling the Securities and Exchange Commission, but figured he'd only come off as a vengeful and slightly deranged felon. He was just a condemned man trying to talk himself out of a hanging.

|||

Pavlo appeared in Judge Tidwell's court for his sentencing in early January, 2001. The same audience of MCI lawyers and a lone *Atlanta Journal-Constitution* reporter sat by. Pavlo had asked that no family members attend. His shame was too great.

He had prepared a statement to read before his sentencing. He'd written about how he'd been driven to his crimes by hatred of MCI. He wanted it to be part of the permanent court record. Morris talked him out of it. Tidwell was a law-and-order judge. He wanted his cons full of remorse and nothing else.

"Are we prepared for me to render a sentence?" Tidwell asked.

Morris rose buttoning his jacket. "Your honor, my client would like to make a statement for the record prior to sentencing."

"Proceed."

"Thank you, Your Honor." Pavlo approached a small podium and read a statement expressing love for his family, acknowledging what he'd done, and his willingness to accept the consequences. "It has been said that the road to a righteous life is narrow but it is nonetheless a road and not a tightrope," he said in closing. "I should have known better and I vow to do better."

Pavlo returned to his table and remained standing. Tidwell sentenced him to three years and five months of prison time and ordered Pavlo to pay $5,766,636.75 in restitution to MCI, AT&T and BTI over the Waltis Enterprises ruse.[5] Along with the $5.5 million judgment the banks won against him, Pavlo was now on the hook for $11.3 million. Morris recommended an alcoholism program in prison that could reduce Pavlo's sentence by up to 14 months.

Their day's work done, client and lawyer headed out to the parking lot for a smoke.

"It was an ingenious plan, I'll give you that," Morris said. "But now that it's all over, I've gotta ask. Why? Why, with so much going for you, did you do it?"

Pavlo paused and lit his cigarette. "I started out hating MCI's customers. Then I hated MCI. Then I hated myself. After that, greed took over. I figured even if MCI caught me, it would keep quiet because it was doing far worse. What I didn't count on was the banks getting involved. That's what killed me. All the shit they dredged up. But I really did hate the bastards. All of 'em."

"That much is obvious, my friend."

Pavlo climbed into his pickup for the ride back to Savannah and popped R.E.M. into the CD player.

> *It's the end of the world as we know it.*
> *It's the end of the world as we know it.*
> *It's the end of the world as we know it,*
> *and I feel fine...*

He wasn't feeling fine, but it was the end of the world as he'd known it, and he was relieved.

26 People Like Me

PAVLO HELD a last pre-prison meeting with Jim Wilkie at the Time Out Sports Bar in Alpharetta. They talked about their impending time and laughed about all the hell they'd raised.

"One day this will all be over and someone's gonna ask me 'Did you steal six million bucks?'" Wilkie said. "I'm gonna look 'em in the eye and say 'You're damn right I did. Every last penny. It was the dumbest thing I've ever done.'"

Pavlo agreed. It had been an exciting ride with lots of fun and laughs. But money, power, and revenge were poor substitutes for the father, husband, son, friend, and mentor Pavlo should have been. It was time to pay the price.

On a Sunday morning in January, 2001, before Pavlo was scheduled to report to prison, he and Rhoda agreed that she'd go on to church alone and he'd have a chat with the boys. "We'll wait for you in the parking lot after the service," Pavlo told her.

Rhoda gave him a long hug and walked toward the doors of the Wilmington Island Presbyterian Church, where the pastor was greeting his congregation. Bubby and Howie looked up at Pavlo with shining faces. It was a rare treat when their mom attended church alone and they spent the morning doing something fun with their dad.

"What're we gonna do?" Bubby asked.

"Let's walk over to the golf course."

He'd known for awhile that he'd probably be headed to prison. But it was only in the past few weeks, with two months until he had to report, that he'd faced up to the fact that he'd have to tell his sons. He and Rhoda had turned to Father Patrick O'Brien for guidance.

Pavlo had known the native Irishman since serving as an altar boy two decades earlier during his masses at Savannah's Cathedral of St. John the Baptist.

O'Brien had since moved to St. Peter the Apostle Church and School on Wilmington Island, where the Pavlo boys were students. The priest listened to his abbreviated description of his crimes and said he thought Bubby, then ten, and Howie, nine, too young to cope with the notion their father was going to prison. Instead, O'Brien advised telling them that Pavlo had to go away to "work for the government."

Rhoda and Pavlo had doubts about Father O'Brien's advice but they were in uncharted waters. They were hoping Pavlo would be assigned to a low-security prison camp, but since neither had ever seen one they had no idea whether they'd be able to pass it off as some sort of remote government facility. At that point almost anything seemed worth a try if it would relieve the boys of the shame, if not the sorrow, of losing their father for a few years. Besides, Bubby and Howie still believed in Santa Claus, so maybe the notion that dad was away "working for the government" wasn't too much of a stretch.

Pavlo was still feeling the shame of having to reveal his fate to the grown-ups in his family. After telling Rhoda, he'd broken the news to his father during a visit to Sistersville the previous September. It hadn't come as a complete shock. His son had been a trouble-free kid growing up, but Walt Sr. had been uneasy about the direction his life had taken ever since he'd moved to Atlanta and gone to work for MCI. In Walt Sr.'s eyes, Pavlo and Rhoda had both become taken with material trappings like fancy vacations, expensive cars, and over-priced restaurants. It was a world he neither knew nor aspired to join.

Still, Walt Sr. couldn't keep his bottom lip from quivering or his hands from shaking when his namesake delivered the news that he was going to prison. He offered a hug that went on longer than any Walt Jr. remembered getting from his father, and a whispered "I love you, son."

Pavlo's mother, Gene, was a different story. A woman whose life began and ended with her family, she knew nothing of the business world or her son's troubles. She had been helping around his house on Wilmington Island when he approached her.

"Mom, I've done something wrong and I'm going to prison," he said, reciting words he'd rehearsed over and over.

His mother looked at him as if he'd round-housed her in the head. Without a word, she buried her face in his shoulder and began crying hysterically.

"I don't understand. I've never understood any of this."

Pavlo's brothers had taken the news better. He'd told his younger brother Chris over lunch with Rhoda. By the time he got to Barry, he just picked up the phone and called him in Cleveland. Pavlo decided to let his friends get word through the grapevine. That left him only the hardest task of all. Telling his sons.

Bubby and Howie were happy as fleas on a dog, walking with their father the few hundred yards from the church parking lot to the eighteenth tee of the Wilmington Island Country Club. Not another soul was in sight. The scene reminded Pavlo of the day after Christmas years earlier when his father had taken Barry and him to a bitterly cold par three course in Belpre, Ohio for their first golf outing. Walt Sr. had always been preparing them to succeed in business. For Pavlo, it hadn't quite worked out.

"I've got to tell you guys something," he started. Bubby and Howie snapped to attention.

"Is something wrong?" Bubby asked.

"Not really. It's just that daddy's going to be away for awhile."

"Where to?" Howie asked.

"To work for the government." It wasn't a total lie. Jesup prisoners cut fire lines for the U.S. Forest Service and grass at Fort Stewart in Savannah. "I'll be fine but I'm gonna be gone a pretty long time."

"How long?"

"Maybe a couple of years. Mom will bring you guys to visit."

The boys were silent. They looked at each other for guidance.

"Why?" Bubby asked.

"It's something I have to do. The important thing is I need you guys to take care of mommy. Can you be big boys and do that for me?"

"Where're you going? Is it far away?"

"No. And I'll be helping people."

"What people?"

"People you don't know."

Howie began to cry. Pavlo gathered him into his arms. Bubby looked off toward the golf course.

"It'll be alright. You have to trust me." He struggled not to cry.

"I don't get it," Bubby said through tears.

"You'll understand in time. We'll be alright. Okay?"

"When do you have to go?"

"March fourteenth. That's not for two months. There's plenty of time to get ready."

"Why's the government making you go away?" Bubby asked.

"It's just one of those things. Look, if it goes well I'll be back after one Thanksgiving and one Christmas. You're big guys. You can take care of your mom that long. Then I'll be home."

"Promise?" Howie asked.

"I promise."

Bubby and Howie were confused and Pavlo had done a lame job of answering their many questions. He wasn't sure how long he'd be gone, how often the family would visit, what they'd tell the boys when they did, or what he would encounter when he got there.

He and Rhoda were confused about how they'd put their family back together when it was all over, if they even could. Pavlo had asked Rhoda if she wanted a divorce. She had insisted she didn't but given the increasing strain on their marriage, they both had their doubts.

Pavlo walked his sons slowly back to the church. Rhoda came out, her face blotchy as if she'd been crying.

"Dad told us," Bubby said, looking down at the parking lot.

"We'll be alright. You okay Howie?" Rhoda asked.

The younger boy ran into his mother's arms and began sobbing. Rhoda looked at her husband. There was nothing he could do. During their last drink together, Wilkie had told Pavlo if people knew ahead of time what their crimes could do to their families, they'd never commit them. Pavlo had learned that lesson too late to prevent his sins as a father from being visited on his wife and sons.

"Let's go home," he said.

|||

The worst moment on the worst day of Pavlo's life came on March 14, 2001 when he kissed Rhoda, Bubby, and Howie goodbye and headed out the door for the ride to prison. His younger brother Chris was waiting in the driveway. Their destination was the federal prison in Jesup, Georgia, two hours south of Savannah.

Pavlo had received fashion advice from a friend of a friend who'd gained expertise after hiring an undercover FBI agent as a deck hand on his marijuana-running shrimp boat. Pavlo had dressed in gray Wal-Mart issue sweat pants, white socks, a T-shirt and white sneakers that he knew met the regulations of the Federal Bureau of Prisons. Otherwise his street clothes would be mailed home in a box marked "Jesup Federal Prison."

Chris waited behind the wheel of Pavlo's pickup. For nearly four years Pavlo had pulled every legal trick he could imagine, and plenty of illegal ones, to try to avoid this day. He'd burned through hundreds of thousands of dollars mounting his legal defense, lied to his lawyers, shredded documents, turned on friends, and felt the sting of friends turning on him.

He'd had his chances and blown them. His fate was sealed. He was about to get locked up with a bunch of street thugs and drug pushers. Part of him felt a cut above. Another felt lower than the lowest. More than anything he was scared shitless.

"I guess I'll just have to take it like a man," he said as Chris drove down the long driveway toward Wilmington Island Road. "Or, if what I've heard about prison is true, I might have to take it like a woman."

Chris managed a wan smile. Good thing he was behind the wheel, Pavlo thought. Drive, hell. He was having trouble breathing. He looked over at Chris whose gaze was dead-ahead. Without a word, his brother fished a fresh pack of Marlboro Lights from his pocket and held it out.

"Ah, a condemned man's last wish!" Pavlo lit up and watched the trees fly by. As the cigarette burned low, he carefully put it out in the ashtray and lit another.

"So," Chris finally asked, "How'd we ever get here?"

For the first time Pavlo realized how hard it must be to drive your big brother to prison. Walt had been the first to go to college, the first to get a graduate degree, and the first to achieve white-collar success. Chris had followed him to engineering school and their brother Barry to business school.

The silence lingered. Pavlo had spun his story so many ways so many times he didn't know where to begin. The longer he thought, the more he felt relief mix with his fear. He had nothing left to lose. He could finally tell his story spin-free.

"In the movies you can tell the bad guys because they wear black hats or capes. In our dreams they're witches or demons. But you know what?"

"What?"

"In real life the bad guys are people like me."

Epilogue

IN JUNE, 2001, three months after Pavlo went to prison, attorney Kenneth Vianale filed a class action against WorldCom, still considered a large, well-respected corporation.[1] His 113-page complaint alleged, among other things, that half the telecom reseller accounts WorldCom had inherited from MCI were three-to-seven years past due.[2]

That meant MCI had sold WorldCom worthless assets that WorldCom was still carrying on its books. Among the one hundred former employees interviewed was a credit manager who described the old MCI carrier accounts as an "absolute shambles."[3]

Judge William H. Barbour of the U.S. District Court in the Southern District of Mississippi, WorldCom's home, tossed out the suit in April, 2002. "The numbers are so large, the stakes so high...that the reader (of the complaint) reacts by thinking that there must have been some corporate misbehavior," he wrote. Barbour went on to describe the allegations of rampant wrongdoing at WorldCom as lacking in "real substance."[4]

The Securities and Exchange Commission also launched an investigation into WorldCom's accounting in the spring of 2002 demanding it hand over, among other things, details of the $685 million in carrier accounts the company had written off in the fall of 2000.[5] Three months later, in June 2002, *Forbes* magazine writer Neil Weinberg published a six-page article on Walter Pavlo, Jr., titled Ring of Thieves. The SEC immediately informed Pavlo's attorney, Bruce Morris, of its interest in interviewing his client.[6] But it never followed up.

A month later, WorldCom, having faked $11 billion in income, filed for the largest bankruptcy in history.[7] Shortly afterward, the scandal-plagued firm changed its name to MCI. The combined company, once worth $151 billion, was sold to Verizon for $6.8 billion in 2005.[8] Thus, the entrepreneurial upstart Bill McGowan had used to topple a telephone monopoly, and transform an industry, ceased to exist.

 # Where Are They Now?

Walter Pavlo Jr.: Pleaded guilty to obstruction of justice, money laundering and wire fraud and served 24 months in federal prison. He was released and divorced from Rhoda Voth, his wife of 15 years, in 2003. He lives in Tampa, Florida and has remarried. He works as a public speaker, addressing university students, law enforcement officials, business people and accountants.

Harold Mann: Pleaded guilty to money laundering, wire fraud and tax fraud. He served 48 months in federal prison. Released in May, 2006, he was deported to Canada.

Sean Hennessy (a pseudonym): Granted immunity by the government in exchange for his extensive cooperation.

James Wilkie IV: Pleaded guilty to one count of wire fraud and served 18 months in federal prison. He lives in Atlanta, Georgia with his wife Becky.

Mark Benveniste: Convicted at trial of bank fraud, mail fraud, wire fraud and making false statements, he was sentenced to 63 months in federal prison. He is living in Atlanta, Georgia.

Rhoda Voth: Divorced from Walter Pavlo in 2003, she is working and raising their two sons.

James Wanserski: Left MCI in October 1998, shortly after the MCI-WorldCom merger, to work for accounting firm Arthur Andersen. He lives in the Atlanta area and works as a consultant.

Ralph McCumber: Retired and living in Atlanta.

Robert Hilby: Moved to San Francisco to set up Internet startup Simple Access, which folded.

Endnotes

Chapter 2 – Big Time

1. Lorraine Spurge, *Failure Is Not An Option. How MCI Invented Competition in Telecommunications* (Encino, California: Spurge Ink!, 1998), p. 41.
2. Ibid, p. 9.
3. Ibid, p. 49.
4. Ibid, p. 155.
5. Ibid, p. 183.
6. Philip L. Cantelon, *The History of MCI: 1968-1988, The Early Years* (Washington, D.C., MCI Communications Corp., 1993), p. 500.

Chapter 3 – Reach Out and Touch Yourself

1. Bob Bentz, *Opportunity is Calling*, (Wayne, Penn., ATS Publishing, 1993), p. 21.
2. Spurge, p. 240.
3. Bentz, p. 23.
4. From an interview with Dick Martin, former AT&T executive vice president, May 19, 2006.
5. Neil Weinberg, "Ring of Thieves," *Forbes*, June 10, 2002.

Chapter 4 – Biting Heads Off Chickens

1. Deposition of Ralph Ray McCumber in the Matter of Manatee Partners, Limited Partnership v. MCI Telecommunications Corporation, 1:97-CV-3782-GET, July 15, 1998.
2. "LCI Rings Up Profit," *Washington Technology*, Apr. 11, 1996.

Chapter 5 – Hedge Hopping

1. Interview with Ralph McCumber, June 27, 2006.
2. Jack T. Hammer's Answer to Plaintiff's Amended Complaint, Counterclaim and Cross-Claim, Nov. 30, 1998, 1:97-CV-3782-GET.
3. "Terms and Conditions" Agreement between MCI Telecommunications Corporation and Telecom Management Systems, Sept. 23, 1996, pp. 1-16.
4. Arbitration Coordinator, Office of the General Counsel, MCI Communications Corp., MCI Arbitration Rule Book, (Washington, D.C., July 1, 1994), p. 3.
5. Deposition of James Bradley Folk in the Matter of Manatee Partners, Limited Partnership v. MCI Telecommunications Corporation, 1:97-CV-3782-GET, Sept 17, 1998.
6. MCI Carrier Financial Services Monthend Statistics, December 1996.
7. MCI Carrier Financial Services – Aging Result Summary Report by Service VP, Dec. 1996 Month End, pp.23-25.
8. McCumber testified in his deposition that "I always like to leave room to make sure that my subordinates hit the target so I do."
9. McCumber deposition.

Chapter 6 – Making The Numbers

1. MCI Carrier Financial Services, Carrier A/R Management, Aug. 1, 1996, p. 3.
2. Spurge, p. 177.
3. MCI Internal Report, TUSA Agings, NASP ID Grand Totals, August 1996 Monthend, pp. 1-6.
4. MCI amortization schedule for VoiceCom, Apr. 1995. VoiceCom repaid MCI in 1996.
5. MCI Carrier Financial Services, Carrier Accounts Receivable Management, Feb. 17, 1997, p. 3.
6. The facts in the following dialogue were taken from: MCI Office of the General Counsel, Litigation Dept., "Arbitration Summary Figures 1994," Jan. 16, 1995.
7. McCumber deposition.
8. James Surowieki, "What Psychic Friends Failed to Foresee," The Motley Fool, Feb. 20, 1998, p. 1.
9. MCI Carrier Financial Services – Aging Result Summary Report, Jan. 1997, p. 11.
10. http://alum.hampshire.edu/~cbdF92/psychic.html
11. MCI Carrier Financial Services – Aging Result Summary Report by Service VP, Dec. 1996, p. 4.
12. News release, *The Spectator*, Hamilton, Ont. Oct. 11, 1994.

13. Robert Brehl, "Struggling TelRoute Fires Back at Bell," *Toronto Star*, Jan. 20., 1995, p. E1.

Chapter 7 – Target Man

1. McCumber deposition.
2. Ibid.
3. http://www.thedigest.com/shame/cherry.html.
4. http://www.thedigest.com/67/67-32.html.
5. www.fec.gov/pdf/record/1997/jun97.
   pdf#search=%22FEDERAL%20ELECTION%20COMMISSION%20
   (FEC)%20FINES.%20The%20FEC%20recently%20fined%20
   Cherry%20Communications%20Inc.%20and%20its%20chai
   rman%20James%20R.%20Elliott%20%22.
6. Michael G. Warner, "Phone Company Barred From State for 2 Years," *Los Angeles Times*, Sep. 8, 1996.
7. Deposition of James H. Wanserski, Manatee Partners, Limited Partnership v. MCI Telecommunications Corporation, 1:97-CV-3311-GET, July 14, 1998.
8. William G. Flannigan and Brigid McMenamin, *Forbes*, Aug. 3, 1992.
9. www.franklinps.com/f-dash.asp?Page=62689.html.
10. Interview with Jim Franklin, Aug. 16, 2006.

Chapter 8 – Change of Command

1. Federal Communications Commission, Memorandum Opinion and Order, Hi-Rim Communications, Inc., v. MCI Telecommunications Corp., Aug. 25, 1997.
2. "MCI Communications Inc.: Cam-Net Communications To Sell 6% Stake to Firm," *Wall Street Journal*, Dec. 1, 1995.
3. Ibid.
4. U.S. Securities and Exchange Commission, Release No. 7357, Oct. 10, 1996.
5. Brent Mundry, "SEC Wins Injunction on Wolfson's Olsen Payne Broker," *Street Wire*, July 17, 2003.
6. http://www.thedigest.com/79/79-17.html, "Primus Buys Cam-Net," *DLD Digest*, Apr. 10, 1997.
7. McCumber deposition.
8. MCI Carrier Financial Services, Carrier Accounts Receivable Management, Feb. 17, 1997, p. 3.
9. Ibid.

Chapter 9 – Young Turks

1. Letter from Mark Benveniste, July 23, 2006.
2. Statement of Undisputed Material Facts in Support of Motions for Summary Judgment by MCI Communications Corporation and James H. Wanserski, Manatee Partners, Limited Partnership v. MCI Telecommunications Corporation, 1:97-CV-3311-GET, Feb. 22, 1999, p. 5.
3. Interview with Mark Benveniste, Sept. 23, 2006.
4. MCI Carrier Financial Services, Carrier Accounts Receivable Management, Feb. 17, 1997, p. 3.
5. "Reorganized AT&T to Cut 40,000 Jobs; Impact on Region May Not Be Severe," *Washington Post*, Jan. 3, 1996.
6. Email from Walter Pavlo, Jan. 4, 1996.
7. Ibid.
8. Wanserski deposition, July 14, 1998.
9. "Not a natural leader" was how Wanserski's boss had described him in an early 1995 job evaluation. "Jim gives people the sense he would prefer to have him and his organization left alone," the report went on. Still, Wanserski's boss described him as having "fully met" his key objectives. Top among them: "Meet or beat the writeoff and aging plan for Business Markets." Job evaluation of Jim Wanserski, Feb. 1995; Wanserski deposition, July 14, 1998.
10. Spurge, p. 182.
11. Email from Wanserski's boss, James Folk, to Nate Davis, Mar. 9, 1997, p. 1, states "His (Wanserski's) weakness was singular reliance on loyalty with his directs (direct subordinates), not sufficiently checking on their performance details."
12. MCI Carrier Financial Services, Carrier Accounts Receivable Management, Feb. 17, 1997, p. 3.
13. TUSA Agings NASP ID Grand Totals, Sept. 5, 1996, p. 2.
14. Jack T. Hammer's Answer To Plaintiff's Amended Complaint, Counter-Claim And Cross-Claim, in the Matter of Manatee Partners, Limited Partnership v. MCI Telecommunications Corporation, 1:97-CV-3782-GET, Dec. 1, 1998, p. 15.
15. Jack T. Hammer's Motion for Summary Judgment, in the Matter of Manatee Partners, Limited Partnership v. MCI Telecommunications Corporation, 1:97-CV-3311-GET, Feb. 22, 1999, p. 6.
16. G. Ernest Tidwell, Judge, United States District Court, in the Matter of Manatee Partners, Limited Partnership v. MCI Telecommunications Corporation, 1:97-CV-3782-GET, Sept. 8, 1999, p. 10.

Chapter 10 – Solutions Provider

1. MCI Carrier Financial Services, East/West Collections, Feb. 7, 1997, p. 17.
2. MCI, East/West/900 Collections report, Collections West, GCI/ General Communications, Dynell Garrett, Feb. 7, 1997.
3. Wanserski deposition, July 14, 1998.
4. MCI Memorandum, Subject: 1st Quarter 1996 Revenue Operations Recognition Program, From James B. Folk to All Employees, Revenue Operations, May 6, 1996, pp. 3-4.
5. MCI Carrier Financial Services, Carrier Accounts Receivable Management, Feb. 17, 1997, p. 3.
6. MCI Expense Report of Walter Pavlo, Feb. 2, 1996.
7. MCI Expense Report of Walter Pavlo, Mar. 1, 1996.
8. Deposition of Robert Hilby, Manatee Partners, Limited Partnership V. MCI Telecommunications Corporation, et al, 1:97 CV-3782-GET, Dec. 17, 1998.
9. Ibid.
10. Notice of Apparent Liability for Forfeiture, Telephone Publishing Corporation and Telemedia Network, Inc. d/b/a International Telnet, Federal Communications Commission, Apr. 18, 1997.
11. Ibid.
12. Testimony of Robert Hilby, National Bank of Canada, et al. v. MCI WorldCom, Inc. Transcript of Trial, Apr. 11, 2000.
13. Hilby deposition.
14. MCI Carrier A/R Management, Aug. 1, 1996, p. 8.
15. Hilby deposition.
16. MCI Carrier Business Management Review, June 19, 1996, p. 7, shows Carrier Financial Services held a note receivable from Caribbean Tel & Tel for $10.25 million.
17. Spurge, p 7.
18. Order and statement of fact by the Court, Manatee Partners, Limited Partnership v. MCI Telecommunications Corporation, 1:97-CV-3782-GET, Sep. 8, 1999, p. 11.
19. Ibid.
20. "Two Companies to Join S&P 500," *Wall Street Journal*, Mar. 26, 1996.

Chapter 11 – Putting the Cat on the Roof

1. Spurge, p. 245.
2. Wanserski testified in a Nov. 20, 1998 deposition that the TNI account preceded him in Carrier Finance and he was not familiar with its details, including how much it had owed MCI.
3. "Mergers ring in a daunting new era for the three independent Baby

Bells," *Wall Street Journal*, Apr. 22, 1996.

4. John J. Keller, "AT&T's Lucent unit files largest-ever IPO in U.S.," *Wall Street Journal*, Mar. 13, 1996.

5. Hilby deposition.

Chapter 12 – Don't Worry Baby

1. Deposition of David Lewis Wickett in the Matter of Manatee Partners, Limited v. MCI Telecommunications Corporation, 1:97-CV-3782-GET, Sept. 14, 1998.

Chapter 13 – Hog Sty Bay

1. Wanserski deposition, July 14, 1998.

2. Testimony of Charles Douglas Dickson, National Bank of Canada, et al. v. MCI WorldCom, Inc., Transcript of Trial, Apr. 12, 2000. James H. Wanserski Renewed Motion To Dismiss Plaintiffs' First Amended Complaint Pursuant to FED.R.CIV.12(b) (6), 1:99-CV-1580-GET.

3. Ibid.

4. Ibid.

5. Ibid.

6. Memorandum in Opposition to Motions for Summary Judgment Filed by Defendants, National Bank of Canada, et al. v. MCI WorldCom, Inc., 1:97-CV-3782-GET, Mar. 17, 1999, p. 11.

7. Dennis said he did not recall discussing Rapid Advance with Pavlo, Neil Weinberg, "Ring of Thieves," *Forbes*, June 10, 2002.

8. MCI Carrier Services presentation, RELI – Reseller Enhanced LEC Interface, Carrier Product Training, Sept. 1996, MCI SensiBILL, Rapid Advance.

9. Folk deposition, Sept. 17, 1998.

10. Jack T. Hammer's Answer to Plaintiff's Amended Complaint, Counterclaim and Cross-Claim, Nov. 30, 1998, 1:97-CV-3782-GET.

11. Spurge, pp. 244-246.

12. MCI Telecommunications Corporation letter from Walter Pavlo to John Spear, Apr. 12, 1996. Spear has stated that he did not receive this document and would not have approved it.

13. Interview with Mark Benveniste, Sept. 23, 2006.

14. MCI Expense Report of Walter Pavlo, May 16, 1996.

15. James Wanserski Calendar, May, 1996.

16. Letter of agreement from Harold Mann, Orion Management, to Robert Hilby, TeleMedia Network, Inc., May 9, 1996, pp. 1-6.

17. Hilby deposition.

18. Ibid.

19. www.webcom.com/offshore/ims2/biographies.htm.

Chapter 14 – This Could Be Ugly

1. MCI Carrier Business Management Review, June 19, 1996, p. 9.
2. MCI Carrier Accounts Receivable Management, Feb. 17, 1997, p. 3.
3. MCI email, Walter Pavlo to John J. Baldino, Jim Wanserski, Pete Cassidy, James B. Folk and M. Andrew Giddings, Subject: ATI, June 25, 1996.
4. MCI email, James B. Folk to John J. Baldino, Subject: ATI plan B, July 1, 1996.
5. MCI Expense Report, Walter Pavlo, July 1, 1996.
6. Swidler & Berlin, Letter from ATI attorney Joel Van Over to Donald J. Elardo, Esq., MCI legal counsel, Mar. 30, 1995, pp. 1-2.
7. MCI Communications Corp. Proxy Statement/Prospectus, Mar. 3, 1997, p. 21.
8. MCI Expense Report, Walter Pavlo, June 24, 1996.
9. Folk deposition, Sep. 17, 1998.
10. Ibid.
11. Deposition of James Bradley Folk in the Matter of Manatee Partners, Limited Partnership v. MCI Telecommunications Corporation, 1:97-CV-3782-GET, Oct. 29, 1998.
12. Folk deposition, Sep. 17, 1998.
13. Cable and Wireless Summary of Outstanding Charges, Nov. 1, 1996; Frontier Communications Summary of Outstanding Charges, Nov. 21, 1996; MCI Carrier Financial Services – Aging Result Summary Report, Jan. 1997.
14. Ibid.
15. Frontier Communications letter, Robert Stegar (Director, Cost Access) to Gene Filocco (MCI Director), July 26, 1996; Cable & Wireless letter, Kenneth J. Wees (General Counsel) to Gene Filocco (MCI Director), Dec. 5, 1996.
16. Commercial Customer Financial Services, Doug Maine Update – Oct. 18, 1996, "Carrier 90 I Agings Deteriorations is in "Big 3" Carriers."
17. "Sports People; McLain Pleads Guilty," *New York Times*, Oct. 19, 1988.
18. "Sports People: Baseball; McLain Indicted on Pension Theft Charges," *New York Times*, May 10, 1996.
19. McLain admitted tipping off Mantle to the pitch, writing "Tell Mickey it's coming right down the pipe." Denny Mclain with Mike Nahrstedt, Strikeout, (St. Louis, Missouri, *The Sporting News*, 1988), p. 44.

Chapter 15 – A Good Back Waxing

1. MCI Carrier Account Receivable Management, Feb. 17, 1997, p. 3.
2. Ibid.
3. Wanserski deposition, July 14, 1998.
4. Teletek Form 10-K, United States Securities and Exchange Commission, June 30, 1996.
5. MCI Carrier A/R Management, Aug. 1, 1996, p. 19.
6. AT&T Form 10-K, United States Securities and Exchange Commission, Dec. 31, 1996.
7. Ibid.
8. Brief for Plaintiffs-Appellants, Harriet Goldstein, et al v. MCI WorldCom, Bernard J. Ebbers, Scott D. Sullivan, Case No. 02-60322, U.S. Court of Appeals for the Fifth Circuit; Scott Woolley, "Bernie at Bay," *Forbes*, Apr. 15, 2002.
9. "$2,000,000 Punitive Damage Award in Slovinski vs. Elliott," *PR Newswire*, June 16, 2004.
10. Ibid.
11. "Prepaid Phone-Card Scams Demonstrate the Risk of Fraud of Misuse of Stored Value," Fried, Frank, Haris, Shriver & Jacobson LLP, July 25, 1996.
12. Wanserski testified in his July 14, 1998 deposition that he led the Chateau Elan discussion and that Pavlo "played very little role in the presentation." This differs from Pavlo's recollection.
13. Folk deposition, Oct. 29, 1998.
14. Lynch's participation is based on Walter Pavlo, Jr.'s recollection.
15. Wanserski deposition, July 14, 1998.
16. "Basic Telecommunications Vendor for the Twenty-First Century," MetroLink, Aug. 1996, p. 6.
17. Letter from Harold Mann to John C. Paulsen, Aug. 14, 1996.
18. Ibid.
19. Manatee Capital, Commissions Payable – By Customer, Dec. 31, 1996.

Chapter 16 – Dead on Arrival

1. MCI Carrier Accounts Receivable Management, Write-offs, Feb. 17, 1997.
2. Manatee Capital, Commissions Payable – By Customer, Dec. 31, 1996.

Chapter 17 – Scamming The Scammers

1. Tel-Central Traffic Analysis, "Current amount due through Aug 96 rebill."

2. Iapps.courts.state.ny.us/attorney/AttorneyDetails?attorneyId=536
4905
3. Investigative Programs, Organized Crime, Mobstocks, www.fbi.
gov/hq/cid/orgcrime/casestudies/mobstocks.htm.
4. MCI Internal Document, "Tel-Central and related transactions, 1.0
Initial Credit of $2,215K to Tel-Central, with offset in 900 Service,
1.1 Detailed credit on Tel-Central, 1.1 – Tel-Central – Batch 4495,"
Aug. 30, 1996.

Chapter 18 – The Mac Daddy Card

1. Letter from Jim Wilkie to Mssrs. Eric and Martin Cherry, Oct. 21,
1996.
2. Ibid.
3. United States of America v. Walter A. Pavlo, Jr., U.S. District Court
for the Northern District of Georgia, Oct. 12, 2000.
4. Annual Report for the Fiscal Year 1997, MCI Communications
Corporation, Apr. 15, 1998.
5. Spurge, p. 183.
6. Ibid.
7. Steven Lipin, "British Telecommunications and MCI Unveil $20.88
Billion Merger Agreement," *Wall Street Journal*, Nov. 4, 1996.
8. Letter from Walter Pavlo, MCI Telecommunications Corp., to
Harold Mann, Nov. 6, 1996.
9. Deposition of James H. Wanserski, Manatee Partners, Limited
Partnership v. MCI Telecommunications Corporation, 1:97 CV
3782-GET, Nov. 20, 1998.
10. Wickett deposition.
11. Letter from Jim Wilkie to Eric Cherry, Nov. 22, 1996.
12. Mann/Pavlo Agenda, Review Issues with Core People, Actions
Taken Since June, Aug. 5, 1997.
13. Orion Management Services, Inc. , Letter from Harold Mann to
Michael Howard (IMS – Grand Cayman), Mar. 12, 1997.
14. Carrier Accounts Receivable Management, Feb. 17, 1997, Carrier
Segment Base, p. 3.
15. Ibid.
16. James Wanserski testified in his Jul. 14, 1998 deposition his "general
recollection" that Hi-Rim's debt was carried into 1997 amid
discussions with its principals about ways to recover the dollars.
17. Tel-Central, Estimated Feb. 1996 SCA Rebill, Jan. 27, 1997.
18. MCI Telecommunications Corporation, Third Amended

Contract between Tel-Central Communications, Inc and MCI Telecommunications Corp., July 1, 1996, pp. 20, 23.

19. MCI internal memorandum from Walter Pavlo to Lisa Guignard, Business Development, Dec. 6, 1996.

Chapter 19 – It's All A Lie

1. MCI internal report, "Tel-Central and related transactions, Section 2.0, 900 Service settlements are replicated, and duplicate JV's are posted, then credits are transferred to TLCN -- $5,205,591.54."
2. Manatee Capital, Commissions Payable – By Customer, FPE Dec. 31, 1996, p. 1.
3. Ibid.
4. Wanserski deposition, Nov. 20, 1998.
5. MCI Telecommunications Corporation letter From Jim Wanserski to Denny McLain, Jan. 13, 1997.

Chapter 20 – Everyone's Nasdaqable

1. James Wanserski stated "I was convinced of fraud, but I had to get him (Walter Pavlo) back into the office to lock it down," *Financial Executive*, Mar. 2006, p. 30.
2. Wanserski wrote in *Financial Executive*, Mar. 2006, that he became concerned about Pavlo's actions in mid-1996 after several sales and business people contacted him; Wanserski's claim was contradicted by the testimony of his boss, James Folk, who testified Wanserski "accepted as true and accurate" the results and numbers Pavlo and Wilkie presented to him and "did not go find another source"; the authors' research found no evidence that supports Wanserski's claim he was suspicious of Pavlo prior to 1997.
3. James Wanserski confirms speaking with Mann about Tel-Central in his Aug. 6, 1998 deposition.
4. Wanserski deposition, July 14, 1998.
5. Brief in Support of Motions for Summary Judgment by MCI Communications Corporation and James H. Wanserski, Manatee Partners, Limited Partnership v. MCI Telecommunications Corporation, 1:97-CV-3311-GET, Feb. 22, 1999, p. 17.
6. MCI Communications Corporation letter from Thomas F. O'Neil, III, Chief Litigation Counsel, MCI Law and Public Policy, to Gary Dupler (WorldCom, Inc.), Dec. 6, 1996.
7. Wanserski deposition, Oct. 21, 1998.
8. Ibid.
9. MCI Communications Corp. sworn letter of proof in insurance claim, July 2, 1997, p. 2.

10. Affidavit of Debra Rader, National Bank of Canada, et al. v. MCI WorldCom, Inc., 1:97-CV-3782-GET, Oct. 12, 1998, p. 2.
11. Ibid, p. 3.
12. Letter from James B. Folk to Walter Pavlo, Feb. 10, 1997.
13. Wanserski Deposition, Oct. 21, 1998.
14. Wanserski deposition, July 14, 1998.
15. Ibid.
16. James Wanserski Calendar, Feb. 1997.

Chapter 21 – Die Like An Aviator

1. Wanserski deposition, Oct. 21, 1998.
2. Deposition of Edward G. McGinty in the Matter of Manatee Partners, Limited Partnership v. MCI Telecommunications Corporation, 1:97-CV-3782-GET, Dec. 15, 1998.
3. MCI email from McGinty to "BlackJim," Feb. 25, 1997.
4. www.melaleuca.com/
5. Folk deposition, Sept. 17, 1998.
6. Ibid.
7. Order and statement of fact by the Court, Manatee Partners, Limited Partnership v. MCI Telecommunications Corporation, 1:97-CV-3311-GET, Sept. 8, 1999, p. 10.
8. Folk deposition, Sept. 17, 1998.
9. McGinty deposition.
10. Ibid.
11. Folk deposition, Sept. 17, 1998
12. MCI Communications Corp. Proxy Statement/Prospectus, Mar. 3, 1997.
13. Email from Jim Folk to Nate Davis, Mar. 9, 1997.
14. Ibid.
15. Ibid.
16. Separate email from Jim Folk to Nate Davis, Mar. 9, 1997, p. 1; Folk deposition, Sept. 17, 1998.
17. CorpAmerica, Inc. letter to Walt Pavlo, "The Certificate of Incorporation for: Corvus Communications, Inc.," Oct. 10, 1997.
18. United States of America v. Walter A. Pavlo, Jr., U.S. District Court for the Northern District of Georgia, Oct. 12, 2000.
19. Brief in Support of Plaintiffs' Motion for Partial Judgment, National Bank of Canada, et al v. MCI Telecommunications, et al, 1:97-CV-3782-GET, Feb. 22, 1999, p. 4.
20. Brief in Support of Motions for Summary Judgment by MCI Communications Corporation and James H. Wanserski, Manatee Partners, Limited Partnership v. MCI Telecommunications Corporation, 1:97-CV-3782-GET, Feb. 22, 1999, p. 19.

21. Ibid, p. 18.
22. Ibid, p. 20.
23. Statement of Undisputed Material Facts, Manatee Partners, Limited Partnership v. MCI Telecommunications Corporation, 1:97-CV-3311-GET, Feb. 22, 1999, p. 3.
24. "Ex-Baseball Star and His Partner Are Convicted of Pension Fraud," *New York Times*, Dec. 14, 1996.
25. Order and statement of fact by the Court, Manatee Partners, Limited Partnership v. MCI Telecommunications Corporation, 1:97-CV-3311-GET, Sept. 8, 1999, p. 20.
26. Plaintiffs' Consolidated Opposition To MCI Telecommunications Corporation's Motion, National Bank of Canada, et al. v. MCI Telecommunications Corporation, 1:97-CV-3782-GET, Jan. 18, 2000, p. 8.
27. Memorandum in Opposition to Motions for Summary Judgment Filed by Defendants, National Bank of Canada, et al. v. MCI WorldCom, Inc., 1:97-CV-3782-GET, Mar. 17, 1999, p 19.
28. Interview with Bruce Morris, June 28, 2006.
29. Brief in Support of Plaintiffs' Motion for Partial Summary Judgment, Manatee Partners, Limited Partnership v. MCI Telecommunications Corporation, 1:97-CV-3311-GET, Feb. 22, 1999, p. 6.
30. Agreement between MCI Telecommunications, signed by James B. Folk, AP, Revenue Operations, and Communications Systems International, Inc., Oct. 9, 1997.
31. Ibid.
32. APCC Compensation Program Agreement, Dec. 17, 1997.

Chapter 22 – The Bert and Bernie Show

1. "British Telecom Cuts Value of MCI Purchase by $5 billion," *Wall Street Journal*, Aug. 25, 1997.
2. Response of MCI Telecommunications Corp. to Plaintiffs' Statement of Material Facts To Which There Is No Genuine Issue To Be Tried, 1:97-CV-3311-GET, Mar. 15, 1999, p. 6.
3. Reply Brief In Support of Plaintiffs' Motion for Partial Summary Judgment, National Bank of Canada, et al. v. MCI WorldCom, Inc., 1:97-CV-3782-GET, Apr. 1, 1999, p. 10.
4. Response of MCI Telecommunications, 1:97-CV-3311-GET, Mar. 15, 1999, p. 6.
5. Ibid, p. 7.
6. MCI email to Carrier Sales & Support, Subject: MCI Rapid Advance on Hold, Mar. 11, 1997.

7. Letter from Bernard J. Ebbers to Bert C. Roberts, Jr., Oct. 1, 1997.
8. Annual Report for the Fiscal Year 1997, MCI Communications Corporation, Apr. 15, 1998.
9. Ibid.
10. Letter from Charles R. Lee to Bert C. Roberts, Jr., Oct. 15, 1997, www.secinfo.com/d17sw.811.d.htm.
11. Kelly Greene, "Wrong Number: How Phone Deal Turned Sour," *Wall Street Journal*, Feb. 4, 1998.
12. www.pbs.org/newshour/bb/business/july-dec97/mci_11-10.html.
13. Order and statement of fact by the Court, Manatee Partners, Limited Partnership v. MCI Telecommunications Corporation, 1:97-CV-3311-GET, Sept. 8, 1999, p. 15.
14. Ibid, pp. 2-3; National Bank of Canada, et al. v. MCI WorldCom, Inc., 1:97-CV-3782-GET, Feb. 22, 1999.
15. Order and statement of fact by the Court, Manatee Partners, Limited Partnership v. MCI Telecommunications Corporation, 1:97-CV-3311-GET, Sept. 8, 1999, p. 3; Brief in Support of Motions for Summary Judgment by MCI Communications Corporation and James H. Wanserski, Manatee Partners, Limited Partnership v. MCI Telecommunications Corporation, 1:97-CV-3311-GET, Feb. 22, 1999, p. 49.
16. Brief in Support of Motions for Summary Judgment by MCI Communications Corporation and James H. Wanserski, Feb. 22, 1999, p. 2.
17. National Bank of Canada et al. Statement of Claim In The Grand Court of the Cayman Islands, Feb. 27, 1999.
18. "From M.V.P. to Federal Prisoner," *New York Times*, Jan. 22, 1998; "Charges Are Dropped Against Ex-Baseball Star," *New York Times*, July 21, 1999.
19. Greene, *Wall Street Journal*, Feb. 4, 1998.

Chapter 23 – Tidying Things Up

1. Presentence Investigation Report, United States of America v. Walter A. Pavlo, Jr., U.S. District Court for the Northern District of Georgia, 1:00-CR-707(01), Dec. 19, 2000.
2. United States of America v. Walter A. Pavlo, Jr., Oct. 12, 2000.
3. United States District Court, Northern District of Georgia, Subpoena to Testify Before Grand Jury, sent to Orion Management Services, Inc. June 12, 1998.
4. Folk deposition, Sept. 17, 1998.
5. Wanserski deposition, Jul. 14, 1998.
6. Employment Termination Agreement between MCI Telecommunications Corp. and James Wanserski, Oct. 1, 1997.

7. Wanserski deposition, July 14, 1998.
8. Ibid.
9. Ibid.
10. Ibid.
11. Folk deposition, Sept. 17, 1998.
12. Ibid.
13. Interview with James Wilkie, June 19, 2006.
14. Ibid.

Chapter 24 – Bring A Bazooka

1. IRS Form 1040X – Amended U.S. Individual Income Tax Return, Tax Year 1996, Walter A. Pavlo, Jr., Dec. 18, 1998.
2. Ibid.
3. Hon. G. Ernest Tidwell, Judge, United States District Court, in the Matter of Manatee Partners, Limited Partnership v. MCI Telecommunications Corporation, 1:97-CV-3782-GET, Sept. 8, 1999, p. 7.
4. The facts and quotes in the following six paragraphs are cited from: National Bank of Canada, et al. v. MCI WorldCom, Inc., Transcript of Trial, Apr. 10, 2000.
5. The facts and quotes in the following eleven paragraphs are cited from: National Bank of Canada, et al. v. MCI WorldCom, Inc., Transcript of Trial, Apr. 11, 2000.
6. The facts and quotes in the following seven paragraphs are cited from: National Bank of Canada, et al. v. MCI WorldCom, Inc., Transcript of Trial, Apr. 12, 2000.
7. Court Order, Manatee Partners, Limited Partnership v. MCI Telecommunications Corporation, 1:97-CV-3311-GET, May 5, 2000.
8. Ibid.

Chapter 25 – The End of the World

1. Court Order, Manatee Partners, Limited Partnership v. MCI Telecommunications Corporation, 1:97-CV-3311-GET, May 5, 2000.
2. Presentence Investigation Report, United States of America v. Walter A. Pavlo, Jr., U.S. District Court for the Northern District of Georgia, Dec. 18, 2000.
3. Ibid.
4. WorldCom, Inc., Form 10-Q for the quarterly period ended Sept. 30, 2000, United States Securities and Exchange Commission.
5. Presentence Investigation Report, p. 9.

Epilogue

1. Neil Weinberg, "Asleep at the Switch," *Forbes,* July 22, 2002.
2. Consolidated Amended Class Action Complaint, WorldCom Inc. Securities Litigation, United States District Court, Southern District of Mississippi, 3:00CV833BN, June 1, 2001, p. 30.
3. Ibid, p 31.
4. Opinion and Order, MCI WorldCom Inc. Securities Litigation, United States District Court, Southern District of Mississippi, 3:00CV833BN, Mar. 29, 2002.
5. Deborah Solomon, "SEC Is Investigating Qwest, WorldCom," *Wall Street Journal,* Mar. 12, 2002.
6. Letter from Bruce H. Morris to Walter Pavlo, June 24, 2002.
7. www.pbs.org/newshour/updates/worldcom_07-22-02.html
8. www.forbes.com/markets/2005/02/14/cx_ab_0214video1.html

Select Bibliography

Bentz, Bob. *Opportunity Is Calling: How To Start Your Own Successful 900 Number.* Wayne, Pa.: ATS Publishing, 1993.

Cantelon, Philip. *The History of MCI: 1968-1988, The Early Years.* Washington, D.C.: MCI Communications Corp., 1993.

Cauley, Leslie. *End of the Line: The Rise and Fall of AT&T.* New York: Free Press, 2005.

Endlich, Lisa. *Optical Illusions: Lucent and the Crash of Telecom.* New York: Simon & Schuster, 2004.

Gilder, George. *Telecosm, How Infinite Bandwidth Will Revolutionize Our World.* New York: Free Press, 2000.

Malik, Om. *Broadbandits: Inside the $750 billion telecom heist.* Hoboken, NJ: John Wiley & Sons, 2003.

McLain, Denny. *Strikeout: The Story of Denny McLain.* St. Louis, Missouri: The Sporting News, 1988.

Martin, Dick. *Tough Calls: AT&T and the hard lessons learned from the telecom wars.* New York: AMACOM, 2005.

Reingold, Dan. *Confessions of a Wall Street Analyst.* New York: HarperCollins, 2005.

Spurge, Lorraine. *Failure Is Not An Option: How MCI Invented Competition in Telecommunications.* Encino, Calif.: Spurge Ink!, 1998.